Lesson Study

A Japanese Approach to Improving Mathematics Teaching and Learning

Clea Fernandez
Teachers College, Columbia University

Makoto Yoshida
Global Education Resources

D1308179

LAWRENCE ERLBAUM ASSOCIATES, PUBLISHERS

2004   Mahwah, New Jersey   London

Lawrence Erlbaum Associates, Inc., Publishers
10 Industrial Avenue
Mahwah, New Jersey 07430

Cover design by Kathryn Houghtaling Lacey

Library of Congress Cataloging-in-Publication Data

Fernandez, Clea, Yoshida, Makoto.
    Lesson Study : A Japanese Approach to Improving Mathematics
    Teaching and Learning
        p. cm. — (Studies in mathematical thinking and learning)
    Includes bibliographical references and index.
ISBN 0-8058-3961-5 (acid-free paper)
ISBN 0-8058-3962-3 (pbk. : acid-free paper)
    1. Mathematics—Study and teaching (Elementary)—Japan—Hi-
roshima-si—Case studies. 2. Lesson planning—Japan—Hiroshima-shi—Case studies. I. Fernandez, Clea. II. Title. III. Series.

QA135.6.Y67 2004
372.7'0952—dc21   2003052861
                                                                   CIP

Books published by Lawrence Erlbaum Associates are printed on acid-
free paper, and their bindings are chosen for strength and durability.

Printed in the United States of America
10   9   8   7   6   5   4   3   2

Lesson Study

A Japanese Approach to Improving
Mathematics Teaching and Learning

STUDIES IN MATHEMATICAL THINKING AND LEARNING
Alan H. Schoenfeld, Series Editor

Artzt/Armour-Thomas • *Becoming a Reflective Mathematics Teacher: A Guide for Observation and Self-Assessment*

Baroody/Dowker (Eds.) • *The Development of Arithmetic Concepts and Skills: Constructing Adaptive Expertise*

Boaler • *Experiencing School Mathematics: Traditional and Reform Approaches to Teaching and Their Impact on Student Learning*

Carpenter/Fennema/Romberg (Eds.) • *Rational Numbers: An Integration of Research*

Cobb/Bauersfeld (Eds.) • *The Emergence of Mathematical Meaning: Interaction in Classroom Cultures*

Clements/Sarama/DiBiase (Eds.) • *Engaging Young Children in Mathematics: Standards for Early Childhood Mathematics Education*

Cohen • *Teachers' Professional Development and the Elementary Mathematics Classroom*

English (Ed.) • *Mathematical and Analogical Reasoning of Young Learners*

English (Ed.) • *Mathematical Reasoning: Analogies, Metaphors, and Images*

Fennema/Nelson (Eds.) • *Mathematics Teachers in Transition*

Fennema/Romberg (Eds.) • *Mathematics Classrooms That Promote Understanding*

Fernandez/Yoshida • *Lesson Study: A Japanese Approach to Improving Mathematics Teaching and Learning*

Lajoie • *Reflections on Statistics: Learning, Teaching, and Assessment in Grades K-12*

Lehrer/Chazan (Eds.) • *Designing Learning Environments for Developing Understanding of Geometry and Space*

Ma • *Knowing and Teaching Elementary Mathematics*

Martin • *Mathematics Success and Failure Among African-American Youth: The Roles of Sociohistorical Context, Community Forces, School Influence, and Individual Agency*

Reed • *Word Problems: Research and Curriculum Reform*

Romberg/Fennema/Carpenter (Eds.) • *Integrating Research on the Graphical Representation of Functions*

Schoenfeld (Ed.) • *Mathematical Thinking and Problem Solving*

Senk/Thompson (Eds.) • *Standards-Based School Mathematics Curricula: What Are They? What Do Students Learn?*

Sternberg/Ben-Zeev (Eds.) • *The Nature of Mathematical Thinking*

Wilcox/Lanier (Eds.) • *Using Assessment to Reshape Mathematics Teaching: A Casebook for Teachers and Teacher Educators, Curriculum and Staff Development Specialists*

Wood/Nelson/Warfield (Eds.) • *Beyond Classical Pedagogy: Teaching Elementary School Mathematics*

Contents

Foreword

James W. Stigler

I will never forget the first time I bought a cookie in a Japanese department store. I looked through the glass bakery case and pointed to the cookie I wanted, much as I might have done in a bakery back home. But that's where similarity to home ended and Japanese culture started to take over. The clerk took my cookie and wrapped it carefully in tissue paper. She gently placed it in a gold paper box, sized perfectly to fit my single cookie. She then took a piece of ribbon and carefully tied it around the box. This elegant package was then placed in a beautiful bag with a handle on top. For Americans, the point is to eat the cookie, not convert it into an artistic masterpiece. We tend to think such details don't matter, but they do. As I later unwrapped my cookie, I enjoyed it in a way I had never enjoyed a cookie before.

It turns out "cookie wrapping" is not an isolated practice, but just another example of the way the Japanese approach many things, including teaching and learning. On that first trip to Japan in 1979, besides eating cookies and riding on trains that departed and arrived exactly on time, I visited an elementary school and observed a Japanese mathematics class for the first time. Impressed by the teaching method, and more so by the teacher, I wondered about the exquisite preparation it must take for someone to learn to teach with such precision and artistry. It was later, after many trips to Japan and many visits to Japanese schools, that I became aware of "lesson study" and the role it might play in the development of teaching in Japan. Just as Japanese cookies are converted into artistic masterpieces, so too are Japanese lessons meticulously planned and teaching improved.

The concept of lesson study seems simple and obvious: If you want to improve education, get teachers together to study the processes of teaching and learning in classrooms, and then devise ways to improve them. Remarkably, lesson study is not only a means of improving the skills and knowledge of teachers, but also a way to improve the knowledge base of the teaching profession. Japanese teachers are not only meeting in groups to improve teaching and learning, but writing books for other teachers in order to share what they have learned. Simple, obvious, and elegant, yet not at all like what teachers do in the United States.

It was Makoto Yoshida, who came to study with me at the University of Chicago, who first told me about lesson study, and who had the wisdom to keep talking about it. It soon became clear that this "lesson study" business warranted further investigation. When Makoto went back to Japan to study the innermost workings of lesson study groups at Tsuta Elementary School in Hiroshima, another of my graduate students (Clea Fernandez) and I started a lesson study group in Los Angeles, and began to explore how it might look in the United States.

Clea and Makoto have gone on to make major contributions to our understanding of lesson study, and this book clearly is one of the most important of these. Clea and Makoto tell the story of lesson study at Tsuta Elementary School in a way that is accurate and true to this Japanese practice, yet accessible and comprehensible to U.S. audiences. I can't think of two people better qualified to tell this story.

Their book is published at a time when, coincidentally, there is great interest in the United States in learning about lesson study. In fact, lesson study is in danger of becoming the latest fad in U.S. education circles, which could well spell its quick demise if we are not careful. Indeed, the history of education in the United States is filled with examples of fads that come and go quickly, never given a chance to really be evaluated or improved or integrated into the lasting fabric of the education landscape. Often, Americans adopt the superficial aspects of some educational idea and miss completely the substance that underlies the idea. A superficial implementation of lesson study is not likely to have any positive impact on the learning of teachers and students, and given our impatient political climate, a lack of immediate results may well lead to lesson study being declared a failure before it is even understood in any deep sense.

What we need to realize is that the devil (and God too) is in the details, which is what makes this book so important for the American audience. This is something the Japanese appear to understand, whether serving cookies or improving teaching. This book is a celebration and exposition of the details of lesson study in Japan. Many Americans who have heard that, in lesson study, teachers meet in groups to collaborate have rushed off to "do" lesson study without ever finding out what, exactly, these groups of Japanese teachers talk about in their meetings. This book presents the details of Japanese lesson study, and these details can take your breath away. We know, for example, that Japanese lesson study groups can spend hours and hours planning a single lesson. But what does it mean to "plan" a lesson? What do they talk about for all those hours? Is it anything like what American teachers talk about?

These details will prove to be critical if we want to learn from lesson study, and if we hope to implement lesson study productively in the United States. Some will think the details do not matter, especially given the vast cultural differences between Japan and the United States. But this confuses the issue. True, we cannot implement lesson study in the United States the same way it is implemented in Japan. But we also cannot implement lesson study unless we understand it in a deep sense. Details are important not because we must copy exactly what the Japanese do, but because we must understand its substance. This understanding will elude us unless we come to terms with the details.

Those of us interested in lesson study, and in improving teaching and learning in U.S. schools, should be grateful for the care and clarity with which Clea and Makoto have presented the substance of Japanese lesson study. There is much to be learned in these pages. Take your time, and enjoy unwrapping this fascinating glimpse into the profession of teaching in Japan.

Acknowledgments

We wish to express our sincerest gratitude to Jim Stigler who helped plant the seed for the initial idea for this project and played a major role in bringing it to fruition. We are also deeply indebted to Alan Schoenfeld for his very able assistance and incisive comments in every step of the writing process. Alan not only helped us substantially improve our manuscript but we both learned a great deal from working closely with him.

Many thanks are also due to the teachers at Tsuta and Ajinadai Nishi Elementary Schools. They not only graciously let Makoto into their inner circle to observe *Lesson Study* practice first-hand, but they welcomed him wholeheartedly. These teachers also spent many tireless hours answering his queries and sharing their stories about lesson study. We thank them for their time, wisdom, and friendship. Without their help, this study never would have been possible.

An invaluable informant and one that Makoto remembers with great fondness is Ms. Reiko Furumoto, who at the time of data collection was the vice-principal at Tsuta Elementary School. She was a caring individual who devoted all her energy and knowledge to helping teachers grow professionally and who cared deeply about students. Unfortunately, Ms. Furumoto passed away this past year when she was still on duty as a principal at Asahara Elementary School. We are greatly saddened that Ms. Furumoto can not celebrate our achievement of publishing this book with us. However, we find comfort in the thought that her commitment to improving education and the professional lives of teachers will be passed on through this book to lesson study practitioners in the United States. We dedicate this book to Ms. Furumoto.

Makoto also thanks his parents for their patience and support since the onset of this project. They have his deepest gratitude for all their sacrifices, hard work, and worry. Without their unwavering belief in his potential, he never would have been able to achieve this milestone. Unfortunately, Makoto's father passed away while this book was still in its final stages of editing. Makoto regrets very much that he wasn't able to show his father a final published copy of this book. He also thanks his wife Miriam, for her endless support. Of all the people mentioned, she is truly the one that made it possible for him to see this project to fruition. Last but not least, he thanks his daughters Maia and Nina. Their precious smiles and laughs have been his encouragement during the long journey of writing this book.

Clea thanks all the residents of 37th street, old and young, who enrich her life and who enthusiastically live with all her "projects."

Introduction

WHY STUDY LESSON STUDY?

During an early afternoon in September 2000 we observed eight Japanese teachers as they sat around a table in their school's staff room planning together a lesson, which was to be the initial lesson in a 12-lesson unit entitled "proportions." In this lesson students would be exploring the idea that variables can covary and would come to see the distinction between linear and nonlinear relationships. Here is a brief excerpt from the 2-hour discussion that these teachers had on that day:

T1: We want students to come up with examples from their daily lives. The issue is, how should we phrase the question so that students can generate varied examples? Mr. Hirano, how did you teach this lesson last year?

T3: I used pictures ... for example I showed a picture of a car on a highway. First the students came up with the notion of time and distance. But when I gave them more time, more diverse ideas came up, such as energy consumption and distance.

T1: So the point was to use a picture to imagine a change in quantity. Okay, any other ideas? First let's just come up with different approaches, let's just exchange ideas.

T4: ... Students have made potato chips at school. The color of each chip is different so we could ask why the colors of these chips are different. The answers could vary form time in the oil, the temperature of the oil, etc. We could discuss how as one of these things changes, the color changes.

T1: So how would you phrase the question: *There are many potato chips, but why are the colors different?*

T6:   … I think it is important to show the real thing, not the picture. It could be putting a bucket under the tap, so that they can see the change in the volume of water.

T8:   But if we bring in objects, students will want to do the experiment themselves. So if we bring objects, I think we should allow students to manipulate them. I would stick to showing the pictures like Mr. Hirano suggested. The point is simply to come up with various examples.

T1:   I find Ms. Sato's idea of potato chips very interesting … However, strictly speaking, burned-ness as represented by color can be quantified, but it is hard. Similarly, we should avoid examples like *the more homework I have, the worse I feel*.

T4:   We also have to be careful that students don't come up with linear relationships only.

On that same afternoon we could have observed many other groups of teachers in Japan having similar conversations about how to plan instruction. These conversations would have taken place in the context of an activity called *lesson study*, which Japanese teachers engage in to improve the quality of their teaching and enrich students' learning experiences. Through lesson study not only do teachers plan lessons together, but they also go on to observe these lessons unfold in actual classrooms and to discuss their observations.

Only a few years ago, lesson study was almost unknown in the United States. This is no longer the case, in great part due to the success of a book entitled *The Teaching Gap: Best Ideas from the World's Teachers for Improving Education in the Classroom* (Stigler & Hiebert, 1999). There, authors James Stigler and James Hiebert describe the essence of lesson study and call for lesson study practice in American schools. Stigler and Hiebert set out "to convince the reader that something like lesson study deserves to be tested seriously in the United States." Judging from the response to the book, the case has been made.[1]

The recognition that U.S. teachers are likely to benefit from an activity that provides them opportunities to work together on their practice and in particular to watch each other teach is not surprising. The question now is how to move forward. We know that Japanese teachers value lesson study highly as a form of professional development—so highly that many of them can not imagine doing without it (Inagaki, Terasaki, & Matsudaira, 1988). Moreover,

---

[1]For a historical account on the growing interest in lesson study in the United States, see Chokshi (2002).

researchers have identified lesson study as being critical to supporting educational change and innovation in Japan (Lewis & Tsuchida, 1997).

However, little has been written about how Japanese lesson study groups function and how they organize their work. For example, how did the group referred to earlier select the lesson it was working on and what guided that decision? Even less is known about the details of what teachers do and discuss as they carry out lesson study. How typical was the conversation reproduced here? What else would a group like this tend to discuss? How is lesson study embedded in teachers' professional lives? What are the structural and contextual elements that support and sustain lesson study practice in Japan? What is it that makes Japanese teachers consider this activity so valuable to them?[2]

This volume sets out to answer these questions by providing a detailed account of the lesson study work conducted by a group of teachers at Tsuta Elementary School, a public school, in Hiroshima, Japan. We describe how the teachers at this school launched, organized, and structured their work, as well as what they discussed, thought about, and struggled with as they jointly worked on lesson study. We also describe how they interfaced with the surrounding educational environment in which they conducted this work, and how they interpreted and thought about their lesson study practice.

Our purpose in writing this book is to offer American educators a rich and grounded understanding of lesson study from which to evaluate what this practice can offer them and from which to shape their own lesson study practice. We hope that this book will also offer insights about the broader issue of what it takes for teachers to learn in and from their practice. Gaining such insights is important given current efforts aimed at encouraging teachers to use their teaching as a site for their own professional learning (Cochran-Smith & Lytle, 1999; Feiman-Nemser, 2001; Lampert & Ball, 1998; Mathematical Science Education Board, 2002; Putnam & Borko, 2000; Schifter, 1998; Seago & Mumme, 2002; Seidel, 1998). It is also our hope that the lesson study work that we describe in this book will vividly illustrate the complexities involved in teaching mathematics—even in the early grades. Indeed, our readers will learn

---

[2]Some of the work written to date in English about lesson study includes: Fernandez, 2002; Fernandez, Cannon, & Chokshi, 2003; Lewis, 2002; Lewis & Tsuchida, 1998; Stigler & Hiebert, 1998; Research for Better Schools, 2002; Yoshida, 1999. Lesson Study Research Group's website at Teachers College, Columbia University (http://www.te.edu/lesson study/) is a good place to find many recent publications related to lesson study. The website also has links to many other lesson study websites such as: Global Education Resources (GER) (http://www.globaledresources.com/), Lesson Study Group at Mills College (http://www.lessonresearch.net/), and Research for Better Schools (http://www.rbs.org/).

about the numerous and difficult dilemmas faced by a group of teachers as they worked together on a first-grade subtraction lesson. We hope that hearing about the struggles of these teachers can serve as a reminder of the respect and support that we owe all of those who tackle the task of teaching our children. Finally, we would like this book to add to the growing number of examples that illustrate how educators in the United States. can find rich ideas in the educational practices of their counterparts abroad. Improving the quality of our schools is too important a prerogative for us to turn our backs, as we have often tended to do, on what education in other countries can teach us, particularly in this age of globalization (Chokshi, 2002).

BOOK OVERVIEW

The Organization of This Book

This book is organized into 15 chapters. In chapter 2 we provide a general description of lesson study practice in Japan. We discuss the basic steps involved in lesson study. We describe how lesson study tends to be organized, structured, and supported in most schools. We give a brief history of the development of this practice and how it came to be so widespread in Japanese elementary schools. In chapter 3 we give background information about Tsuta Elementary School, the setting for the lesson study activities that we describe in this book. We also provide a history of lesson study in the region in which this school is located and we describe the lesson study work Tsuta teachers had been engaged in for several years prior to the activities described in this book. In the next 10 chapters we describe in detail the conversations and activities that the first- and second-grade teachers at Tsuta carried out as they jointly planned, observed, revised, and retaught a first-grade lesson on subtraction with regrouping. We also describe how other teachers at the school supported and took part in key aspects of this work. We explain how the lesson study activities of these first- and second-grade teachers were related to other lesson study work carried out at the school. In particular, we devote an entire chapter to describing a lesson study open house that involved all the teachers at Tsuta. We recount how the teachers got ready for this event, what happened during this open house, and how this work was related to other lesson study work carried out at the school. In the two concluding chapters of this book we describe the mechanisms that schools like Tsuta employ to make the most out of their lesson study experiences, and we discuss what teachers actually gain from these experiences and how.

A Note on Data Sources

This book is based on observations that Makoto Yoshida carried out between October 1993 and March 1994 at Tsuta Elementary School, Hiroshima, Japan, as a part of his doctoral dissertation (Yoshida, 1999a; Yoshida, 1999b). Yoshida sat in on all the lesson study meetings and activities that the first- and second-grade teachers at this school took part in. This yielded 94 hours of observations for us to draw on, 32 of which were videotaped and the rest of which were recorded via detailed field notes.

In addition, throughout this book we refer to interviews that Yoshida regularly conducted with Tsuta teachers and administrators. The more formal of these interviews were audio taped, and in the case of more informal exchanges careful notes were taken. These interviews were carried out in order to answer questions and clarify issues that came up during the observations made at this school. For example, questions were asked about past meetings that were not observed and about the organization of lesson study at the school. Inquiries were made about the meaning of certain technical words used in the meetings or classrooms. Finally teachers were asked to discuss their reactions to certain events observed and their feelings about participating in lesson study.

In order to supplement and put in context our description of lesson study at Tsuta, we plan to draw on two other data sources collected as part of this research effort. First, throughout the book, we quote from 10 background interviews conducted with administrators from schools other than Tsuta, education officials, and a number of Japanese researchers. Second, we will also present results from two separate surveys. The first was a school survey designed for either a principal or vice-principal to complete. In this survey administrators were asked to describe what they saw as the purpose and motivation for supporting lesson study in their buildings. They were also queried about the scope and organization of lesson study in their schools as well as the support and financial assistance made available to them for doing lesson study. Administrators were also asked if they would grant permission for their teachers to receive a separate survey. This teacher survey asked teachers about the frequency and intensity with which they typically engaged in lesson study, why they did this, how they felt about doing it, and whether they encountered any difficulties in organizing and conducting lesson study with their colleagues. The school survey was mailed to all 40 public elementary schools in the western region of Hiroshima, where Tsuta is located. A total of 35 of the 40 administrators who received this survey completed it, and 22 of them granted permission for their teachers to be surveyed. Out of the 232 teacher surveys that were mailed, 129 were returned.

The year these data were collected there were 3 elementary schools out of the 40 schools within the western region of Hiroshima that were doing lesson study in the area of mathematics. Fortunately, two of these three schools, Tsuta and Ajinadai Elementary School, agreed to participate in the study. The third school declined due to opposition from the teachers, who did not feel comfortable having an outsider scrutinizing their work. Of the two schools that gave their consent, only Tsuta was planning to hold a lesson study open house that year, an aspect of lesson study that schools only engage in from time to time. Tsuta was therefore chosen as the main research site in order to be able to study the role that open houses play in the lesson study process. Nevertheless, 17 hours of observations of lesson study work were also carried out at Ajinadai. These observations have also informed the description of lesson study that we provide in this book.

Although, as we discuss later, Tsuta is in most respects a typical Japanese public elementary school, we are well aware that no school can represent a nation accurately. What we describe in this book is therefore not meant to represent modal lesson study practice, assuming there could be such a thing. Rather we offer a description of the lesson study work conducted at Tsuta in order to paint a portrait of what lesson study can be like. It is our hope that this portrait can enrich discussions about how the ideas of lesson study can be profitably used to enhance the education of students in the United States.

2

An Overview of Lesson Study

Lesson study is a direct translation for the Japanese term *jugyokenkyu*, which is composed of two words: *jugyo*, which means lesson, and *kenkyu*, which means study or research. As denoted by this term, lesson study consists of the study or examination of teaching practice. How do Japanese teachers examine their teaching through lesson study? They engage in a well-defined process that involves discussing lessons that they have first planned and observed together. These lessons are called *kenkyujugyo*, which is simply a reversal of the term *jugyokenkyu* and thus literally means study or research lessons, or more specifically lessons that are the object of one's study. Study lessons are "studied" by carrying out the steps described next in an attempt to explore a research goal that the teachers have chosen to work on (e.g., understanding how to encourage students to be autonomous learners).

THE LESSON STUDY PROCESS

Step 1: Collaboratively Planning the Study Lesson

Work on a study lesson begins by teachers coming together to plan the lesson. This planning is of a meticulous and collaborative nature. Teachers share their ideas for how best to design the lesson by drawing on their past experiences, observations of their current students, their teacher's guide, their textbooks, and other resource books. The end product of this first step is a lesson plan that describes in detail the design that the group has settled on for their lesson.

Step 2: Seeing the Study Lesson in Action

The next step is for one of the teachers in the group to teach the lesson to his or her students. This implementation is of a public nature because it involves the other teachers as observers. These observers come to the lesson with the lesson plan in hand, which they use as a tool to guide what they look for in the lesson.[1]

Step 3: Discussing the Study Lesson

The group next comes together to reflect on the lesson now that they have seen it unfold in a real classroom. The teachers share what they observed as they watched the lesson and provide their reactions and suggestions.

Step 4: Revising the Lesson (Optional)

Some groups will stop their work on a study lesson after they have discussed their observations of it, but others will choose to go on to revise and reteach the lesson so that they can continue to learn from it. This revision process leads to the creation of an updated version of the lesson plan that reflects all the changes that the teachers have decide to make to the design of their lesson.

Step 5: Teaching the New Version of the Lesson (Optional)

A second member of the group will next publicly teach the new version of the study lesson to his or her students, while colleagues again come to observe. Sometimes if teachers cannot attend both lessons, they will choose to observe the second implementation, which generally represents the culmination of the group's work for a particular study lesson.

It is very rare to see the same teacher teach the lesson twice to the same class, or even to a different class. One reason for this tendency is that varying the teacher and the students provides the group a broader base of experiences to learn from. It also gives as many teachers as possible a chance to teach in front of others.

It is also rare for a group to choose to revise and reteach the lesson a third time because there is only so much a group can learn from examining a particular lesson. It is generally considered more productive to move on to working on an entirely new lesson than to keep revising the same lesson over and over again with diminishing returns. Also it becomes logistically difficult to keep working on the same lesson as time goes by and children are progressing through the curriculum.

---

[1]Teachers surveyed reported that during the 1993–1994 school year they observed on average six study lessons at their school and four study lessons at other schools. Teachers also reported being observed by other teachers at their school at least once or twice. Moreover, about half of the teachers reported having had the opportunity to be observed by teachers from outside their school.

Step 6: Sharing Reflections About the New Version of the Lesson

The teachers will next come together to discuss their reactions to what they saw transpire when the second version of the study lesson was taught. This conversation again centers on teachers sharing their observations, comments, and suggestions.

It is common during all the lesson study meetings, and in particular when teachers share reflections about a study lesson they have observed, for a group member to be assigned to take detailed minutes. This way the group can have available for future reference a good record of all the ideas that were generated during their work together. As we shall discuss later, such a record is very useful when the teachers later turn to writing a report of their work.

VENUES FOR CONDUCTING LESSON STUDY

Teachers conduct lesson study in many different venues. For example, teachers participating in government or local board of education supported designated school research programs often engage in lesson study as part of their research and professional development. Preservice teachers are also very often involved in lesson study during student teaching. They will prepare a study lesson in collaboration with their university-based mentors and the teacher that they have been assigned to work with in their school site. They will then teach the lesson in this school, and all the teachers in the building, the university mentors, and other student teachers will come observe. Similarly, first-year teachers are generally assigned a mentor with whom they often choose to do a lesson study. The teacher and the mentor will collaboratively plan a study lesson, which the first-year teacher will teach and to which all teachers in the building are invited. As we discuss in detail in a later chapter, groups of teachers from across schools also come together to carry out lesson study either in regional study groups that are systematically organized by the teachers of the district or clubs that are organized voluntarily by teachers with a particular interest.

Perhaps the most popular venue for doing lesson study is within a single school as part of an activity called *konaikenshu*. The term *konaikenshu* is also made up of two Japanese words. The first, *konai*, means "in school" and the second, *kenshu*, means "training." Thus, the term *konaikenshu*, which in essence refers to a form of school-based in-service has been translated as "in-service education within the school" (Nakatome, 1984), "in-house workshops" (Shimahara, 1991), and "in-house study workshops" (Sato, 1992). However, we have chosen to use the Japanese word *konaikenshu* in order to emphasize the uniqueness of this type of training. In our minds, what makes *konaikenshu* unique is that it is a form of in-service professional development that brings together the entire teaching staff of a school to work in a sustained and focused manner on a schoolwide goal that all teachers have agreed is of critical importance to them.

Typically, in order to select a *konaikenshu* goal, teachers will gather to think about the mission statement of their school (see Box 2.1) and what it implies about the qualities that they should aim to foster in students. They will then take stock of their actual accomplishments with students and will try to identify gaps they perceive between their aspirations and the outcomes they are seeing in their students. Once they have found a gap that they all agree is troubling and widespread, they move to selecting a *konaikenshu* goal, which will represent an attempt to narrow this gap. For example, teachers might notice that although they want to help foster children who are curious and have a desire to learn, instead, as students progress through the grades, they are actually becoming less inquisitive. In such an instance the teachers might select a *konaikenshu* goal that focuses on fostering curious and inquisitive children.

As is illustrated by the example just provided, *konaikenshu* goals tend not to target the development of specific academic skills in students. Rather these goals aim at developing in children broader dispositions toward learning, school, peers, and themselves (see Box 2.2). An analysis of words used to describe *konaikenshu* goals conducted by Lewis and Tsuchida (1997) illustrates this feature nicely (see also Lewis, 1995). These researchers found that *autonomy* was the most commonly employed word in these goals. Similarly, a focus on specific academic skills was quite rare when we analyzed the *konaikenshu* goals described by the 35 Hiroshima schools surveyed as part of this investigation.[2]

Although *konaikenshu* goals target broad dispositions, the majority of schools will pursue these goals in the context of studying a particular academic subject area (Kitayama & Yamada, 1992; Nakatome, 1984).[3] For instance, in the example that we provided earlier of setting as a goal to foster curious and inquisitive students, the school in question might choose to focus on developing these dispositions in students as they learn science.

---

[2]Only 5.7% of the schools surveyed mentioned that they had goals related to developing students' academic abilities. The rest of the goals mentioned were related to, for example, fostering students' expressive abilities (*hyogenryoku*); cultivating a group that listens, talks, understands, and helps each other (e.g., *shudanzukuri, gakkyuzukuri,* or *nakamazukuri*); fostering students' autonomy (*shutaisei*); discovering and developing students' individuality (*kosei*); kindling children's desire to learn (*iyoku*); and fostering children's understanding and tolerance for each other's differences (*hitori hitori no chigai*).

[3]The school survey confirmed this tendency to ground lesson study in the examination of a particular academic area of content. Seventy-six percent of schools reported conducting *konaikenshu* with a focus on an academic subject such as Japanese Language, Mathematics, Social Sciences, or Daily Living.

Box 2.1
Japanese Schools' Mission Statements

Every school in Japan has a mission statement, which generally outlines goals for children's academic, moral and physical development. These statements represent the core values that are to guide both the teaching and the management of the school. Here are examples of mission statements for two schools in the western region of Hiroshima, including Tsuta.

Tsuta Elementary School's Mission Statement:

A. Overall Goal:
Fostering students who base their lives on a policy of human respect and who have the following characteristics: a generous spirit, excellent academic ability, healthy mind and body, and an urge to live vigorously.

> An ideal student is one who thinks hard and whose actions are influenced by his or her thinking; who helps and learns from others; and who cares about life and is healthy.

> An ideal school is one that is strict, yet thoughtful; beautiful and enriching; fun and full of life.

B. Specific Goals (to achieve the school's overall goal):
(1) To foster students' desire to learn autonomously and to develop strong academic ability in them.
(2) To promote creativity and the ability to implement it.
(3) To teach students basic living habits, including greeting others cheerfully. To develop a generous spirit in students that includes showing gratitude and a desire to help others.
(4) To develop students who understand and encourage others and who have the ability to recognize and prevent discrimination and contradictions.
(5) To teach students to take care of their own health and pay attention to safety, as well as to care about their lives and that of others.
(6) To encourage students to improve and maintain their own physical strength autonomously.

(continued on next page)

Hatsukaichi Elementary School Mission statement:

1. Fostering knowledge—Students who study hard.
    Students who seek wider knowledge, have the desire to learn autonomously, who understand and learn from others, and who are sensitive to others.
2. Fostering healthy hearts and minds—Students who can help others.
    Students who encourage other students, who can think about other people's points of view and feelings, and who can help others in order to grow together.
3. Developing a healthy body—Students who have strong/healthy bodies.
    Students who have a strong willpower and bodies and who are tenacious in accomplishing their goals.

Box 2.2
Examples of *Konaikenshu* Goals

Here are examples of some of the *konaikenshu* goals that schools in the western region of Hiroshima were working on during the 1993–1994 school year.

Making a circle of friends in order to grow together: focusing on a Japanese language class in order to foster students' expressive ability.

Using a Japanese language class to foster students' ability to wrestle with topics they discover on their own.

Fostering students' lively and autonomous behavior by developing their physical strength and health.

Developing lessons that encourage students to learn from each other.

Developing well-thought-out mathematics lessons that provide students a feeling of satisfaction and enjoyment of mathematical activities, while fostering their ability to have good foresight and logical thinking.

Fostering students who have a generous heart and a strong sense of motivation by providing them with guidance that recognizes their individuality.

In addition, it is typical for a school to maintain the same *konaikenshu* goal for a period of several years (Lewis & Tsuchida, 1997).[4] This prolonged focus is meant to provide enough time for the school to make significant progress in moving closer to attaining its chosen goal (see also Maki, 1982). It is not unusual, however, for a school to focus on different aspects of its goal, or to take different perspectives on this goal, from one year to the next.

Lesson study is by far the most common activity that is carried out as part of *konaikenshu*.[5] In other words, it is often the case that the *konaikenshu* goal chosen by a school is explored through the conduct of lesson study. This provides lesson study with an umbrella goal that is well motivated and carefully selected, and of concern to teachers. Conversely, this combination of *konaikenshu* and lesson study provides a concrete process (i.e., working on study lessons) for thinking about how to bring a school's selected *konaikenshu* goal to life. As one of the teachers interviewed explained:

> We have a school goal. So, I think lesson study gives us opportunities for everybody to think about how the school as a whole should tackle that goal. I think if all the teachers at a school do not think about the school goal and make an effort to reach it, the school will never change.

The Organization of *Konaikenshu*-Based Lesson Study

In order to work effectively, teachers engaged in *konaikenshu*-based lesson study at their school will break into subgroups of four to six members that take responsibility for planning study lessons. In a large enough school these subgroups may bring together teachers who teach the same grade level. In smaller schools, teachers from similar grades might come together to form one of these subgroups (e.g., the first- through third-grade teachers).

In order to maintain a smooth and school-wide conduct of lesson study, many schools in Japan establish a *konaikenshu* promotional committee (*kenshu-sokushin-soshiki* or *kenshu-soshiki*).[6] The role of this committee is to help plan and organize *konaikenshu* and to keep it on track. This committee tends to be composed of a few teachers who are highly committed to doing *konaikenshu* and who play a critical role in helping others maintain interest and enthusiasm for this activity. In most cases these committees do not include administrators in order to keep the work teacher led and teacher run. However, generally both the principal and vice-principal also help support

---

[4]The schools surveyed reported spending an average of 3.96 years on their *konaikenshu* goals.

[5]All schools surveyed reported that they conducted lesson study during *konaikenshu*.

[6]All the schools surveyed reported having such a committee in place.

konaikenshu, which is recognized as an important part of school management (e.g., Maki, 1982; Nakatome, 1984).

Schools also often solicit the help of an outside advisor to help them with their lesson study. All the schools surveyed reported asking an outside advisor to help them with their lesson study work. The advisor does not attend all meetings but might visit on key days and in particular on days when study lessons are taught. Outside advisors can sometimes be experienced teachers who are on leave from teaching for a year and who are hired by the regional education office to provide staff development to schools. The outside advisor can also be a university-based expert. However, this advisor is most often an instructional superintendent. Instructional superintendents are appointed by prefectures or prefectural regional offices and generally are assigned to cover schools in one of the regions within the prefecture.[7] In most cases they specialize in a particular content area (e.g., mathematics or Japanese language) and their job is to regularly visit schools, where they observe lessons, talk to teachers and principals, and deliver lectures. They do this as a way of providing ongoing professional development and advice to schools. Instructional superintendents visit their assigned schools regardless of whether or not these are doing *konaikenshu* in the superintendent's content area of specialty. However, when a school chooses to conduct *konaikenshu*-based lesson study that focuses on the content area that the superintendent specializes in, this provides the instructional superintendent a rich context for working with the school.[8]

It is also not unusual for schools to organize their *konaikenshu* work around planning a lesson study open house (*kokai jugyo* or *kokai kenkyujugyo*).[9] This involves inviting teachers and other educators from neighboring schools to come see and discuss a set of study lessons and to present to them the *konaikenshu* work that the school has been pursuing. Generally, this is done after a school has been working on a *konaikenshu* goal for a while so that the school can have well-developed ideas to share and is-

---

[7]Japanese elementary and middle schools (i.e., schools that provide compulsory education) are divided among 47 administrative regions called prefectures. Prefectures in turn are divided into regions, each with its own regional education office. All prefectures function under the umbrella of a national Ministry of Education (*Monbusho*).

[8]All the schools surveyed reported inviting at least one outside advisor to help with their *konaikenshu*. Eighty percent of these schools invited an instructional superintendent, 31% invited a university professor, 14% invited an experienced teacher, 11% invited a retired principal, and 3% invited a subject specialist from the ministry of education.

[9]Eighty percent of the schools surveyed reported conducting an open house, although at varying scales. Some schools invited a handful of guests and others hosted a large event to which many teachers and administrators from numerous schools were invited.

sues to discuss with its guests. Given the purpose of these open houses, it is not surprising that these events are sometimes referred to as "Learning Research Presentation Meeting" (*gakushu kenkyu happyokai*).

Schools often produce, at the end of each year, a written report about their *konaikenshu* work. These reports, which are called "Summary of the Study" or "Research Bulletins" (*Kenkyukiyo no Matome*),[10] can vary widely in format. However, their focus is always on providing a description of the work carried out at the school and teachers' reflections about the key lessons learned from this work. Research bulletins typically assemble the lesson plans for all the study lessons taught at the school during the course of the year and summarize the ideas and insights that working on these lessons provided the teachers. On years when schools hold an open house, or when they work on a goal for the last time before moving on to a new area of focus, more detailed and extensive summative research bulletins are often produced.

It should be noted that all the work described above (except teaching the study lessons) is generally done after school. Children in Japan finish school between 2:40 and 3:45 p.m., depending on their age and the day of the week. However, teachers are hired to work until 5 p.m. and are expected to remain in the building. It is during these afternoon hours that most *konaikenshu* meetings are conducted, although these meetings often also spill into after-hours.

A BRIEF HISTORY OF LESSON STUDY

The origins of lesson study can be traced back to the early 1900s (Nakatome, 1984). Although *konaikenshu* is a newer practice, dating back only to the beginning of the 1960s, the strategy of combining *konaikenshu* and lesson study was already well established by the middle of the 1960s. A decade later the Japanese government, seeing the value of *konaikenshu*, began to encourage schools to engage in this practice, which at the time was solely a grassroots activity. During this period the Japanese government created small pockets of financial assistance and other incentives for schools to conduct *konaikenshu*, all of which still exist to this day.[11] It is estimated that today the vast majority of elementary schools and many

---

[10]Seventy-seven percent of the schools surveyed reported producing a research bulletin at the end of the 1993–1994 academic year.

[11]Twenty-three of the 35 schools surveyed reported receiving some kind of financial support for their *konaikenshu* activities. Of these 23 schools, one received support from the National Ministry of Education and the others received support from the regional or prefectural boards of education. The amount of assistance varied from as little as about $70 (10,000 yen) to as much as $3,600 (500,000 yen) per school year. On average schools received about $1,000 (140,000 yen).

middle schools conduct *konaikenshu* (Nakatome, 1984).[12] In contrast, very few Japanese high schools carry out this activity today or have ever engaged in it in the past.[13]

Despite the Japanese government's clear interest and support for *konaikenshu*, this activity has always remained voluntary. In principle, schools do *konaikenshu* because they choose to. In reality, however, many schools see *konaikenshu* as quasi-required (Kitayama & Yamada, 1992). A principal from an elementary school explained this situation as follows:

> For whatever reason, almost all schools around here are conducting *konaikenshu*. As you said, none of the laws say that we [schools] must conduct *konaikenshu*, but it is highly recommended. Also, because almost all schools are doing *konaikenshu*, we feel we have to do so as well.

Another principal interviewed explicitly linked the popularity that *konaikenshu* enjoys today with the incentives provided by the government:

> There are some incentives to do *konaikenshu* these days. There is some financial support available for schools to run *konaikenshu* from the local Board of Education. Although the Board of Education does not provide money to teachers [as additional salary] the money can be used to invite outside people, for example, curriculum or subject specialists, university professors, et cetera; as well as sending some teachers to other schools to observe what other schools are doing; and making a study bulletin at the end of the school year.

A second equally important reason for the popularity of lesson study might have to do with the fact that Japanese teachers find participation in *konaikenshu*, and in particular lesson study, very helpful to them (Inagaki, Terasaki, & Matsudaira, 1988). Although lesson study work is time-consuming, it allows, among other things, for teachers to have a clear idea of their strengths and weaknesses, and for them to gain vital information that can be used to improve their teaching skills (Nakamura, Takahashi, & Kurosawa, 1989). In the words of three teachers and one principal:

---

[12]All the schools surveyed reported that during the 1993–1994 academic year they were involved in this type of work. Furthermore, both the director of the National Institute for Educational Research in Japan and Dr. Manabu Sato of the Graduate School of Education at the University of Tokyo confirmed during interviews (6/24/94 and 3/26/97) that most elementary teachers in Japan engage in lesson study.

[13]The absence of this activity at the high school level has to do with the fact that Japanese high school teachers focus a great deal of their attention on preparing students for college entrance exams. Moreover, high school teachers attend to their students' needs by taking on the role of guidance or career counselors. In principle, however, there is nothing about lesson study that makes it less suitable for teachers at the high school level.

Developing a great lesson is an ideal thing but I think the best thing about the lesson study experience is that it gives you a chance to reflect about and re-think your own teaching.

I think even if it is a short period of time, having a place where everybody gets together and discusses instruction very seriously is an extremely valu-able experience.

I also think that the experience [doing lesson study] gives us a chance to build good relationships among teachers. I think strong relationships (*kizuna*) can be built when teachers get together and very seriously think about what we do, teaching ... Anyway, lesson study can help teachers de-velop strong relationships, something I think is really important for all teachers.

Also, this on-the-job problem-solving process [lesson study] requires teach-ers' seriousness, intensity, and responsibility as professionals, because ev-erything you try to do at school always influences the students. The work environment, this feeling of seriousness is the advantage of doing profes-sional development in the school.

All this should not be taken to mean that the lesson study work of all schools is of equal quality. As would be expected, the quality of *konaikenshu* activities varies widely depending on the caliber of the school leadership, the quality to the teachers in the building, the bonds that exist between them, and their inherent interest in *konaikenshu*. One principal explained:

Of course we think it is important to conduct *konaikenshu* but I can't say all schools are doing very well if I think about the quality of the training.... How you make the *konaikenshu* more meaningful depends on the condition of leadership and togetherness of teachers at the school.

The bulk of this book is devoted to describing in detail how teachers at Tsuta Elementary School, in Hiroshima, Japan, conducted *konaikenshu-*-based lesson study. Tsuta represents both a typical Japanese public ele-mentary school and one whose *konaikenshu* was carried out with serious-ness and commitment. As such, Tsuta provides a window into what lesson study can look like without taking us to a unique setting. We now invite the reader to take a look through this window with us.

3

Lesson Study
at Tsuta Elementary School

In this chapter we set the stage for our description of *konaikenshu*-based lesson study at Tsuta. We begin with a brief history of *konaikenshu* in the region where this school is located. We provide basic background information about the school itself. We next summarize the *konaikenshu* work in progress at this school when the observations, on which we will base our subsequent descriptions, began in October 1993. We conclude with an overview of the *konaikenshu* work carried out at Tsuta between the start of these observations and their conclusion in March of 1994.

KONAIKENSHU IN THE WESTERN REGION
OF HIROSHIMA

There are no historical documents that trace the development of *konaikenshu* in the western region of the Hiroshima Prefecture, where Tsuta is located. However, an interview with Mr. Harada, a well-respected and long-standing principal in the region, provided information on this topic. Mr. Harada recalled that in the early 1960s a group of teachers from Itsukaichi Elementary School who were interested in mathematics education decided to start meeting regularly and eventually began to do lesson study under Harada's leadership, a teacher at that time. Their goal was to develop mathematics lessons that fostered mathematical thinking (*sugakuteki kangaekata*) among students. Gradually as other teachers at the school showed interest in this work it expanded into a whole-school *konaikenshu*. Harada could not recall exactly when this expansion was completed, but he believed that it was two or three years before 1966, when he was relocated to another school. According to him, between 1965 and 1970 many schools in the region started to conduct *konaikenshu*. During this period the work at Itsukaichi served as a model for these schools, which started to send their teachers to Itsukaichi to observe mathematics study lessons taught there. Another factor that helped spread the work done through *konaikenshu* at Itsukaichi was the population

18

growth that was taking place at the time in this region. Many new schools had to be built and teachers from Itsukaichi were gradually transferred to some of these schools, bringing with them a tradition of *konaikenshu* that slowly took root where they went. It is interesting to note that when the data described in this book were collected in 1993, many of the principals and vice-principals in the western region of Hiroshima had been teachers at Itsukaichi in the 1960s.

ABOUT TSUTA ELEMENTARY SCHOOL

Tsuta is located in the suburbs of Hiroshima City, which is the prefecture's biggest city, with a population of over one million people in 1993 (see Fig. 3.1). Hiroshima Prefecture is divided into four administrative regions, of which the Western Region is one. This region includes two small cities, and in 1993 it had a population of about 170,000 and was served by a total of 40 elementary schools, which enrolled 13,523 students and employed 626 teachers (Hiroshima Education Office, 1993).

Tsuta is located in the town of Saeki, about a 1-hour bus ride northwest of the city of Hiroshima (see Fig. 3.2). The town of Saeki is in a mountainous region and as a result, many students at Tsuta have parents who work in small-scale farming and forestry. In addition, because this town is not far from Hiroshima, many Tsuta parents commute to this city to work. The mountain areas neighboring the town of Saeki have suffered from depopulation, which has resulted in the integration over the past 20 years of many small schools into Tsuta. As a result, some students are required to travel long distances to come to Tsuta every day. Unlike American schools, Japanese schools do not provide school buses, so parents have to drive their children or students have to take public transportation.

During the 1993–1994 academic year, Tsuta had 261 students, 21 staff members, and 11 classrooms. The school had six grade levels with two classes at each level, except for the third grade, which had only one class. The average class size was 24 students, which at the time was less than the Japanese national average of 29 (Hiroshima Education Office, 1993). Each class had its own homeroom and a teacher in charge of the class. The 21 staff members included 1 principal, 1 vice-principal, 11 assigned homeroom teachers (for 11 classes), 1 music teacher, 1 special education teacher, and 6 other supporting staff (e.g., general affairs staff and school lunch preparation staff).

Despite being small in size by Japanese standards for public schools, Tsuta had a gymnasium, a 25-meter swimming pool, a playground the size of a soccer field, a music classroom, a science laboratory, a computer room, and a staff room. These facilities are in fact quite common in Japanese elementary schools. Indeed, except for its relative small size, Tsuta was in every respect a typical Japanese public school served by typical teachers.

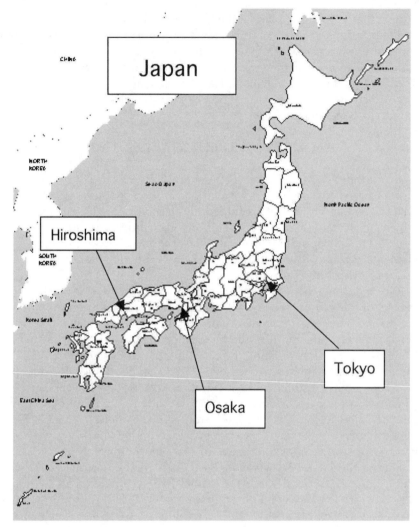

FIG. 3.1   Map of Japan.

LESSON STUDY AT TSUTA ELEMENTARY SCHOOL
BETWEEN 1991 AND 1994

The lesson study work observed at Tsuta took place during the third year of a cycle of *konaikenshu* that was started during the 1991 academic year. Next we provide a brief account of each of these 3 years of *konaikenhsu* (see Fig. 3.3). This account is based on interviews with Tsuta teachers and ad-

FIG. 3.2   Tsuta Elementary School; Hiroshima, Japan.

ministrators, as well as a review of a number of records about *konaikenshu* available at the school.

Summary of 1991–1992 *Konaikenshu* Activities at Tsuta

The 1991–1992 academic year represented a transition year for *konaikenshu* at Tsuta. The school was in the midst of working on mathematics study lessons, which targeted the goal of promoting students' ability to think autonomously, invent, and learn from each other. In fact, during the course of that year eight study lessons were developed with this goal in mind.

However, there was a growing sense of dissatisfaction with this work, and early in this academic year teachers began to voice doubts about the quality of *konaikenshu* and associated lesson study activities at Tsuta. Many complained about lack of seriousness and poor communication among those involved. Some teachers were actually worried that these problems might ultimately affect student learning.

Eventually, during a schoolwide faculty meeting, a small group of teachers and the vice-principal proposed that they continue to focus on mathematics but that they present the results of their work at a lesson study open house. These teachers felt that having an open house would make participants more serious about lesson study. Some of the teachers present at this staff meeting opposed this proposal, not because they did not see the value in lesson study or in a continued focus on mathematics, but rather because they were concerned about the time commitment that adopting this proposal would imply. One of the teachers at Tsuta remembered this meeting

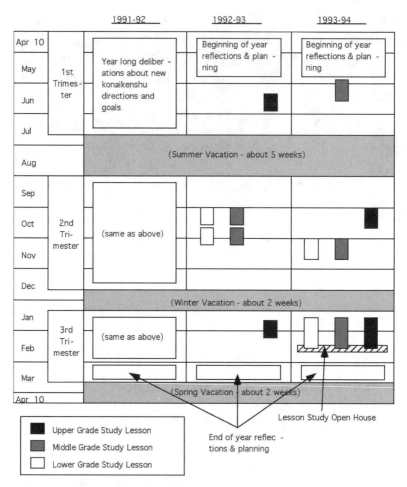

FIG. 3.3   Tsuta Elementary School's 1991–1994 *konaikenshu* activities.
Note: During the 1991–1992 academic year, while the teachers deliberated about new directions for their work they also conducted eight study lessons that are not included in this figure because we consider these lessons to be part f a previous *konaikenshu* cycle.

well and explained that he was one of those opposed to the idea of presenting the results outside of the school. He said that a school he had previously taught in had had a lesson study open house at the end of its *konaikenshu*. He remembered that many teachers stayed at the school until 8 or 9 o'clock nearly every night during the 2 months prior to this event. Another teacher described the staff meeting as having been a very heated one where neither side wanted to compromise. She said that in fact several long schoolwide faculty meetings were devoted to discussing the issue of lesson study before eventually all the teachers at Tsuta agreed to continue working on mathematics and to carry out an open house as well.

This consensus was reached in part because several conditions were set by the teachers in order to keep their work from becoming too intense. First, it was agreed that teachers would not force or pressure others to stay at lesson study meetings after 6 o'clock, regardless of the amount of unfinished work. Teachers would just have to do their best to work cooperatively and efficiently in the limited amount time available to them. The teachers also decided to invite a mathematics instructional superintendent from the regional office of education, Mr. Saeki, to play the role of outside advisor to the school. They also committed to keeping to a same *konaikenshu* goal for the next 4 years and to holding an open house at the end of the 1993–1994 academic year, their third year of this work.

The deliberations required to reach the consensus and ground rules described above took place during the first two thirds of the 1991–1992 academic year. The remainder of that year was devoted to thinking about the school's new *konaikenshu* goal. The teachers began by investigating the kinds of mathematics learners that were developing at their school. This exploration took on two forms. They evaluated results of various tests given to students during the course of that year (e.g., teacher-designed end of unit and end of trimester tests, as well as end-of-year mathematics tests that were available on the market from several educational publishers).[1] Second, they conducted careful observations in each other's classrooms as students worked on mathematics tasks.

The results of their evaluations showed that students in the lower grades (first and second) were weak in reading comprehension of word problems, knowledge stability of already learned material, ability to use previous knowledge, and desire to learn. Students in the middle grades (third and fourth) were weak in reading comprehension of word problems, knowledge of the concept of numbers, knowledge about geometrical figures, ability to think mathematically, and conversion of units. Students in the higher grades (fifth and sixth) were weak in comprehension skills for diagrams, charts, and graphs. They too were found to be lacking in their reading com-

---

[1]These tests usually included story problems that required students to show their work (e.g., writing out expressions and explaining how to find solutions). The teachers at Tsuta explained that multiple-choice question formats were very rare in these tests. Moreover, according to Tsuta's vice-principal, children at this school were not required to take any standardized test. This should come as no surprise because standardized tests are not at all common in elementary schools in Japan.

prehension for word problems. In addition, they had trouble constructing expressions, diagrams, and/or charts from the sentences in story problems.

The Tsuta teachers concluded that students at all grade levels were having trouble comprehending word or story problems and that this should be taken into account in selecting a goal to work on. This weakness seemed all the more important given that 1992 revisions to the national curriculum (*Gakushu Shido Yoryo*)[2] identified skills in solving word problems as an important area to target in the teaching of mathematics at all grade levels.

Summary of 1992–1993 Lesson Study Activities at Tsuta

The Tsuta teachers chose their actual *konaikenshu* goal at the beginning of the 1992–1993 academic year.[3] They used their desire to try to come closer to the aspirations they had for their students as word problem solvers and the mission statement of their school (see Box 2.1) to guide their goal selection. Ultimately they settled on the following *konaikenshu* goal: "Focusing on problem-solving-based learning (*Mondai-kaiketsu-teki-gakushu*) in mathematics in order to promote students' ability to think autonomously, invent, and learn from each other" (see Box. 3.1). The reader will note that this was an expanded version of the goal that the teachers had previously been working on and which it turned out they did not want to totally abandon. Based on their past year's observations of students, the teachers also decided that they would focus on study lessons from units that dealt directly with the topic of "numbers and calculations" and that they would focus their attention on children's thought processes. More specifically, they wanted to examine the process students used to solve word problems on there own and in particular when manipulatives were used to aid them.

The rest of that year the teachers worked on study lessons. They broke into three subgroups in order to do this—a first- and second-grade group (the lower group), a third- and fourth-grade group (the middle group), and a fifth- and sixth-grade group (the upper group). There were four or five teachers in each of these groups, two from each grade level (except for third grade) plus one special subject teacher (e.g., music teacher). The lower group worked on a total of two study lessons, one from September 29 to October 13 and the other from October 23 to November 4. During

---

[2]For more information please refer to Shogakko Gakushu Shido Yoryo [Elementary School Course of Study], published by Monbusho in 1989, and Shogakko Shidosho—Sansu-hen [Elementary School Instructional Manual—Mathematics Edition], published by Monbusho in 1989 (Monbusho, 1989a, 1989b).

[3]The Japanese school year is divided in to three trimesters. There is a 40-day summer vacation between the first and the second trimester, about 2 weeks of winter vacation between the second and the third trimester, and about a week of spring vacation between the end of the school year and the beginning of the next school year.

Box 3.1
History of Problem-Solving-Based Learning in Japan

The expression problem-solving-based learning (*mondaikaiketsu-teki-gakushu*) used at Tsuta Elementary School originates from the concept problem-solving learning (*mondaikaiketsu gakushu*), which became popular in Japan after World War II as part of the New Education Movement.

The New Education Movement began in Japan during the Taisho period (1912–1926) and is sometimes referred to as the Taisho New Education Movement (*Taisho Shin-Kyoiku Undo*). This movement, which focused on the concept of *child-centered education*, had many critics and eventually lost most of its supporters as fascism emerged in Japan during the 1930s and 1940s. Its critics asserted that "the movement is neglecting the importance of transmitting cultural heritage and assets in an organized fashion," and "the movement does not correspond to the society's need."

The New Education Movement was rekindled in Japan after World War II when the First United States Education Mission (*Dai-ichi-ji Beikoku Kyoiku Shisetsudan*) came to Japan. During this second wave of the New Education Movement, concepts such as unit learning (*tangen gakushu*), problem-solving learning (*mondai-kaiketsu gakushu*), and the project method were introduced to Japan.

Problem-solving learning, which was one of the core concepts of this movement, has its roots in John Dewey's reflective thinking. Problem-solving learning appealed to Japanese educators because it emphasized the importance of knowledge and practice and promoted students' active learning through solving problems encountered in everyday life.

However, during the postwar era when this concept of problem-solving learning was being integrated, students' national achievement scores showed a decline. As a result, problem-solving learning was criticized. People said "it does not fit into learning sciences," and "it makes it difficult to establish a systematic curriculum." Nevertheless, efforts to adapt this concept quietly survived in Japan, particularly in mathematics education.

As it turned out the NCTM [National Council of Teachers of Mathematics] standards, published in the United States in 1986, spurred Japanese mathematics teachers and educators to vigorously reexamine problem solving. This eventually led to national recommendations in the early 1990s about the need to improve children's

(continued on next page)

ability to think deeply about mathematics problems. The revised course of study published at the time stated that in order to focus on improving problem solving processes, it was necessary to prepare activities that matched children's developmental stages and which included the use of manipulatives [to facilitate learning] (*sosa*).

The new textbooks introduced in 1992 followed suit, emphasizing the importance of fostering problem-solving skills among students. For example, the *Elementary School Arithmetic Teacher's Instructional Manual* (1992) discusses in its introduction the importance of problem-solving skills and devotes a whole chapter to this topic. Although this chapter provides a lot of information, teachers are explicitly encouraged to conduct actual experimentation and research on this topic through, among other things *kounaikenshuu*.

This is exactly what the Tsuta teachers were doing through their study of what they referred to as *mondaikaiketsu-teki-gakushu*. It is interesting to note that they used a slight variation of the term problem-solving learning by adding the middle term *teki*, which literally means "like" and which we have translated using the word English word "based." The Tsuta teachers explained this slight variation in language as a way for them to personalize the term in order to emphasize that they were trying to develop their own understanding of this concept through the experimentation in their own classrooms and with the population of students that they served.

identical time periods the middle group also worked on two study lessons. The upper group worked on one study lesson between June 1 and June 23 and another one between January 21 and February 3. This amounted to a total of 12 public teachings because each of these study lessons was taught in both an original and a revised version. During that year, Mr. Saeki, the outside advisor, visited the school during four separate occasions. All of these visits were scheduled on days when study lesson were taught and discussed.

Before any of the work just described actually began, all the teachers first carefully planned when each subgroup would be working on each study lesson, when these lessons would be taught, who would be responsible for doing the teaching, and when Mr. Saeki would be invited.

The Tsuta *konaikenshu* promotional committee played a key role in this planning. This committee had four members: a lower, middle, and upper teacher and the school's head teacher.[4] This group met twice a month in order to guarantee the smooth management of *konaikenshu* and also kept track of time spent on lesson study in order to make sure that things did not get out of hand. Moreover, this committee, with the help of the vice-principal, spent a lot of time making sure that the *konaikenshu* goal satisfied all the teachers' interests. In particular, they made sure that this goal was based on the everyday realities of the school and was clear to all the teachers. The vice-principal explained that if the teachers' everyday issues and *konaikenshu* activities diverged, the teachers would most likely lose motivation in this work.

Summary of 1993–1994 Lesson Study at Tsuta

At the end of the previous academic year the teachers at Tsuta had gotten together to reflect about what they had accomplished through *konaikenshu*. The first 2 months of the 1993–1994 academic year were devoted to continuing these reflections as well as to planning. This planning included, as it had in the previous year, carefully setting the lesson study schedule, but it was more involved because that year the school was to host an open house.

After reflecting about their past year's lesson study work, the teachers decided to focus their *konaikenshu* goal on fostering students' ability to share and evaluate solution strategies during a part of the lesson that they referred to as *neriage*. *Neriage* is a term created by Japanese teachers and made up of two words—*neru* and *ageru*. The word *neru* in this case means to polish, to refine, or to elaborate. And the word *ageru* means to finish, complete, or be through with. So the word *neriage* means to polish or refine to completion (see also Appendix A). It is used by Japanese teachers to describe the part of the lesson where students present and discuss their ideas for solving a problem they were first asked to struggled with during a preceding period of seatwork (*jirikikaiketsu*). The purpose of *neriage* is for students to ultimately identify and understand both what are correct and optimal solution strategies to a problem. In other words, *neriage* is a whole-class discussion aimed at building, based on the collective ideas introduced by the students, consensus about optimal solutions. This process is critical in Japanese lessons because these lessons center on students working on rich problems, which they then discuss as a whole class with the teacher playing the role of facilitator.

---

[4]In the Hiroshima region head teachers are senior teachers who help oversee the academic affairs of the school and in particular its proper implementation of the curriculum. During the 1993–1994 school year a sixth-grade teacher, Mr. Mizuno, filled this function.

A focus on *neriage* was chosen for lesson study because after conducting *konaikenshu* during 1992–1993, the teachers realized that their students did not have good listening, presentation and discussion skills. In particular, they had trouble understanding solutions presented by others and lacked the skills needed to differentiate between better and less sound solution strategies presented during the course of lessons.

After this focusing of the school's *konaikenshu* goal, Mr. Saeki, was invited to a schoolwide meeting at Tsuta on June 3, 1993. Mr. Saeki lectured the teachers on the importance of incorporating *konaikenshu* into school management. He also gave a presentation entitled "Theory and Training on the New Outlook of Academic Ability (*Atarashii Gakuryokukan*) and Problem-Solving-Based Learning" because he was aware of the *konaikenshu* goal the teachers at Tsuta were pursuing. The work that the teachers did from that point onward tried to incorporate the suggestions and ideas provided by Mr. Saeki. Mr. Saeki returned to the school on five separate occasions during the course of that school year. During the first three of these visits he observed at least one study lesson and took part in the discussion that followed. His fourth visit to the school was for the open house, an event that Mr. Saeki not only attended in full but also at which he gave a speech. The last time Mr. Saeki came to the school that year was for a final meeting held by the teachers in order to reflect about their *konaikenshu* experience.

During this year the teachers worked on 7 study lessons, which were all implemented twice, resulting in 14 lessons taught at the school for other teachers to observe. The lower group was responsible for three of these study lessons. The upper and middle groups each worked on two study lessons, respectively. The first study lesson conducted that year was one planned by the lower group between June 3 and June 17, 1993. The next study lesson was one that the upper group worked on between October 1 and October 21—the day that the observations reported in this book were initiated. Between October 25 and November 18, the lower group worked on a study lesson, which is the one that we plan to describe in detail. During this same time period the middle group also prepared a study lesson. Finally, between January 3 and February 17, all three groups worked on their last study lessons for the year. The final versions of all three of these lessons were taught and discussed at the lesson study open house that Tsuta held on February 17.

Illustrating the Lesson Study Through the Work of 5 Tsuta Teachers

This chapter is the first of the eight chapters we devote to describing in detail the work that the lower grade teachers carried out for their October–November 1993 study lesson. In this chapter, we introduce the teachers in the lower group, the lesson that they chose to work on, and how they organized and structured their work on this lesson. In the chapters that follow we recount the major conversations and key activities that these teachers engaged in as they planned, observed, discussed, revised, and retaught this lesson. We realize that many of the specifics of our portrayal pertain only to the lesson in question. However, as we discuss in the two concluding chapters of this book, the types of conversations and activities that the lower grade teachers engaged in are very typical of lesson study. We focus on this particular group and their study lesson merely to provide a concrete illustration.

THE LOWER GRADE PARTICIPANTS

The following four teachers were members of the lower grade group:

Ms. Tsukuda:	First-grade teacher, 11 years teaching experience, second year at Tsuta. Had a strong interest in the teaching of elementary mathematics.
Ms. Nishi:	First-grade teacher, first year of teaching, first year at Tsuta. Had a strong interest in the teaching of physical education.
Ms. Chijiiwa:	Second-grade teacher, 21 years teaching experience, first year at Tsuta. One of the more experienced teachers at the school
Ms. Maejima:	Second-grade teacher, 5 years teaching experience, second year at Tsuta. She had a strong interest in

konaikenshu because she wanted to improve her teaching skills. She was one of the teachers who had pushed for having an open house.

Ms. Furumoto, the vice-principal of the school, was the fifth member of this group.[1] That year was her first at Tsuta. She had 24 years of teaching experience and had a long-standing interest in the teaching of mathematics. Despite her seniority, Ms. Furumoto behaved as an equal member of the lower group. When interviewed about this, she explained that her role, like that of the principal, was to guide, support, and motivate all teachers to participate in *konaikenshu*. However, she warned that administrators like her needed to be careful not to intervene in the teachers' activities. According to her, it was critical for teachers to feel total autonomy in their lesson study work without having any sense of being controlled from above.

In addition to being a member of this lower grade group, the vice-principal served as a liaison to the school's outside advisor, Mr. Saeki. She not only arranged meetings between Mr. Saeki and the principal of the school for them to talk about *konaikenshu* issues, but she herself also regularly spoke with Mr. Saeki on the phone. This allowed Mr. Saeki to stay informed on how *konaikenshu* was progressing, what the teachers had discussed in their meetings, and what their concerns were. Without such communication it would have been hard for Mr. Saeki to give proper advice to the teachers at Tsuta when he visited with them.

THE ORGANIZATION OF THE LOWER GROUP'S WORK

The members of the lower group had decided at the beginning of the school year that they would work on a first-grade lesson for their October–November cycle of lesson study. However, they selected the actual lesson that they would work on during the break at the end of the first

---

[1]The principal, in contrast, was not a member of any particular group but came to observe all the study lessons taught at his school and attended all the facultywide meetings devoted to *konaikenshu*. He also tried to spend as much time as possible participating in grade level meetings. In addition he occasionally met with Mr. Saeki to consult with him about the *konaikneshu* work that his school was doing. His other important responsibility related to *konaikneshu* was to secure funding for this activity.

trimester. These teachers decided to study the first lesson from a 12-lesson unit on subtraction. The lesson in question was meant to introduce students to the concept of subtraction with regrouping (*kurisagari*).

The lower grade teachers generally got together to plan a study lesson on Mondays from 4 to 5 p.m., a time that had been set aside by the school for *konaikenshu*. These Monday meetings were on occasion used to bring together the entire teaching staff of the school to discuss lesson study, but more often the various grade level groups used this time to meet separately. Each grade level group also had an hour reserved for lesson study meetings on three out of five Friday afternoons (from 4 to 5 p.m.). In addition, one of these five Friday afternoons was left open for optional meetings, which if needed could focus on lesson study. Finally, on two out of every five Thursdays, 3-hour schoolwide faculty meetings were scheduled. Although these meetings were devoted to discussing various school-related issues, whenever necessary *konaikenshu* would be included as part of the agenda for these meetings.

In addition to the officially scheduled meetings, it was not uncommon for extra time to be tacked on to the end of other school days to work on *konaikenshu*. However, as we have already discussed, teachers at Tsuta Elementary School had agreed to stop any *konaikenshu*-related meetings by 6:00 p.m. in order to avoid becoming overburdened by this activity. The lower grade teachers generally stuck to this rule.

These teachers went through the basic steps of planning, teaching, discussing, revising, and reteaching that are generally carried out when a group works on a study lesson (see Fig. 4.1).

They began planning their subtraction lesson on October 25 and tried it out for the first time on November 15. They then discussed and revised this lesson during the 3-day period that preceded its second implementation on November 18. A 2-hour debriefing meeting followed this second teaching.

In the next three chapters we describe the planning and preparation that the teachers engaged in to create a first version of their study lesson. In chapter 8, we describe what happened when this lesson was actually taught to students. In chapter 9 we describe the teachers' reactions to the lesson. In chapter 10 we go over the modifications the teachers chose to make to this lesson and we describe the new lesson plan that they drew up. In chapter 11, we describe what happened when a second group member taught the revised study lesson. Finally, in chapter 12, we describe the conversations the teachers had about this second version of the lesson.

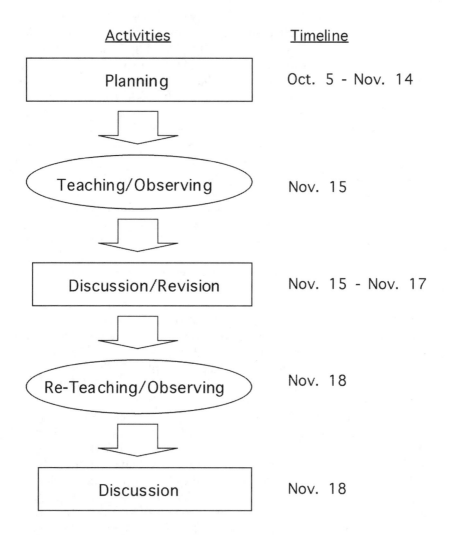

Activities   Timeline

Planning   Oct. 5 - Nov. 14

Teaching/Observing   Nov. 15

Discussion/Revision   Nov. 15 - Nov. 17

Re-Teaching/Observing   Nov. 18

Discussion   Nov. 18

FIG. 4.1 Schedule of activities carried out for the lower grade subtraction study lesson.

Drawing Up a Preliminary Lesson Plan

Planning and preparing to teach a first version of the lower grade subtraction study lesson was carried out in several steps (see Fig. 5.1).

First, between October 25 and October 30, Ms. Nishi and Ms. Tsukuda, the two teachers who would be teaching the first and second versions of this lesson, drew up a preliminary lesson plan to present to the rest of their group. The group then got together on November 1 and then again on November 5 to discuss the plan and suggest changes or refinements to it. The group also received feedback from others at the school during 30 minutes of an all-staff meeting held on November 4. This feedback was elicited by giving everyone, in advance of the meeting, a copy of the preliminary plan that the two first-grade teachers had drafted.

There were no other formal group meetings between November 5 and November 15, the day that Ms. Nishi taught this lesson. However, during

Planning Activities	10/25-30	Two first grade teachers developed a preliminary lesson plan.
	11/1	Lower grade teachers discussed the proposed lesson plan. (2 hours)
	11/4	Lower grade teachers presented their lesson plan at the all staff meeting and received feedback. (0.5 hours)
	11/5	Lower grade teachers discussed the lesson. (1 hour)
	11/5-14	Two first grade teachers (with some help from the other lower grade teachers) finalized the lesson plan, created lesson materials, and prepared to teach the lesson.

FIG. 5.1   Working on the lower grade subtraction lesson: Planning phase.

this time period there were many informal discussions about the impending study lesson. Teachers in Japan all have desks, teaching materials, and supplies in a common staff room (*shokuinshitsu* or *kyoinshitsu*) where they spend most of their time when they are not teaching (i.e., planning lessons, correcting homework, holding meetings, relaxing, and socializing). Some have argued that these staff rooms facilitate an ongoing exchange of ideas among teachers (Stevenson & Stigler, 1992), and this was certainly the case for the lower grade teachers with respect to lesson study. On the cold November days preceding Ms. Nishi's lesson, they often stood around the gas heater in the middle of the staff room sipping tea and discussing their ideas for this lesson. They talked about issues they felt were still unresolved and the materials they needed to prepare to implement this lesson. They also discussed the nervousness of Ms. Nishi, a first-year teacher. Although they were preoccupied about the upcoming lesson implementation, they joked around and laughed; it seemed as if they were truly having a good time.

By November 14, Ms. Nishi and Ms. Tsukuda had revised their lesson plan so that it would reflect both the formal and informal discussions that had taken place at the school about their lesson during the preceding 2 weeks. Once this next version of the plan was created, necessary preparations were made for Ms. Nishi to teach this study lesson to her students while other teachers at the school observed.

We devote three chapters to describing the planning process outlined above. In this chapter we describe the preliminary lesson plan that Ms. Nishi and Ms. Tsukuda initially presented to their group, as well as the process that these two teachers carried out in order to create this plan. In the chapter that follows we summarize the discussion that they had with their peers about this plan. The subsequent chapter is devoted to going over the revisions that these two teachers made to their proposed lesson plan. In that chapter we also briefly recount what they did to prepare Ms. Nishi to teach this lesson.

Between October 25 and October 30, Ms. Tsukuda and Ms. Nishi met several times at school to prepare a first draft of the lesson plan (*shidoan*) for the subtraction lesson they would be working on with their lower grade colleagues. These meetings were held in an informal fashion, between classes or after work, whenever time was available. As they worked on this lesson plan, the two teachers consulted numerous resources, including their teachers' manuals, other instructional materials, and lesson plans that had been stored over the years in the school's staff room.

They decided that Ms. Tsukuda would actually write the lesson plan because she is the one teaching the lesson at the second time after Ms. Nishi's implementation of the lesson and had more years of teaching experience (11 years) than Ms. Nishi (a new teacher). In addition, Ms. Nishi was enrolled in mandatory beginning teacher training organized by the government while also teaching full-time, and therefore had a much fuller schedule than Ms. Tsukuda. However, Ms. Tsukuda made sure to share what she was writing with Ms. Nishi so that she would feel included in the process of drafting this plan. These two teachers gave out their first draft of the lesson plan to the other members of their lower group on October 30.

THE LESSON PLAN: A COMPLEX
THREE-PART DOCUMENT

Despite the short 5-day period available to them, the plan distributed by Ms. Nishi and Ms. Tsukuda was a complex and meaty document that had three main sections: a introductory section, a section about the unit containing the lesson, and a section about the lesson itself (see Fig. 5.2). Although we next outline the contents of each of these sections, we encourage the reader to look over this document with care, as familiarity with this plan is essential for understanding what we describe in subsequent chapters.

Section 1: An Introduction to the Lesson Plan

The lesson plan begins with an introductory section that provides some basic descriptors about the lesson and the unit containing this lesson (e.g., grade, time, date, and unit name). Several paragraphs of background information then follow. These paragraphs frame the plan by describing the children in the class, the current state of their knowledge, their abilities, and their interests.[1] The remarks made in this introductory section also help shed light on the thinking that guided the development of the lesson. For example, the reader learns that in order to motivate students, the lesson will use a story problem that draws on a class field trip. The reader also learns that in subsequent lessons students will be guided towards solving subtraction problems like the one covered in the lesson (i.e., 12–7) by using what is referred to as the subtraction–addition and subtraction–subtraction methods.

Section 2: Information About the Unit

The next section of the plan focuses on providing information about the subtraction unit from which the lesson was selected. This section is divided into three subsections. The first subsection lists the five main goals for the unit. For example, one of the goals listed is for students to confidently and reliably calculate subtraction with regrouping by using the related concept of addition of two single-digit numbers involving carrying

---

[1]Even though Ms. Nishi was going to teach the lesson first, the descriptions provided here were about Ms. Tsukuda's class because she had written out this lesson plan. Ms. Nishi had not had the time to create a version of the plan that was tailored to her own students.

Mathematics Learning Lesson Plan

Instructor: Keiko Tsukuda

1. Date & Time: November 18, 1993 (Thursday), Second Period
2. Grade: First grade. Ume Class: 11 boys, 8 girls, total of 19 students
3. Name of the Unit: Subtraction (2)
4. Reasons for Setting up the Unit:

Up to this point, the students have been studying the concept of subtraction in situations where regrouping is not necessary. Moreover, by composing and decomposing numbers, the students have been able to notice the different forms in which a number can be expressed. Also, by using the versatility of numbers, the students have been thinking about various ways to add numbers when carrying (advancing numbers to the next denomination) is involved.

In this lesson, the students will encounter subtraction problems (such as 10 to 19 minus 1 to 9) that cannot be solved without regrouping (i.e. by subtracting the number from the number in the ones position). Students will see that by using concepts learned in previous lessons, it is possible to solve these problems by taking the one from the ten's position to make ten (i.e. regrouping). The students will realize that once this step is taken, they can proceed to solve the problem by using strategies they have learned in past. In addition, this lesson hopes to deepen the students' understanding of the 10 decimal system (place value). Furthermore, through this lesson, the students should be able to perform subtraction with regrouping by choosing the most efficient method given the numbers involved

The students in this class, except for student M, understand the concept of subtraction without regrouping and can use manipulatives to solve this type of subtraction problem. In addition, they can find the correct answer to such problems. However, the time it takes to solve this type of problem varies greatly among the students, and a great number of them still immediately try to use their fingers rather than using the manipulatives provided to them, such as blocks. Moreover, there are large differences in the students' ability to process these calculations. There are students who can calculate the answers in their heads by using difficult methods such as composition and decomposition of numbers, which is considered the foundation of addition with carrying and subtraction with regrouping. Others can draw on the concept of supplementary numbers of 10 (*ju no hosu*); and the calculation of three (single digit) numbers (*3-kuchi no keisan*). In contrast, there are students who take a long time to obtain the answer, even when they use a concrete object to aid them in their calculations.

Even under these circumstances, the number of students who say "I like arithmetic" is comparatively high. When asked why they feel this way students respond with comments like: "It's fun to do activities using manipulatives like

FIG. 5.2　First lesson plan draft produced by Ms. Tsukuda and Ms. Nishi.

blocks and tiles," or, "It is fun because it is like a quiz game," or, " It is fun because you get to report your answers (in front of the class)."

In this lesson I plan to use problems based on the children's everyday life in order to motivate them to tackle the subject. Moreover, when I use manipulatives to facilitate student learning in this lesson, I plan to devise materials that will leave a record of the children's thought processes. It is my hope that having students solve these types of problems (problems based on the children's everyday life) will help in achieving the goal of this unit.

As for the numbers to use in the problem for this lesson, I decided on [12 minus 7] because I believe it will elicit many different ideas for how to solve the problem. Not only do I expect the *subtraction-addition method* (*genkaho*), but also the *subtraction-subtraction method* (*gengenho*), the *counting-subtraction method* (*kazoehiki*), and the *supplement-addition method* (*hokaho*) to come up.

In the next lesson, while thinking about the most efficient calculation method, the students will attempt to master the subtraction-addition method and the subtraction-subtraction method. In order to do this, I will make the students repeatedly practice through such activities as reflexively finding the supplementary numbers of 10 (*ju no hosu*). I will also have them practice decomposing the number that is subtracted in order to match the number in the one's position with the number that is being subtracted from (in subtraction with regrouping).

5. The Goals of the Unit:
    (1) To deepen students' understanding of the situations where subtraction is used.
    (2) To deepen students' understanding of how to formulate and read subtraction expressions written in symbolic form.
    (3) To foster students' understanding of how to calculate subtraction with regrouping by using the opposite concept of addition with carrying of two single digit numbers. (i.e. 6+7=13 —> 13-7=6)
    (4) To foster students' ability to confidently and reliably calculate subtraction with regrouping by using the related concept of addition of two single-digit numbers involving carrying (i.e. 6+7=13 —> 13-7=6).
    (5) For students to be able to represent a number as the difference between various pairs of numbers. (i.e. 5=11-6, 5=12-7, 5=13-8, etc.).
6. Related Items:
    (this section of the lesson plan was not complete at this time)
7. Plan for the unit (12 lessons)
    Section 1: To understand how to *formulate an expression* (*risshiki*) for subtraction when regrouping (*kurisagari*) is involved, and how to calculate this type of subtraction through the use of concrete manipulaitves ——— (4 lessons)

(continued on next page)

1st lesson: To think about calculation methods for subtraction when regrouping is involved —— (This period)

2nd lesson: To foster a better understanding of the *subtraction-addition method* (*genkaho*) by calculating 12 minus 9 (12-9).

3rd lesson: To foster a better understanding of the *subtraction-subtraction method* (*gengenho*) by calculating 13 minus 4 (13-4).

4th lesson: To learn how to select the most efficient method of subtraction depending on the given numerical values.

Section 2: To apply subtraction with regrouping to different situations in problems —(3 lessons)

1st - 3rd lessons: To increase proficiency in solving problems using subtraction with regrouping when you have differences and remainders.

Section 3: To make cards containing subtraction with regrouping problems and practice using the cards when calculating —— (3 lessons)

1st - 3rd lessons: To master the calculation process by enjoying playing games and using the calculation cards.

Section 4: Review —— (2 lessons)

1st - 2nd lessons: To review what the students have learned by doing exercises.

8. Perspectives on Evaluation (of Students' Understanding of the Material)

a. Interest • Attitude:

(How well do the students) attempt to progress in calculating subtraction while using concrete objects. (How well do the students) attempt to present their ideas.

b. Way of Thinking:

Ability to solve problems by using previously learned concepts and/or the idea of breaking numbers into tens.

c. Expression • Processing of Concepts:

Ability to calculate subtraction with regrouping by using the opposite concept of addition with carrying of two single digit numbers (i.e. 6+7=13 —> 13-7=6)

e. Knowledge • Skills:

To understand how to calculate subtraction with regrouping by using the opposite concept of addition with carrying of two single digit numbers (i.e. 6+7=13 —> 13-7=6) and what it means.

9. Things to Prepare

(this section of the lesson plan was not complete at this time)

10. Objective of this Lesson

(this section of the lesson plan was not complete at this time)

11. Progression of the Lesson

FIG. 5.2 *continued*

Learning Activities and Questions [hatsumon]	Expected Student Reactions	Teacher Response to Student Reactions/ Things to Remember	Evaluation
1. Grasping the Problem Setting "The other day we went leaf collecting, didn't we? What kind of leaves did you get?" "That's right. You drew the faces of the people in your family on the leaves, didn't you?"	• "Ginkgo Tree" • "Red and brown leaves" • "We also collected acorns." • "The pictures turned out pretty funny." • "I collected so many leaves that I have some left over."	• Give praise to the students who did a great job reporting their answers and raising their hands at various points during the lesson. • Check out beforehand how many leaves each student collected and how many people are in their family.	(the teacher did not prepare this column at this time)
"How many leaves did you collect, Student A?" "How many leaves did you collect, Student B?" "How many leaves did you collect, Student C?" "How many people are in your family, Student C?"	A: 18 leaves. B: 15 leaves. C: 10 leaves. C: 4 people. Oh, wait, my mom had a baby the other day, so 5 people.	• Make students understand the problem setting and that the teacher is looking for students to answer the questions by using subtraction. • Remind them of the supplementary numbers of 10.	
"How many leaves did you have left, Student C?" "Did everyone have leaves left over?"	• "5 leaves." • "(Yes) there were (leaves) left over." • "I had 12 leaves left over." • "I had a lot of leaves left over."		
2. Presentation of the Problem Format 1.) Present the format and use it on previously learned subtraction situations (without regrouping).			

(continued on next page)

"Wow, you guys are great! You were studying math even during your Life Studies (a mixture of Social Studies and Science) lesson. What kinds of calculations (of the four: addition, subtraction, multiplication or division) were you doing?
"Were the problems you did in your head like this one?"

****

"Child _____ collected _____ number of ginkgo leaves. S/he drew _____ pictures of her/his family on the leaves. How many leaves are left over?"

****

"What do you think?"
"What should we write in the blanks?"

"What would you write in the blanks if you were Student C?"

• "It's great, isn't it?"
• "Um, subtraction."

• "I don't know what will be in the blanks."
• "Oh, I don't understand."
• "It must be the name of the student who collected the leaves."
• "They are the number of leaves collected and the number of pictures drawn."
• It's "Student C collected 10 Ginkgo leaves. And then s/he drew 5 pictures of his/her family on the leaves. How many leaves are left over?"

• Point out to the students that they are using arithmetic not only during the arithmetic period, but in a lot of other situations too.

• While presenting the problem and practicing subtraction problems they already learned, use conversation with the students to help them understand the problem.

• When you present the problem, confirm what the necessary conditions are.

FIG. 5.2 *continued*

40

"What is the expression for this problem?"	• "It's 10 minus 5."	
"What is the answer?"	• "It's 5."	
	• "No, it's 5 leaves."	
"Now let's do Student D. How many leaves did Student D collect? How many pictures of his family did he draw?"	D: Collected 19 leaves, drew 4 pictures.	• Change the numerical values in the problem little by little and confirm that you want them to use subtraction when they have a situation where they have to find the remainder.
"Make the problem for Student D."	• It's "Student D collected 19 Ginkgo leaves. And then he drew 4 pictures of his family on the leaves. How many leaves are left over?"	
"Do you understand? What expression did we use to get the answer?"		
"How did we find the answer?"	• It's 19 - 4.	• Remind them of subtraction of two digit numbers without regrouping and confirm that in this case they subtracted the numbers in the ones positions from each other to find the answer.
	• We subtracted 4 from the 9 of 19.	
	• 9 is made of 5 and 4 so you know right away the answer is 5.	
	• We divided 19 into 10 and 9 and then calculated it.	
2.) Using this format to set up the main problem of the lesson		
"Now let's do it from Student E's perspective. How many leaves did Student E collect? How many pictures of his family did he draw?"	E: Collected 12 leaves and drew 7 pictures of his family.	

(continued on next page)

"Let's make this the problem."	• It's "Student E collected 12 Ginkgo leaves. And then he drew 7 pictures of his family on the leaves. How many leaves are left over?"	
"O.K. Now, let's write this on the handout 'What we know' and 'What we're asking', find these and write them down.		• Prepare a handout and have them write on it.
3. <u>Solving the Main Problem</u> 1.) Thinking about formulating an expression. "Think about making an expression from 'What we know' and 'What we're asking'."	• 7-12. • 12-7. • You can't subtract 7 from 2.	
2.) Understanding what the problem is asking "That's right. But if you compare 12 and 7, which one is bigger?" "Well, then, it seems like you should be able to subtract it." "Today we're going to think about how to find the answer to 12- 7."	• 12. • It seems hard. • That's easy.	• Make the students notice that you can't subtract using these two one digit numbers (2-7), make them think about how to do this type of calculation.

FIG. 5.2   *continued*

3) Solving the problem individually "How did you find the answer? Think about it as if you were trying to teach it to your little sister who will be starting first grade next year"

A. "Counting-Subtraction" Method.
(1) Take them one by one from 12 and find the remainder.
(2) Break up 12 into 10 and 2, take them one by one from 10 and count the remaining numbers.
(3) Since it's 12 minus 7, it's the same until 7, then you count on your fingers 8, 9, 10, 11, and 12. ("Supplement-Addition" Method)
B. "Subtraction-Addition" Method
(4) Break 12 up into 10 and 2, then subtract 7 from 10. The answer to that (10 - 7) is 3, then you take the 2 you broke up and add that to get 5.
C. "Subtraction-Subtraction" Method
(5) Break 7 up into 2 and 5, and subtract 2 from 12. Then you take the answer 10 and subtract 5 from it to get the answer, 5.
(6) It can't be done.

• Find out which students are of the following 3 types when it comes to addition with carrying. Give extra individual help especially to type C students.

Type A: Composition and decomposition (breaking down) of numbers is simple for this type of student. Able to calculate it in his/her head.

Type B: Can find the answer by manipulating some sort of half concrete object.

Type C: Finds it difficult to calculate unless he/she uses some sort of concrete object or his/her fingers.

• Using blocks, tiles, expressions, sentences, egg cartons, etc. help each student learn to explain how they came up with the answer on their own.

(continued on next page)

4. <u>Polishing and Reporting Individual Solution Methods</u> "Teach the other students in your group how you came up with the answer and chose one method to report in front of the class." ("Why did you break 12 up into 10 and 2?") ("Why did you break 7 up into 2 and 5?") "Are there any other ways to find the answer?"		• Have the students in the group explain until all the students understand, even the ones who haven't come up with an answer yet. • Have the students decide on one solution method and report it as a group. • Have the students ask questions about the group solution methods that they don't understand. If the students don't ask any questions, the teacher should pose questions.
	• Yes, there are.	• Report the other solution methods you noticed and wrote down while walking around the classroom.
5. <u>Summary and Announcement of Next Lesson</u> "Let's try to solve 12-9, it doesn't matter what method you use." "O.K., then, let's try to use solution method B in the next lesson."	• "Solution method B is the fastest way." • "9 is just one away from 10 so 1 and 2 makes the answer 3. " • et cetera.	• Try to lead the students who are still using the "counting- subtraction" method to use solution method A. (2).

FIG. 5.2 *continued*

(i.e., $6 + 7 = 13 \rightarrow 13 - 7 = 6$). A second goal listed is for students to be able to represent a number as the difference between various pairs of numbers. (i.e., $5 = 11 - 6, 5 = 12 - 7, 5 = 13 - 8$, etc.).

The teachers did not write anything in the next subsection, which is entitled "related items." They included this heading as a place marker to remind themselves that eventually they would provide a description of the connections existing between this subtraction unit and other units taught to children in Grades 1 through 5.

In the third subsection the sequence for the entire unit is outlined. In this section the teachers explain that the unit in question is made up of 12 lessons, of which the one described in the plan is the first. They also explain that the unit can be further divided into four subunits. For example, the second subunit is made up of three lessons and focuses on having children apply subtraction with regrouping to situations represented in different word problems. The purpose of this subunit is described as "to increase students' proficiency in solving problems using subtraction with regrouping when you have differences and remainders."

Section 3: Information About the Lesson

In the next section of the plan the focus shifts to the lesson itself. It begins by listing the dimensions along which students' reactions to this lesson will be evaluated. These dimensions are students' interest and attitude, their ways of thinking, how they process concepts, and their knowledge. Under ways of thinking, for example, the teachers plan to look at students' ability to solve problems by using previously learned concepts and/or the idea of breaking numbers into tens.

The next two subsections are entitled "things to prepare" and "objectives for the lesson." These headings were also left as place markers for sections to be completed later when the teachers had a chance to continue working on the lesson plan.

The next subsection, which is quite extensive and constitutes the heart of the lesson plan, is entitled "Progression of the Lesson" (*Jugyo Katei*). It describes the lesson blow by blow in a four-column chart. The first column of this chart contains an explanation of the learning activities that will be carried out in the lesson as well as of the key questions (*hatsumon*) that the teachers intend to ask at different points in the lesson. This column also includes verbatim lines for the teacher to deliver during key moments in the lesson. By reading this first column, one can see that the lesson will be made up of five parts. In the first part, called "grasping the problem setting," the teacher will make sure that children understand the field trip context selected for the lesson, which was an outing to the park to collect gingko leaves on which children later drew their family members. In the next part, entitled "presentation of the problem format," the lesson shifts to introducing the problem format that will be used, which is a word problem that reads as follows: *Child _____ collected _____ number of ginkgo leaves. S/he drew _____ pictures of her/his family on the leaves. How many leaves are left over?* Next, the teacher will ask students to work on a few examples with this format, none of which will involve regrouping. In the third part of the lesson, "solving the lesson problem," children will be introduced to the central problem for the day, $12 - 7$.

The teacher will make sure that the children understand this problem. In particular she will verify that they see that it involves subtraction and that it is represented as $12 - 7$, and not $7 - 12$. The teacher will next allow the children time to try to solve this problem on their own. After the children have worked on the problem, the next part of the lesson, called "polishing and reporting individual solution methods," is the *neriage,* where students present and discuss their solution strategies. The purpose will be for the class to compare and contrast the range of ideas generated for how to find the answer to the problem 12 minus 7. The children will then work on the practice problem $12 - 9$ so that they can see that here the subtraction–addition method (decompose 12 into 10 and 2; subtract 9 from 10 and add the left over 1 to 2) is the most efficient solution strategy. In "summary and announcements," the final part of the lesson, the teacher will conclude the lesson by saying that next time they will practice how to use the subtraction–addition method.

In the second column of the lesson chart, which is entitled "Expected Student Reactions," the teachers describe ideas, answers, and reactions they are expecting from their students. For example, in this column the different solution strategies that children could come up with when asked to solve for $12 - 7$ are outlined and labeled according to the basic solution method that they represent. Figure 5.3 provides a schematic representation we have created in order to help the reader understand what is meant by the solutions mentioned in this part of the plan.[2]

The next column in this chart outlines how to respond to different student reactions and also lists important things for the teacher to remember. For example, at one point it is noted that the teacher should remember that children who use certain methods find it difficult to do this without the aid of concrete objects or their fingers. It is also noted in this area that other methods can be carried out by children by simply manipulating some sort of half concrete object (i.e., tiles or counters used to represent leaves).

The last column in this lesson chart is entitled "Evaluation" and is meant to be a running commentary about how the teachers will assess the success of different parts of the lesson. The column was not filled out because the teachers had run out of time. It too was left as a place marker for subsequent completion.

When queried about why they developed such a detailed lesson plan, the teachers provided several insights. Ms. Tsukuda explained that anticipating student solutions and how to react to them is excellent preparation for teaching a lesson. Feeling prepared helps allay the nervousness that the teacher doing the teaching is likely to experience. Second, these anticipations prepare the teacher for understanding the student responses and solutions that

---

[2]Appendix B provides a quick reference guide to the solution strategies included in the lesson plan and continually referred to by the teachers during their discussions.

A. Methods Involving Counting

1. Counting-Subtraction Method

Version 1: Take away 7 objects one by one from 12 objects by counting and then find the remainder by counting the number of left over objects.

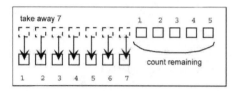

Version 2: Break up 12 objects into a group consisting of 10 objects and a group consisting of 2 objects, then take away 7 objects one by one from 10 and count the remaining objects

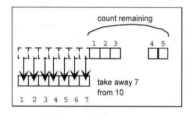

Count up from the 8th object onwards. This method is often combined with finger counting so that the child counts the objects with his or her finger by saying "8, 9, 10, 11,12" and then finds out the number of fingers that were folded.

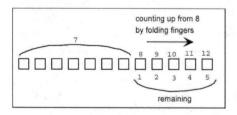

FIG. 5.3 Various subtraction methods anticipated by the teachers calculating 12 minus 7. *(continued on next page)*

B. Methods Do Not Involve Counting

1. Subtraction-Addition Method (Genkaho)

> Decompose the number 12 into 10 and 2 and then subtract 7 from the 10 to get an answer of 3. Then add the 2 that and the 3 to get an answer 5.

2. Subtraction-Subtraction Method (Gengenho)

> Decompose 12 into 10 and 2. Decompose 7 into 2 and 5. First, subtract one 2 from the other. Second, subtract 5 from the remaining 10 to get the answer 5.

FIG. 5.3.   *(continued)*

occur in the classroom and equip the teacher with appropriate reactions to these. Finally, providing this detail in the lesson plan prepares the teacher to be better able to make use of student responses to lead the class to the desired outcome in terms of their thinking and understanding. Several of the other teachers explained that this detailed planning was essential groundwork for conducting effective discussions during lesson study meetings. The vice-principal of the school seconded this opinion. She even said that preparation of such a thorough plan was the key to the success of lesson study. She also pointed out that such detailed lesson plans could eventually also serve as a tool for communicating with teachers outside of the group or school. Ms. Tsukuda added that while the teachers did not prepare such detailed lesson plans for everyday lessons, making them provided them a good opportunity to think deeply about how students learn. Certainly, as we see in the next chapter, the conversations that the teachers had about the lesson being planned were rendered efficient, detailed, and focused on student thinking in part due to the availability of this lesson plan.

6

Refining the Lesson Plan

Two lower grade meetings were held to discuss the lesson plan prepared by Ms. Nishi and Ms. Tsukuda. The first of these meetings took place on Monday November 1 from 3:00 to 5:00 p.m. and the second on Friday November 5 from 4:00 to 5:00 p.m. There was also an all staff meeting on November 4 during which Ms. Tsukuda took 30 minutes to walk all the teachers at the school through the proposed lesson plan. Although at this meeting there was no time for extended discussions about the lower grade lesson, everyone thought that what Ms. Tsukuda presented was a good start and they encouraged the lower group to continue developing their ideas.

Both the November 1 and November 5 meetings were held in Ms. Tsukuda's classroom and were attended in full by all the members of the lower grade group. Ms. Tsukuda led the meetings and Ms. Nishi was assigned to take notes. In preparation for the first of these meetings, all the group members carefully read the lesson plan, which they brought with them to both meetings and often referred to as they discussed various aspects of the lesson (see Fig. 6.1).

During the course of these meetings Ms. Tsukuda and Ms. Nishi provided details about the design of their lesson. They talked about the rationale behind certain decisions they had made and they also highlighted aspects of the lesson that had given them difficulty. Their initial work and their commentaries stimulated a rich discussion, which we summarize below according to the main threads of conversation that came up, rather than by taking the reader through the two meetings in chronological order.

WHAT PROBLEMS SHOULD STUDENTS WORK ON?

The teachers spent a good deal of time discussing the problems to be presented during the lesson. Ms. Tsukuda first provided the group with the rationale behind selecting 12 – 7 gingko leaves as the main problem for the lesson. She explained that she and Ms. Nishi wanted students to use a real-world situation to think about various ways for solving subtraction

FIG. 6.1   Lower grade teachers planning the subtraction lesson. Teachers are discussing the lesson using the lesson plan proposed by the two first-grade teachers. Copies of this plan are spread on the table in front of the teachers.

problems with regrouping. In addition, they wanted the real-world situation selected to connect with students' own experiences. Ms. Tsukuda described her thoughts in trying to come up with appropriate problems and situations:

> I looked all around my classroom and couldn't think of any ideas. This lesson is subtraction with regrouping. My class has nineteen students, so I thought I would start with using the number nineteen. Also, there are eight girls in my class. So, to start the class, I would ask: "What is 19 minus 8?" Then, we would get 11. Then, I thought, subtract something from 11. So I tried to find 6 students (among the 11 students) who have the same number of brothers and sisters to subtract from 11. That was what I tried to do at first. But, I thought I was forcing the situation to make a story problem and I thought it wasn't quite right.

Ms. Tsukuda next described the strategy that she and Ms. Nishi settled on. They decided to use numbers derived from an autumn leaf collecting field trip. In order for the story problem to be more meaningful to the students, they thought that it would be a good idea to first do a drawing project in a life study lesson (*seikatsu-ka*).[1] In life study they were working on a unit called "Role of the Family," so they planned to integrate into this unit a project that would ask the students to draw faces of their family members on gingko leaves. Then the leaves would be pasted on a larger piece of paper that was shaped like a gingko tree (see Fig. 6.2).

In addition, they would use a problem format (see Fig. 6.3), which Ms. Tsukuda described as follows:

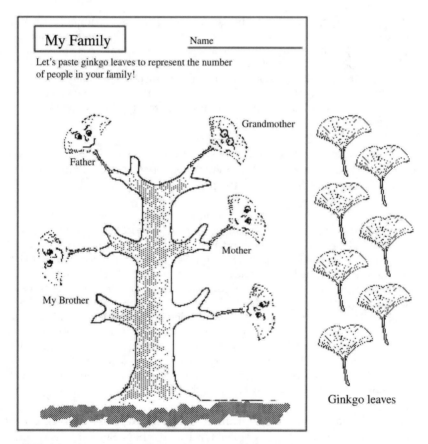

FIG. 6.2   An example of a student's gingko tree collage.

---

[1]Life study (*seikatsu-ka*) is a first- and second-grade subject that was introduced in Japan in 1990. It is a combination of science and social studies.

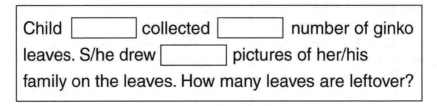

Child [ ] collected [ ] number of ginko leaves. S/he drew [ ] pictures of her/his family on the leaves. How many leaves are leftover?

FIG. 6.3   Story problem developed for the lesson.

As for making up the story problem, Mr. Saeki [the instructional superintendent] has been telling us over and over since last year that we can include blanks in a story problem and let the students plug in some numbers to make up their own problems. So that is why we used the blanks in this problem … Instead of just throwing out a problem [without blanks] to the students and saying "in a case like this problem you have to use subtraction," it really comes alive if you introduce the problem in this new way.

Ms. Tsukuda also explained how she and Ms. Nishi had settled on the numbers 12 and 7, a decision about which she felt group feedback would be useful. Ms. Tsukuda began with the following comments:

Not long ago, the vice-principal showed me several textbooks. All of those textbooks used 12 and 9 ($12 - 9 =$) and 13 and 9 ($13 - 9 =$). Most of the textbooks started out by introducing the subtraction–addition method (*genkaho*) [We remind the reader that in Appendix B we provide a quick reference guide to the solution strategies included in the lesson plan and continually referred to by the teachers during their discussions. This guide will help the reader keep track of these various methods.] In the case of 13 minus 9, first, subtract the number 9 from 10 ($10 - 9 = 1$) and add what is left over in the one's position ($1 + 3 = 4$). I thought that if you narrow it down like that [by teaching the subtraction–addition method], it's not very interesting. So on Saturday, I suggested using 15 minus 8, or 15 minus 7. I thought that these are a little harder than 12 minus 9 and 13 minus 9. Using these numbers should bring out a lot more ideas from students about ways to solve the problem.

Ms. Tsukuda added that she wanted to use the number 7 because one of her students happened to have seven family members. She said she wanted to choose this student for the story problem because he was a low achiever. She thought that making him the focal point for the lesson might help him gain more confidence. The teachers in the group all supported this idea and the use of the number 7 was treated as a given.

The discussion then moved to trying to decide whether the best number to subtract 7 from was 12. The teachers all felt that 12 was a good choice because regrouping would be needed whenever the number of people in any of the students' families was chosen as the subtrahend. This was because there were no students who had less than three people in their family. However, the teachers could not find a good reason for why the students would collect just 12 leaves. Finally, Ms. Furumoto suggested that students could be allowed to collect more leaves, but that later the teacher would ask them to select only 12 clean leaves for making the ginkgo tree collage.

Ms Tsukuda mentioned that in choosing 12 she and Ms. Nishi had taken another issue into account. She explained:

Tsukuda:	Well, I was thinking. I also thought of using 13 minus 7, but it's really hard to break down 7 into 3 and 4 ...
Maejima:	I see, you mean conceptually ...
Tsukuda:	Right, conceptually, it's easy to break 6 down into 5 and 1, and it' s easy to break down 7 into 2 and 5, but it's really hard to break 7 down into 3 and 4 for the first-grade students.

Ms. Tsukuda and Ms. Nishi were interested in how children might decompose the numbers in the problem because they wanted to make sure that a range of solution strategies emerged during this lesson. At one point Ms. Maejima asked Ms. Tsukuda if she really thought that the children would come up with all the different solutions listed in the plan. Ms. Maejima mentioned that as a second-grade teacher who had never taught first grade, she was not sure what could be expected from first graders. Ms. Tsukuda conceded that the supplement–addition method was the one method that perhaps would not come up during the class. However, Ms. Furumoto was more optimistic. She mentioned that one of the students in the middle grade at the school still used this method frequently.

The group also discussed that it would be important for kids to work on specific review problems before tackling the main problem of the lesson. In particular they talked about presenting the problems 10 minus 5 and 12 minus 2. The problem 10 minus 5 was suggested because it dealt with the concept of supplementary numbers (*ju no hosu*), and the problem 12 minus 2 was suggested because it involved the number 12 but did not require regrouping. The teachers discussed whether these review problems might provide too great a hint for how to solve 12 minus 7, because 12 can be decomposed into 10 and 2, and 7 can be decomposed into 5 and 2. Despite these concerns the teachers decided to use these review problems.

The teachers also made sure to create scenarios that connected these two review problems to the leaf collecting activity. The scenario for the first problem, 10 minus 5, would use Ms. Nishi's family: "Ms. Nishi collected 12 ginkgo leaves, but she needed to give 2 leaves to a student, so she had 10 leaves left over. Therefore, Ms. Nishi collected 10 ginkgo leaves. Then she drew pictures of her 5 family members on the leaves. How many leaves are left over?" The scenario for the second problem, 12 minus 2, would use Ms. Tsukuda's family: "Ms. Tsukuda collected 12 ginkgo leaves. Then she drew pictures of her two family members on the leaves, since Ms Tsukuda and her husband are the only family members. How many leaves are left over?"

The teachers also discussed the practice problems that would be used at the end of the lesson. Although children would not be asked to use any particular solution method, the practice problem 12 minus 9 had been chosen in order to encourage the use of the subtraction–addition method. Ms. Tsukuda thought that because the number 9 was very close to the number 10, the students would decompose the number 12 into 10 and 2 to proceed with the calculation, instead of decomposing the number 9 into 2 and 7 thus using the subtraction–subtraction method.

Ms. Tsukuda wondered if it was all right to use 9 as the number to be subtracted because there were no students who had 9 people in their family. Everybody thought that it would be better to have a number representing the number of family members for at least one of the students. Ms. Furumoto, Ms. Maejima, and Ms. Chijiiwa also thought that the problem 12 minus 9 was a little too easy for the practice problem because 9 is very close to 10. Ms. Furumoto suggested that instead 6 would be a better number to use. This idea was rejected because 6 is close to 7 so the smart students could guess the answer based on the answers they found for 12 minus 7. Ms. Tsukuda suggested 4 because there were many students who had 4 people in their family; however, that number was also rejected because 4 could easily be decomposed into 2 and 2; thus, the problem might lead the students to the subtraction–subtraction method. Finally, Ms. Chijiiwa suggested the number 5, because she thought that it was less likely for them to try to decompose 5 into 2 and 3, than 4 into 2 and 2. She also thought that it would be much faster to decompose 12 into 10 and 2, and then subtract 5 from 10, because 10 was easy to think of as the sum of 5 and 5. Everybody agreed with this, and it was decided that the practice problem would be 12 minus 5. In the end, in addition to this problem, the problem 12 minus 9 was kept as a second practice problem, just in case the fast learners needed more work while other students were still working on the first problem.

WHAT MANIPULATIVES SHOULD STUDENTS
BE PROVIDED?

The teachers also discussed at length the issue of what manipulatives to use during the lesson. This discussion was in part prompted by a comment made by Ms. Furumoto, who mentioned that the range of student solutions obtained during the lesson would depend on the kind of manipulatives that the students would work with. She felt that for this lesson it was important to develop a manipulative that would help students come up with a variety of solutions. Ms. Tsukuda said that she and Ms. Nishi had tried to do this, but felt that they had not been successful. The lower grade teachers decided to help them by examining the various manipulatives available at their school (see Fig. 6.4).

During this examination the teachers mentioned a number of qualities they liked in each manipulative. They thought that the tiddlywinks would help students not only see the base 10 structure of numbers but also how to decompose numbers into fives. They also thought that the colored tiles were appealing to young children and easy to see. In addition, their magnetic nature made it easy for children to bring this manipulative up to the board to share their ideas. They liked the flip tile board because all its parts were attached and thus children would not be dropping or losing pieces while working either at their desks or at the board. They also thought that this manipulative helped children learn the various ways of decomposing the number 10 into pairs of complementary numbers. They liked the fact that both the number blocks and the blocks emphasized the base 10 structure of numbers and helped children think about what it means to regroup (i.e., by breaking a 10-block into individual units).

Some immediate concerns were also raised about each manipulative. A major problem with the tiddlywinks was that when children were finished subtracting, one would know nothing about which solution method had been employed. Also because there were only six sets of tiddlywinks in the school, teachers would not be able to give each child an individual manipulative. Their main concern about the flip tile boards was that this manipulative did not support a varied array of solution strategies but rather encouraged simple counting strategies. They thought that the number blocks were hard to use because they were magnetic and tended to stick together. This made it hard for children to manipulate these blocks and also encouraged them to play at sticking the blocks together. This concern also applied to the tiddlywinks. The teachers thought that the blocks were hard for children to transport to the board in order to share their ideas. Also, only a few sets of these blocks were available to them.

Tiddlywinks Board *(Ohajiki-ban)*

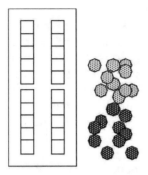

This manipulative has a magnetic board on which are drawn four rectangular strips, which are each broken into five squares. Individual tiddlywinks can be placed in each of these 20 squares. The tiddlywinks supplied are magnets that are covered on both sides with plastic of different color.

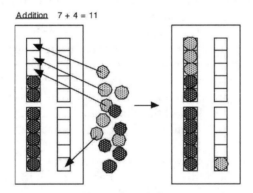

In the case of adding seven and four, students first place seven tiddlywinks on the board, all with the same colored face exposed. They then add four more tiddlywinks with the other colored face exposed. The answer can then be read off by seeing the total number of tiddlywinks on the board.

FIG. 6.4   Student manipulatives discussed during the lower grade meetings.

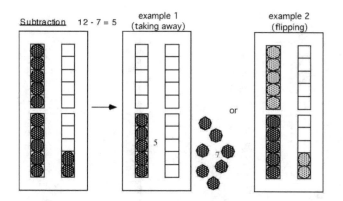

In the case of subtracting seven from 12, students first place 12 tiddlywinks of the same color on the board. They then either remove (example 1) or flip over (example 2) seven of the tiddlywinks. The number of tiddlywinks left over, which are the same color as the original 12, represents the answer to the problem.

Flip Tile Board (*Pata Pata Tairu*)

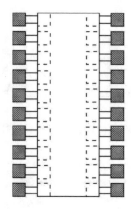

This tool consists of a cardboard center to which 20 tiles are connected with electrical tape (10 on each side of the cardboard). The face of each of these tiles is red and its back is blue. Tiles can be folded in towards the cardboard or left open away from the cardboard (as shown above). This manipulative is used as a counter with the number of tiles opened away from the cardboard representing the current count. In the diagram above the number 20 is depicted.

FIG. 6.4 *continued*

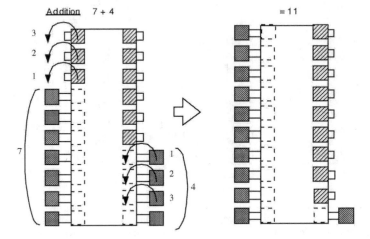

In the case of adding seven and four, students first open up seven tiles on the left side and four on the right side. They then close back three tiles on the right side and open up three corresponding tiles on the left side that had originally remained closed. The number 11 is shown on this counter as the final answer.

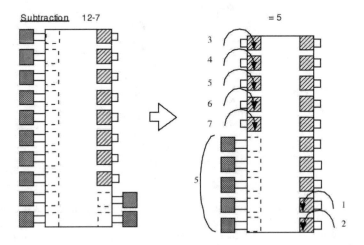

In the case of subtracting seven from 12, the students first open up 12 tiles (10 on the left and two on the right). They then close back seven tiles starting on the right side and then moving up to the left side. The number five is shown on the counter as the final answer.

FIG. 6.4   *continued*

Blocks

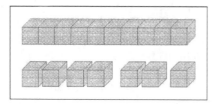

Blocks are made of wood and consist of either individual blocks or rectangular prisms that assemble 10 individual blocks. As children add and subtract, they can trade in 10-blocks for individual blocks or vice-versa.

Number Block (*Kazu no Burokku*)

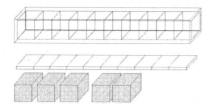

This manipulative works similarly to the wooden block described above. It has individual magnetic cubes that each represents the quantity one. Up to 10 of these cubes can be placed onto a flat rectangular metal board, which in turn slides into a transparent plastic sheath that holds together the 10-block thus created. When children want to "trade" a 10-block for 10 individual blocks, rather than doing a substitution they simply disassemble to 10-block by pulling it out of the sheath.

FIG. 6.4   *continued*

Ms. Chijiiwa felt that in choosing among these four manipulatives they would need to think about the extent to which each might support children's varying conceptualizations of the number 12. By conceptualization she meant whether they would think of 12 as being made up of 10 and 2; or 5, 5, and 2; or 12 individual ones. Ms. Chijiiwa argued that if children were given the blocks, for example, they would be free to represent 12 by lining up 10 blocks and then 2 others, or instead by creating two lines of 5 blocks with 2 blocks left over. Ms. Furumoto agreed that one should not assume that all students would line up the blocks in the same way. She went on to say: "[If teachers] really want to understand how a student's mind works in order to solve a problem, we need to avoid giving too much structure or too many restrictions to the manipulatives we use."

Ms. Furumoto felt that this quality could be achieved with the tiddlywinks by making various grids for students to lay their tiles on. In particular, there could be 10 by 2, 12 by 1, and 5 by 3 grids for children to choose from. However, Ms. Furumoto's idea was rejected because the teachers recognized that first-grade students might have a difficult time deciding which grid to use.

Ms. Tsukuda mentioned that, like Ms. Chijiiwa, some textbooks also proposed using individual blocks as a manipulative. In contrast, she thought that for the students to understand the importance of place value, it was better to give them a manipulative in the form of a group of 10 and two individual ones. Having a group of 10 would help the students realize that they needed to regroup numbers in order to solve the problem. Alternatively, if the number was presented in the form of 12 ones, the students might limit themselves to using the counting–subtraction method. Ms. Maejima agreed that using a manipulative in the form of one 10 and two ones would be the best choice. Ms. Tsukuda suggested that perhaps they could use the number blocks. She said that her class had never used them before but that she could ask the students to take out the flat rectangular metal board, which represents 10, and two cube-shaped tiles, which represent ones. Then she could ask the students to take 5 from 12. Her hope would be that some students would say things like "I can't take 5 from 2," or "Can I exchange this bar for 10 tiles?" However, Ms. Furumoto was concerned that the rectangular metal board was flat in comparison to the cube-shaped tiles, which could cause the students to get confused. This comment reminded Ms. Maejima about an experience that she had using number blocks. She described it as follows:

Maejima:	Well, it was a long time ago. It happened in my class … It was a second-grade lesson so the numbers used in the subtraction problem were much bigger than the first grade ones, but it was a problem that required regrouping. I don't remember the exact numbers in the problem but let's say it was 12 minus 5. A student used another five blocks and placed them on top of the blocks on the desk that represented 12 …
Furumoto:	Oh, I see, she took them away one by one.
Maejima:	Well, she took the five away by placing five blocks on the 10 block and two blocks.

Furumoto:	I see, then she counted the remaining blocks [those that did not have the five blocks on them].
Maejima:	She took away five, using these five blocks. She took five away by placing another five blocks on them, and counted the remaining, 1, 2, 3, 4, 5, 6, 7. So the answer was 7. I was surprised to see how she did it.
Tsukuda:	It is kind of like the counting–subtraction method.
Maejima:	Yes, it was kind of like the counting–subtraction method.
Furumoto:	I think so, too.
Maejima:	Because we used the 10 block [the rectangular metal board that represents 10], I had anticipated that the students would trade in the 10 block for ten blocks, but this student didn't …
Everybody:	I see …
Maejima:	So, there are some students who try to solve the problem, somehow, without trading the 10 block in for 10 individual blocks.
Everybody:	I see …

Ms. Chijiiwa suggested that in order to avoid something like this, they could make sure that children used the transparent sheath that came with the number block set. The flat rectangular metal board with all 10 magnetic tiles placed on it could be inserted into this sheath. Ms. Furumoto liked this idea because neither the tiles nor the rectangular metal board had the same thickness unless they were in the plastic sheath. Thus, if the precaution suggested by Ms. Chijiiwa was not taken, the students in the class might use a counting–subtraction method like the one Ms. Maejima had observed in her second-grade lesson. Ms. Furumoto cautioned, however, that in order to ask the students to think about regrouping, they needed to use a set of 10 that could not be taken apart, like in the case of the blocks. In contrast, the 10 number blocks could easily be removed from the plastic sheath.

Despite this extensive discussion, the teachers were making little progress in determining which manipulative to use, so at one point they decided to look for something else besides the four manipulatives already suggested. The conversation went as follows:

| Maejima: | If we can come up with a manipulative that consists of the group of numbers that add up to the number 10 (*ju no katamari*) and two ones, the students would |

	somehow try to subtract 5 from 12. I wonder if there is such a manipulative close at hand.
Tsukuda:	If we are talking about something close at hand, the egg carton is one I can think of.
Furumoto:	Yeah, yeah, a carton for 10 eggs.[2]
Maejima:	I see …
	[Everybody joined in the laughter because the conversation was not going anywhere.]
Maejima:	I think something like the egg carton makes more sense to use for this problem. Ginkgo leaves are in pieces in terms of the organization of the number 12. They are not like the group of numbers that add up to the number 10 (*ju no katamari*) and two ones. If we want to get solutions like the subtraction–addition method and the subtraction–subtraction method, I think it is better to use a manipulative like the egg carton. If we use materials like gingko leaves, the students would come up with the counting–subtraction method because they are in pieces. What would be a good manipulative that satisfies the condition of a bunch of ten?
Furumoto:	Yes, but we need think if it is OK for us to fix the organization of numbers as a bunch of ten and two ones. Think about it. If the number 12 is represented in pieces, the students can think of the number 12 as 10 and 2 and 12 all together, etcetera.
Chijiiwa:	Yeah, they can line them up in one line.
Furumoto:	Yeah, that is one way, also they can organize the number as 5, 5, and 2. Thus, we need to think about whether or not to narrow how the number is represented. Yes, our goal is not to confuse the students, but to see how the students think or their ideas. I wonder whether we should narrow how the number is represented. I think it is OK to narrow things sometimes, but I think that in this case it is better to give some choices for the students to choose the manipulatives they want in order to solve the problem on their own.

The teachers were intrigued by the possibility suggested by Ms. Furumoto of giving students a choice of manipulatives. Ms. Tsukuda ex-

---

[2]In Japan egg cartons contain 10 eggs instead of 12 eggs like in the United States.

plained that although she wanted to have one manipulative for the whole class to use, she also thought that the lower achievers should use the flip tile board, which they had been accustomed to using during addition lessons. She described how during her last addition lesson she had asked her students to choose among three manipulatives, the flip tile board, the number blocks, and egg cartons. Ms. Furumoto suggested that Ms. Tsukuda could set up a table near the entrance to her classroom with different manipulatives on it. The corner could be called the "hint corner." In fact, students could be given the choice of whether or not to use any of these tools at all. They could instead choose to solve the problem using just *shiki* (expressions)[3] or by drawing on paper. Ms. Furumoto was of the opinion that if they were going to follow this route, they would have to teach the students how to use the hint corner in advance of the lesson. She said that if the students took something from the hint corner, they should know they would be expected to use it for their problem solving and class presentations. However, Ms. Chijiiwa was concerned that the students would become restless if they were allowed to walk around the classroom to go to the hint corner. Ms. Tsukuda added that she was worried that students would fight with each other over manipulatives and that it might take too much time for the students to decide what manipulative they wanted to use.

Ms. Tsukuda raised the issue of how to handle group members using different manipulatives. Ms. Furumoto explained that she was planning to have only individual work (*jiritsukaiketsu*) in this lesson because she thought that there would not be enough time to allow kids to think about the problem on their own and then in groups. She reflected that if there were to be group work, then she would need to ask group members to come to a consensus about the manipulative that they wanted to use. However, she feared that making such a decision might be difficult and time-consuming for first graders. In the end, Ms. Tsukuda and Ms. Nishi were not convinced to do the lesson either by giving students a choice or without manipulatives at all.

The discussion about manipulatives moved in a different direction when Ms. Tsukuda brought up the idea that the manipulative used should meet certain conditions. According to her, Mr. Saeki told her and other attendees at a county and city educational study meeting (*Gun Shi Kyoiku Kenkyukai*, or *Gun Shi Kyoken* for short) that a good student manipulative

---

[3]Teachers in Japan often ask students to write down *shiki* (expression, or mathematical sentence) to show their solution process to a problem because they believe this provides important information for understanding students' solution strategies. *Shiki* requires the students to write their solution using numbers and mathematical symbols. *Shiki* does not include diagrams (*zu*), pictures (*e*), tables (*hyo*), and common algorithms (*hissan*) (vertical calculation method).

should meet four conditions. It should help leave a record of the thought processes used by students' to solve problems. Students should be able to readily understand its use. It should allow students to easily explain their solutions. It should be easy to put back into its original position or shape when the students need to reconsider their ideas.

One condition that the teachers went on to discuss at length was the idea that the manipulative should help leave a record of students' thought processes. The teachers all agreed that this was critical in a lesson designed to focus on students' thinking and solution strategies. Ms. Chijiiwa mentioned that in commenting about a study lesson conducted the previous year, Mr. Saeki emphasized that having a record of student thinking not only was useful for teachers to understand how their students tackled certain problems, but also was important for the students. She recalled that Mr. Saeki had explained that students need a record of all solutions presented during a lesson, if they are to use these solutions during *neriage* to build a deep understanding of concepts targeted in the lesson.

In response, Ms. Tsukuda described her experience at her last school using a manipulative similar to tiddlywinks for an addition lesson. Students were given grids on which they pasted stickers that looked like tiddlywinks. It was easy to understand how students moved their tiddlywinks because they were told to use different colored stickers to represent the two numbers being added. Ms. Maejima commented that although such a manipulative would probably work well in the case of addition, for subtraction it would be very difficult to infer the students' solution strategies because at the end one would only see on the paper the stickers remaining. Ms. Maejima suggested that perhaps they could make tiddlywinks stickers constructed in two layers. First, students would lay down the number of stickers representing the minuend. Then, they would take away the number of top layer stickers that represented the subtrahend. Therefore, the remaining top layers would represent the answer and the teachers could see the students' thinking processes. However, Ms. Tsukuda worried that it was a lot of trouble to make the double-layered stickers. In addition, she thought that if students separated the top and bottom layer of the stickers, the total number of stickers would be more than 12, which might be very confusing for the students. Ms. Furumoto reminded everyone that a second important condition was that the manipulative be simple to use so that children can spend their time concentrating on solving the problem, not on figuring out how the tool works.

At this point Ms. Furumoto suggested just sticking with the standard number blocks. She said that although this manipulative would not leave a permanent record of students' thinking processes, children could be encouraged to also draw how they solved the problems. Students could bring their work with the number blocks to the front of the class and present their ideas. However, Ms. Tsukuda mentioned that there were not enough number blocks for students in her class to work individually.

The teachers discussed the possibility of making their own version of the number blocks. These new number blocks could be made out of paper tiles. Ms. Tsukuda thought that it would not take much time to make one set for each student. Although the teachers did not seem totally convinced, they decided to go ahead and try this homemade manipulative because they did not have time to continue discussing this issue. Moreover, they reminded themselves that although they were not fully convinced about their decision, by trying out the lesson they would stand to learn a great deal about the dilemmas they were having. They would then have a chance to incorporate their learning into the second version of the lesson.

The teachers next moved on to talking about design specifics for the manipulative that they would make. They ultimately settled on a paper manipulative that combined features from the tiddlywinks and the number blocks (see Fig. 6.5).

Various considerations went into finalizing this design. First, the teachers talked about the size of the drawing paper on which students would put their paper tiles. Because the students' desktop space was very limited and first-grade students' attention can be easily distracted by objects falling off their desks, these teachers thought it was important to discuss how the desk

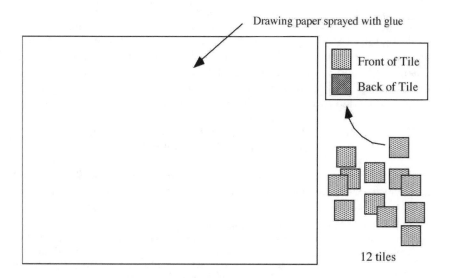

FIG. 6.5   The manipulative developed by the teachers.

space would be used.[4] Ms. Furumoto argued that the length or the width of the paper should be at least 12 tiles in length so the students could line up all the tiles in one line if they wanted to. In addition, Ms. Tsukuda pointed out that because the drawing board had to be more than 12 tiles in length first-grade students would have difficulty lining up all 12 tiles without any space in between them. Therefore, Ms. Maejima added that space would also be needed for students to set aside the tiles that they had removed. Ms. Tsukuda said the size of each tile should be at least 2 centimeters by 2 centimeters in order for all the students in the classroom to see the tiles on the blackboard during the student presentations. Ultimately, the teachers decided to use 11 × 17-inch sized drawing paper (about 30 centimeters by 43 centimeters) and tiles 2 centimeters by 2 centimeters.

Second, for the construction of the tiles, the teachers decided to use cardboard paper with red on one side and pink on the other. Ms. Maejima and Ms. Chijiiwa suggested that it was important to have two different colors on the tiles in order to understand the students' thinking process when they were working on the problem. Maejima described the method for doing this:

> First, the teacher asks student to put all 12 tiles on the left side of the drawing paper. The teacher makes sure to instruct the students to show only one color facing up. Then the teacher asks the students to subtract 7 tiles by turning them over, and putting them on the right side of the paper. In this way we can see how the students subtract the 7 tiles. I guess there are still some problems understanding the students' thinking processes because we will see only the students' finished work.… But I guess we can learn something from it.

Third, the teachers decided to use spray glue to make the surface of the drawing paper sticky so the tiles could be pasted on and peeled off easily and so that the paper could be transported to the board with the tiles on it. Also, they decided to use a thicker drawing paper so the students could bring it to the blackboard without worrying about the drawing paper either falling off or dangling from the blackboard.

HOW WILL STUDENTS BE ENCOURAGED TO DISCUSS THEIR WORK?

The teachers also spent a good amount of time planning how to support a rich classroom discussion of the various ideas children would come

---

[4]When the teachers discussed students' limited desktop space, they also talked about what the teacher should ask the students to put on top of their desks. In this lesson, the students needed a space to put the manipulative (drawing paper) and a handout. This left little room for anything else. Therefore, the teachers decided to ask students to put away their textbooks, notebooks, and pencil cases, and leave only a pencil and an eraser before the class started.

up with for solving 12 minus 7. Ms. Maejima asked Ms. Tsukuda about first graders' ability to explain things in writing by using either words or mathematical expressions (*shiki*). Ms. Maejima wanted to know about this because she felt that students might have trouble reporting their answers and solution methods in front of the class unless they first wrote them down. She said that in her experience, even her second graders had trouble reporting without first writing something down. Ms. Furumoto agreed and suggested that students receive a handout with very clear instructions. All teachers quickly agreed with this idea, but there was less clarity about exactly what this handout might look like. Ms. Tsukuda provided some ideas by sharing with the group her experience using handouts:

> I have tried two or three times this method during mathematics class. First I ask students to write "something you already know" about the problem. Then, I ask them to write "what the problem is asking." Next, students are asked to write the *expressions* (*shiki*). Finally, I ask students to write "how they solved it" in words using words like "to begin with" and "next."

Ms. Maejima responded by raising concerns about time. If the handout had too many parts to be completed, it might take up too much of the 45 minutes available for the lesson. Ms. Tsukuda, however, felt that students could complete a handout like the one she described in about 10 minutes and that this would be time well spent.

The teachers next decided to look at notebooks of Ms. Tsukuda's students to get a sense of their writing abilities. Ms. Maejima noticed that the students' explanations were weak and might not be clear to others. Ms. Tsukuda mentioned that some of the students' explanations included "I did it using my hands" instead of a more accurate statement such as "I used my fingers to count." Some of the teachers felt that when students provide weak explanations the teacher needs to follow-up by asking, "Please show me how you did it." Ms. Furumoto, however, warned against giving students instructions that were too prescriptive and instead suggested having about half of the handout be a large blank space where students could freely draw pictures and provide explanations like "I drew circles and counted them to find the answer." She explained her thinking as follows:

> Giving a format, including some steps to answer, is one way to do it, but it may narrow the students' ability to express their ideas for solving the problem. The students may not grow into and acquire skills such as expressing their ideas using charts, pictures, diagrams, etc. Standardizing the wording [by providing steps] does not help extend students' ideas.

Ms. Chijiiwa mentioned that giving children the task of writing as many solutions as possible on a sheet of paper would be another approach to eliciting a variety of ideas from the students. However, Ms. Tsukuda did not like this idea because she thought first graders tended to get confused when they had more than one idea on a sheet of paper.

Ms. Maejima recommended having a picture of the 12 ginkgo leaves on the handout; Ms. Chijiiwa thought that this would be a good tool for slow learners, akin to giving them a hint card. However, she noted that the pictures of the leaves needed to be scattered around on the handout in order to avoid any a priori clustering. This idea was abandoned when Ms. Tsukuda mentioned that having the drawing of the leaves would encourage students to use the counting–subtraction method. Ms. Furumoto said that the picture of the ginkgo leaves should be given only to the students who needed help, just like when hint cards were used. She also pushed for not abandoning the idea of a blank space where the students could freely draw pictures, word expressions (*kotoba no shiki*), and numeric expressions (*shiki*). Ms. Tsukuda, who also was in favor of this idea, said that she could use the following instructions: "Let's explain how to find your answer clearly so that your little sister who is starting first grade next year can understand it." Ms. Furumoto suggested a slightly different wording: "Let's explain how to find your answer clearly so that you can teach it to someone at home." She also thought that adding the sentence "Let's practice before we go home" might be a good way to encourage children. In addition, she said that for homework it would be interesting to assign the students to teach someone at home how they found their solution. Ms. Tsukuda said she was leaning toward dividing one sheet of paper in half. One half would be blank and the other half would contain a few words like "*Shiki*" (expression), "Sentences," "How did you find the answer?" Ms. Furumoto added that the blank half should have a sentence like "It is OK to draw pictures" to informally suggest to students what they could do with the blank space.

Although many ideas were discussed, the teachers did not have time to settle on a design for the handout. Instead, Ms. Tsukuda and Ms. Nishi agreed to continue thinking about this and to solicit feedback from group members as needed. Ms. Furumoto again reminded everyone that they should not worry too much about unresolved issues. After all, if they made bad decisions, they would simply learn from these mistakes, and could redress them during the second implementation of the lesson.

In addition to examining how a handout could be used to support rich discussions, the teachers also debated whether having students work individually or in small groups might better support such discussions. One of the teachers initiated this debate by saying that she had seen a sixth-grade study lesson where children worked individually and then presented their ideas. She felt this was good for the kids who understood things well, but those who were confused got little out of working alone. For this reason she thought working in small groups was better. She reflected:

> When children work in small groups they can teach each other about solving the problem and come up with a group opinion on how to solve the problem. But, I guess that would be kind of hard to do for first graders. If you do the grouping, it might just end up like what Mr. Mizuno [a sixth-grade teacher at the school] described before, where some kids just think, "Even if I don't do anything someone is going to do the thinking for me, so I'll just do it without thinking at all." So, in the end, they just copy somebody else's answer and the exercise is over for them.

In response, Ms. Tsukuda shared an experience she had during a first-grade addition lesson:

> All the groups came up with the same solution using the method of decomposing the number that is being added to (*hikasu-bunkai*). This solution is much more sophisticated than the method of the counting–addition (*kazoetashi*). So, when I asked the students if there were any other solutions, no one wanted to say that they just used the counting–addition method because the students know that the counting–addition method is a low-level solution strategy compared to decomposing the number that is being added to. For this reason, I think it may be difficult to get various solutions when students work in groups.

Ms. Furumoto, however, felt that if students were encouraged to help each other as they worked in groups, many solutions, including very low-level ones would emerge. She believed that conducting group work in this way would be good for first grade. The teacher could then organize the presentations by first having one group describe one of the solutions it discussed. Because each group would most likely have discussed more than one solution, the teacher would then ask a second group to present a different solution and so forth. This way it would be possible to have some low-level solutions such as the counting–subtraction method presented, even though the more advanced solutions might emerge first.

Ms. Furumoto mentioned that although it was important to have many solutions presented by the students, if the students did not understand each solution, then the presentations would end up being meaningless. The teachers therefore needed to think about how to make sure the students understood each solution, and considered which one was the best. Ms. Tsukuda described how in her class if certain of her students openly agreed with an idea presented by a peer, then other students did as well without really understanding what they were agreeing with. For this reason Ms. Tsukuda was beginning to favor Ms. Furumoto's suggestion of having students discuss their ideas in their small groups. She thought that this might encourage them to speak more openly with each other about what they were really thinking or were confused about. Ms. Furumoto agreed that if these small group conversations could be encouraged, the teacher could at least know what the students really thought about the merits of each of the solutions. However, Ms. Tsukuda pointed out that in this configuration discussions would happen in small groups and as a result the teacher would not be able to hear all of the students' conversations. Ms. Maejima added that it was very difficult for lower grade students to carry on a group discussion using a format that they were not familiar with. Therefore the teachers would need to start practicing right away in their classrooms if they wanted to explore a new method of encouraging discussion.

Ms. Chijiiwa expressed some concern, commenting that there was a tendency for first-grade students to think that their own way was the best, thus impeding their understanding of other solutions. Ms. Tsukuda and Ms. Maejima agreed with Ms. Chijiiwa. Ms. Tsukuda expressed some frustration because she thought that the idea of group work might not work after all. This prompted Ms. Chijiiwa to ask her to describe what she thought would happen if she had group presentations in her class. Ms. Tsukuda replied immediately that the group presentations would lead to the subtraction–addition method or the subtraction–subtraction method. She seemed convinced that although there were five groups in the class they would all present the same ideas because the students who used the counting–subtraction method would recognize that this method was not as advanced and would not want to share it with other members of their group. For this reason Ms. Tsukuda was again leaning toward individual work rather than group work. Ms. Maejima asked if Ms. Tsukuda's students would shy away from presenting their ideas if they thought that their solutions might be less advanced than other solutions. Ms. Tsukuda thought that would be less the case if they had worked alone, but she did expect low achievers to have difficulty explaining their solutions even if the solution methods were as simple as the counting–subtraction method. She recalled an experience that illustrated this:

> I asked one of the students, "How did you do that?" He said "I did it with my fingers." So I said to him, "How did you do that with your fingers?" Then he said, "I used my hand." So I said "OK. Could you show me how you did it with your hand?" "I forgot how I did it."

Ms. Maejima said that if students were not swayed by the advanced solutions presented and would still be willing to share their less advanced solutions, the teacher would only need to worry about how to organize these presentations on the blackboard. However, in light of Ms. Tsukuda's comments about how easily children were swayed by their peers while working in small groups, Ms. Maejima thought it was critical to think about the order of the presentations. Ms. Tsukuda agreed.

Ms. Maejima was also concerned about the lower grade students' ability to differentiate between the solutions presented by other students and their own ideas. She said that children at this level tend to think that their ideas are different from those of others simply because they vary in surface features or are expressed somewhat differently. She said that this often happens when children use different manipulatives to express the same ideas. In order to address this problem, Ms. Furumoto suggested that the teacher should attempt to arrange the solutions and the manipulatives on the blackboard in some organized manner. In addition, she said the teacher should write a few simple explanatory words above each solution presented. Ms. Chijiiwa suggested that the teacher could prepare ahead of time some cards with simple explanations on them. Ms. Furumoto thought that by looking at such cards most of the students would be able to make a better decision about whether their ideas were similar or different. All the teachers agreed to the preparation of these cards.

Ms. Tsukuda shifted the conversation by asking what she should do when the students' explanations were not clear enough for the other students to understand. Ms. Tsukuda commented as follows:

Tsukuda:	When one of my students explains a solution in front of the class, the other students who are listening often say, "Yes, I understand," even though they did not understand. For example, if my students were working on this problem, 12 minus 7, ... then ... one of the students might explain to the class "I divided 12 into 10 and 2 and I subtracted 7 and got the answer." However this explanation is not detailed enough to understand how he got the answer after he divided 12 into 10 and 2.
Chijiiwa:	Oh, I see. If the solution that was used was the subtraction-subtraction method, the explanation is not enough if the student did not explain it like "I divided 12 into 10 and 2 and 7 into 5 and 2, then ..."
Tsukuda:	If it was the subtraction-addition method, you subtract 7 from 10. So you can think of the explanation using either method.
Chijiiwa:	I see, I see ...

After listening to this conversation, Ms. Furumoto suggested that in a case like this, the teacher needs to help the student explain the solution more clearly. If all the students said, "Yes, I understood," even though the explanation was not clear, then the teacher could act a little stupid. She could say, "I did not understand," "I am very surprised you can understand better than me," "Can you explain one more time so I can understand or is there anybody who can help explain it to me?" Ms. Furumoto reminded everyone that if the teacher acts a little stupid, this often motivates students to explain their ideas again with more confidence.

After some more discussion, the teachers decided to have the students work and present individually. Although all the teachers were not convinced that this would be better than group work, they followed Ms. Tsukuda's instincts because the lesson would ultimately be taught in her classroom and she was the one who knew the students better than anybody else. Ms. Nishi was also happy to teach the lesson this way.

HOW TO CONCLUDE THE LESSON?

The teachers also discussed how to conclude the lesson. This discussion first focused on deciding how much time to allocate to the review problems and the end of the lesson relative to the rest of the activities that would take place in the lesson. Ms. Furumoto had a number of suggestions. She thought that the lesson planned was very packed and might need to be extended by 10 to 15 minutes if it was going to be completed in its entirety.[5] She said she had seen such extended study lessons at the Saeki and Yoshiwa districts. There was another possibility, which was to split the lesson into two 45-minute lessons. The first lesson would end after the students finished solving the problem on their own (*jiritsukaiketsu*). After having a short break the second lesson would begin, starting with the student presentations. She proposed making the second lesson the actual study lesson. Ms. Furumoto said she had seen a two-period study lesson like this a couple of years before when she was teaching at a different school and that she found the quality of students' discussion to be quite different from what is typically seen in a regular-length lesson. Ms. Furumoto liked the idea of using lesson study as an opportunity to be experimental and also pointed out that the second-grade teachers were thinking of trying an extended lesson for an upcoming research lesson in February 1994. Ms. Maejima, however, worried that if the lesson was divided right before the students' presentations, the students' thoughts might be interrupted. She thought that making the lesson 10 minutes longer would tire first-grade students. Ms. Tsukuda thought that the lesson would not need to be so

---

[5]In Japan, the length of a lesson at this grade level is usually 45 minutes.

long to warrant extending it to two periods. She thought that having 10 to 15 minutes extra would be enough to complete the lesson. Ms. Furumoto said that the lesson would be taught during the second period, which was to be followed by a 20-minute recess. They could extend the lesson into recess as long as the other classes were quiet. Everybody agreed that they would extend the lesson time and they would make an announcement to the other classes to be quiet during recess. Figure 6.6 shows the time allocation plan that the teachers settled on.

Ms. Tsukuda then mentioned that when she would give the practice problem at the end of the lesson, she would tell the students that it didn't matter what method they used to solve it. She thought that at this point it was not important for students to use one particular method; her goal was simply for students to understand that there were a variety of ways to solve the problem. Ms. Chijiiwa added that if the goal of the lesson was the exploration of various ways to solve the problem, the lesson could be concluded by the teacher saying, "Please do it the way you think is best." However, if the goal of the lesson was to have students understand and move toward using the subtraction–addition method, the teacher needed to organize a discussion designed to get the students to come up with a verdict on what was the best solution. In this latter case, the lesson should end with the teacher saying, "Let's try to do it using the subtraction–addition method from now on." According to Ms. Chijiiwa the decision for how to end the

---

1. Grasping the Problem Setting *(5 minutes)*

2. Presentation of the Problem Format *(10 minutes)*
    (1) Presenting the format and using it on previously learned subtraction situations-- situations without regrouping *(5 minutes)*
    (2) Using this format to set up the main problem of the lesson *(5 minutes)*

3. Solving the Main Problem *(13 minutes)*
    (1) Thinking about formulating an expression
    (2) Understanding what the problem is asking
    (3) Solving the problem individually

4. Polishing and Reporting Individual Solution Methods *(12 minutes)*

5. Summary and Announcement for Next Lesson *(5 minutes)*

FIG. 6.6   Time allocation plan for the study lesson.

lesson hinged on what the teacher wanted to do and what she wanted the students to learn from this lesson.

Ms. Tsukuda preferred ending the lesson by saying, "Please do it the way you think is best." Her inclination was to reserve a good discussion about the best solution for the next lesson. She would facilitate such a discussion by reviewing the solutions that were presented during this study lesson. Ms. Furumoto agreed with Ms. Tsukuda, saying that at first it was not necessary for students to be limited to one way of solving the problem but that rather the students needed to develop their confidence by solving it in their own way. Although Ms. Tsukuda agreed with this, she was hoping that some of her students would say, "The subtraction–addition method is the best way to do it," which would provide a good lead into the next lesson. If that happened, her plan was to say, "Do you really think so? Let's think about it in the next math lesson and let's try using that method next time."

As just illustrated, the lower grade teachers had rich and thought provoking discussions during the course of the two meetings that they devoted to going over the lesson plan proposed by Ms. Nishi and Ms. Tsukuda. Although they did not resolve many of the issues raised, as we see in the next chapter, their conversations served as the basis for a number of the revisions that the two first-grade teachers made to their proposed lesson plan.

7

Preparing to Teach the Study Lesson

TOUCHING UP THE LESSON PLAN

Before Ms. Nishi taught the study lesson on November 15, she and Ms. Tsukuda took care of revising their lesson plan. These revisions included detailing certain parts of the plan that they previously did not have a chance to work through, as well as modifying this plan based on ideas that came up when discussing it with other members of the lower group. Their revised plan is presented in Fig. 7.1 with changes relative to the first draft highlighted in gray. Interestingly, one modification missing from this plan was to revise the introductory part where the students and their past learning experiences were described. This new version of the plan was still based on Ms. Tsukuda's class because Ms. Nishi had not had the time to change this section. Although next we briefly point out some of the more noteworthy changes that the teachers did make to the plan, we encourage the reader to study this document to uncover the other minor alterations made by these two teachers.

The first major change made by these teachers was that they included a diagram in the section called "related items," which had previously been left blank for later completion. The diagram, which was constructed using the reference section of the *Teacher's Instructional Manual* (Gakkotosho, 1992), placed this lesson in the context of 5 years of elementary curriculum. More specifically, it showed how units on addition and subtraction taught in the first grade relate to other units taught between second grade and fifth grade, allowing all the teachers to situate the lesson relative to the material that they were responsible for teaching.

Second, the teachers added a section entitled "The Goals of this Lesson," and deleted the section called "Perspectives on Evaluation," which was incorporated into the new section about goals. Once the teachers had specified their objectives for this lesson, it made sense to evaluate the lesson based on these lesson goals.

Mathematics Learning Lesson Plan

Instructor: Keiko Tsukuda

1. Date & Time: November 18, 1993 (Thursday), Second Period
2. Grade: First grade. Ume Class: 11 boys, 8 girls, total of 19 students
3. Name of the Unit: Subtraction (2)
4. Reasons for Setting up the Unit:

Up to this point, the students have been studying the concept of subtraction in situations where regrouping is not necessary. Moreover, by composing and decomposing numbers, the students have been able to notice the different forms in which a number can be expressed. Also, by using the versatility of numbers, the students have been thinking about various ways to add numbers when carrying (advancing numbers to the next denomination) is involved.

In this lesson, the students will encounter subtraction problems (such as 10 to 19 minus 1 to 9) that cannot be solved without regrouping (i.e. by subtracting the number from the number in the ones position). Students will see that by using concepts learned in previous lessons, it is possible to solve these problems by taking the one from the ten's position to make ten (i.e. regrouping). The students will realize that once this step is taken, they can proceed to solve the problem by using strategies they have learned in past. In addition, this lesson hopes to deepen the students' understanding of the 10 decimal system (place value). Furthermore, through this lesson, the students should be able to perform subtraction with regrouping by choosing the most efficient method given the numbers involved

The students in this class, except for student M, understand the concept of subtraction without regrouping and can use manipulatives to solve this type of subtraction problem. In addition, they can find the correct answer to such problems. However, the time it takes to solve this type of problem varies greatly among the students, and a great number of them still immediately try to use their fingers rather than using the manipulatives provided to them, such as blocks. Moreover, there are large differences in the students' ability to process these calculations. There are students who can calculate the answers in their heads by using difficult methods such as composition and decomposition of numbers, which is considered the foundation of addition with carrying and subtraction with regrouping. Others can draw on the concept of supplementary numbers of 10 (*ju no hosu*); and the calculation of three (single digit) numbers (*3-kuchi no keisan*). In contrast, there are

FIG. 7.1   Lesson plan used for Ms. Nishi's lesson.

students who take a long time to obtain the answer, even when they use a concrete object to aid them in their calculations.

Even under these circumstances, the number of students who say "I like arithmetic" is comparatively high. When asked why they feel this way students respond with comments like: "It's fun to do activities using manipulatives like blocks and tiles," or, "It is fun because it is like a quiz game," or, " It is fun because you get to report your answers (in front of the class)."

In this lesson I plan to use problems based on the children's everyday life in order to motivate them to tackle the subject. Moreover, when I use manipulatives to facilitate student learning in this lesson, I plan to devise materials that will leave a record of the children's thought processes. It is my hope that having students solve these types of problems (problems based on the children's everyday life) will help in achieving the goal of this unit. As for the numbers to use in the problem for this lesson, I decided on [12 minus 7] because I believe it will elicit many different ideas for how to solve the problem. Not only do I expect the *subtraction-addition method* (*genkaho*), but also the *subtraction-subtraction method* (*gengenho*), the *counting-subtraction method* (*kazoehiki*), and the *supplement-addition method* (*hokaho*) to come up.

In the next lesson, while thinking about the most efficient calculation method, the students will attempt to master the subtraction-addition method and the subtraction-subtraction method. In order to do this, I will make the students repeatedly practice through such activities as reflexively finding the supplementary numbers of 10 (*ju no hosu*). I will also have them practice decomposing the number that is subtracted in order to match the number in the one's position with the number that is being subtracted from (in subtraction with regrouping).

5. The Goal of the Unit:
   (1) To deepen students' understanding of the situations where subtraction is used.
   (2) To deepen students' understanding of how to formulate and read subtraction expressions written in symbolic form.
   (3) To foster students' understanding of how to calculate subtraction with regrouping by using the opposite concept of addition with carrying of two single digit numbers. (i.e. 6+7=13 —> 13-7=6)
   (4) To foster students' ability to confidently and reliably calculate subtraction with regrouping by using the related concept of addition of two single-digit numbers involving carrying (i.e. 6+7=13 —> 13-7=6).
   (5) For students to be able to represent a number as the difference between various pairs of numbers. (i.e. 5=11-6, 5=12-7, 5=13-8, etc.).

(continued on next page)

6. Related Items:

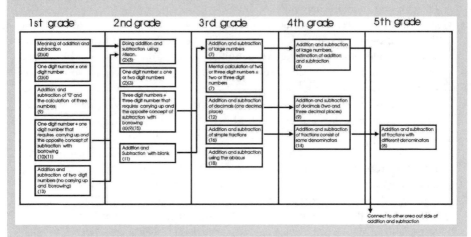

1st grade	2nd grade	3rd grade	4th grade	5th grade

Flowchart boxes:

1st grade:
- Meaning of addition and subtraction (3)(4)
- One-digit number ± one digit number (3)(4)
- Addition and subtraction of "0" and the calculation of three numbers (9)
- One digit number + one digit number that requires carrying up and the opposite concept of subtraction with borrowing (10)(11)
- Addition and subtraction of two digit numbers (no carrying up and borrowing) (13)

2nd grade:
- Doing addition and subtraction using Hissan. (2)(3)
- One-digit number ± one or two digit numbers (2)(3)
- Three-digit numbers + three-digit number that requires carrying up and the opposite concept of subtraction with borrowing (6)(9)(15)
- Addition and Subtraction with blank (11)

3rd grade:
- Addition and subtraction of large numbers (7)
- Mental calculation of two or three digit numbers ± two or three digit numbers (7)
- Addition and subtraction of decimals (one decimal place) (12)
- Addition and subtraction of simple fractions (16)
- Addition and subtraction using the abacus (18)

4th grade:
- Addition and subtraction of large numbers, estimation of addition and subtraction (4)
- Addition and subtraction of decimals (two and three decimal places) (9)
- Addition and subtraction of fractions consist of same denominators (14)

5th grade:
- Addition and subtraction of fractions with different denominators (8)

Connect to other area out side of addition and subtraction

7. Plan for the unit (12 lessons)

    Section 1: To understand how to *formulate an expression* (*risshiki*) for subtraction when regrouping (*kurisagari*) is involved, and how to calculate this type of subtraction through the use of concrete manipulaitves —— (4 lessons)

        1st lesson: To think about calculation methods for subtraction when regrouping is involved (This period)

        2nd lesson: To foster a better understanding of the *subtraction-addition method* (*genkaho*) by calculating 12 minus 9 (12-9).

        3rd lesson: To foster a better understanding of the *subtraction-subtraction method* (*gengenho*) by calculating 13 minus 4 (13-4).

        4th lesson: To learn how to select the most efficient method of subtraction depending on the given numerical values.

    Section 2: To apply subtraction with regrouping to different situations in problems —— (3 lessons)

        1st - 3rd lessons: To increase proficiency in solving problems using subtraction with regrouping when you have differences and remainders.

    Section 3: To make cards containing subtraction with regrouping problems and practice using the cards when calculating —— (3 lessons)

        1st - 3rd lessons: To master the calculation process by enjoying playing games and using the calculation cards.

    Section 4: Review —— (2 lessons)

        1st - 2nd lessons: To review what the students have learned by doing exercises.

8. The Goals of This Lesson:

    a. Interest • Attitude:

FIG. 7.1 *continued*

(How well do the students) attempt to progress in calculating subtraction while using concrete objects. (How well do the students) attempt to present their ideas.

b. Way of Thinking:

Ability to solve problems by using previously learned concepts and/or the idea of breaking numbers into tens.

c. Expression • Processing of Concepts:

Be able to do the calculation of "12-7"

e. Knowledge • Skills:

Understand the meaning and method of the calculation of "12-7"

9. Things to Prepare

A drawing paper coated with spray glue (19), Tiles (12 x 19)

Handouts (19)

Paper cutout Ginkgo leaves — for a hint

Note: Student M., who is a mildly mentally retarded child, does not usually stay in the classroom with the other students during Arithmetic lessons because he receives individual lessons; however, during this lesson, he will stay in the classroom so all the teachers can observe how he is doing. I would like to plan an activity that will help him learn one-to-one correspondence using Ginkgo leaves and the faces of his family members during the time I'm walking around and observing the students to see how they are doing (*kikanjyunshi*).

10. Progression of the Lesson

Learning Activities and Questions [hatsumon]	Expected Student Reactions	Teacher Response to Student Reactions / Things to Remember	Evaluation*
1. <u>Grasping the Problem Setting</u> "The other day we went leaf collecting, didn't we? What kind of leaves did you get?" "That's right. You collected 12 leaves from the big Ginkgo tree at the Shinto shrine and drew the faces of the people in your family on the leaves.	• Red and brown leaves • There were miscanthuses and persimmon trees, too. • I collected chestnuts, too. • "The pictures turned out pretty funny." • "I collected so many leaves that I have some left over."	• Give praise to the students who did a great job reporting their answers and raising their hands at various points during the lesson. • Remind the studa.ents that they collected only 12 Ginkgo leaves after they changed the location. • Check out beforehand how many people are in each student's family.	a. Are the students positively trying to recall the event?

(continued on next page)

"How many leaves did you use for drawing faces, Student A?" "How many leaves did you use for drawing faces, Student B?" "How many leaves did Ms. Nishi use for drawing faces?" "Ms. Nishi collected 10 leaves and drew 5 faces." "How many leaves are left over?"	A: 4 leaves. Oh, we had a new baby the other day, so 5 leaves. B: Because my family is 4 people, so 4 leaves. Ms. Nishi: 5 leaves. • 5 leaves • Well, (by using fingers) it is 5 leaves.	• Make sure that all the students know that Ms. Nishi collected only 10 leaves. • Make students understand the problem setting and the teacher is looking for students to answer the questions by using subtraction. • Remind them of the supplementary numbers of 10.	b. Do the students understand they can solve these problems using subtraction? c. Were the students able to solve the problem 10-5?
"Did everyone have leaves left over?"	• (Yes) there were (leaves) left over. • I had a lot of leaves left over. • I had 8 leaves left over.		
2. Presentation of the Problem Format 1.) Present the format and use it on previously learned subtraction situations (without regrouping) "Wow, you guys are great! You were studying math even during your Life Studies (a mixture of Social Studies and Science) lesson.	• It's great, isn't it? • Well, what calculation do I need to use?	• Point out to the students that they are using arithmetic not only during the arithmetic period, but in a lot of other situations too.	

FIG. 7.1   *continued*

80

What kinds of calculations (of the four: addition, subtraction, multiplication or division) were you doing?	• Subtraction.	• Based on the conversations with the students, present some subtraction problems that they already know how to solve. By reviewing these problems, help students understand the situation of the subtraction problem.	
"Were the problems you did in your head like this one?" ********************* "Child _____ collected _____ ginkgo leaves. S/he drew _____ pictures of her/his family on the leaves. How many leaves are left over?" *********************			
"What do you think?" "What should we write in the blanks?"	• I don't know what will be in the blanks. • I don't understand. • It must be the name of the person who collected the leaves. • They are the number of leaves collected and the picture drawn.	• When you present the problem, confirm what the necessary conditions are.	b. Did the students understand what would be in the blanks in order to complete the problem? b. Were the students able to fill in the blanks with appropriate numbers and think about the problem?
"What would you write in the blanks if it is Ms. Nishi's case?"	• It is "Ms. Nishi collected 10 Ginkgo leaves. And she drew 5 pictures of her family on the leaves. How many leaves are left over?"		
"What is the expression (shiki) for this problem?" "What is the answer?"	• It is 10-5. • It's 5. • No, it's 5 leaves.		

(continued on next page)

Teacher Activity	Expected Student Response	Teaching Notes	Evaluation
"Now let's do Ms. Tsukuda's family. Ms. Tsukuda collected 12 leaves just like everybody did. Ms. Tsukuda's family has 2 members so she drew faces on 2 leaves." "Could you make a problem with Ms. Tsukuda's family?"	• It is "Ms. Tsukuda collected 12 Ginkgo leaves. And she drew 2 pictures of her family on the leaves. How many leaves are left over?"	• Change the numerical values in the problem little by little and confirm that you want them to use subtraction when they have a situation where they have to find the remainder.	b. Were the students able to fill in the blanks with appropriate numbers and think about the problem?
"Do you understand? What expression did we use to get the answer?" "What is the answer?" "How did we find the answer?"	• It is 12 - 2. • It is 10. • I subtracted 2 from the 2 of 12.	• Remind them of subtraction of two digit numbers without regrouping and confirm that in this case they subtracted the numbers in the ones positions from each other to find the answer.	c. Were the students able to do the calculation of 12-2?
2.) Using this format to set up the main problem			
"Now let's do Student C's family. How many faces did Student C draw on the leaves?"	• C: I drew 7 faces on the leaves.		
"Let's make this the problem."	• It is "Student C collected 12 Ginkgo leaves. And then he drew 7 pictures of his family on the leaves. How many leaves are left over?"		b. Were the students able to fill in the blanks with appropriate numbers and think about the problem?

FIG. 7.1   *continued*

"O.K. Now, please find out 'what you already know' and 'what the problem is asking'."	• The numbers we know are 12 and 7. • The numbers we know are the number of leaves collected (12) and the number of faces drawn on the leaves (7). • What the problem asking is "how many leaves are left over?"		

3. Solving the Main Problem

1.) Thinking about formulating an expression (*shiki*). "Think about making an expression from 'what we already know' and 'what the problem in asking'." 2.) Understanding what the problem is asking.	• 7-12. • 12-7. • You can't subtract 7 from 2.	• Ask students to write the expression on the handout.	d. Could the students construct the right expression?
"That's right. But if you compare 12 and 7, which one is bigger?" "Well, then, it seems like you should be able to subtract it." "Today we're going to think about how to find the answer to 12- 7."	• 12. • It seems hard. • That's easy.	• Make the students notice that you can't subtract using these two one digit numbers (2-7), make them think about how to do this type of calculation.	

(continued on next page)

3.) Solving the problem individually "Well, we already used the leaves for the drawing, let's think about the problem using these tiles today. We will be telling each other how each of you solved the problem so please write how you did it using words, too."

(a) It looks like I can do the subtraction, but what can I do?
(b) Counting-Subtraction Method.
- Take them one by one from 12 and find the remainder.
- Break up 12 into 10 and 2, take them one by one from 10 and count the remaining numbers.
- Since it's 12 minus 7, it's the same until 7, then you count on your fingers 8, 9, 10, 11, and 12.
(Supplement-Addition Method)
(c) Subtraction-Addition Method
- Break 12 up into 10 and 2, then subtract 7 from 10. The answer to that (10 - 7) is 3, then you take the 2 you broke up and add that to get 5.
(d) Subtraction-Subtraction Method
- Break 7 up into 2 and 5, and subtract 2 from 12. Then you take the answer 10 and subtract 5 from it to get the answer, 5.

- Let the students paste the tiles freely on the drawing paper and observe how the students conceptualize the number 12. Moreover, ask students to turn the tiles over and leave them on the drawing paper when they subtract in order to understand where the numbers were subtracted from.
- Ask the students to write down their own solution using words on the handout.
- Find out which students are the following 3 types when it comes to addition with carrying
  Type A:
    Composition and decomposition (breaking down) of numbers is simple for this type of student. Able to calculate it in his/her head.
  Type B:
    Can find the answer by manipulating some sort of half concrete object.
  Type C:
    Finds it difficult to calculate unless he/she uses some sort of concrete object or his/her fingers.

a. Are the students positively trying to do the subtraction calculation using concrete objects?

c. Did the students understand the meaning and the method when calculating 12-7.

c. Could the students do the calculation 12-7?

FIG. 7.1   *continued*

84

		Give extra individual help especially to type C students when the teacher walks around to observe the students. Provide Ginkgo leaves if the type C students need them to think about the problem.	
4. Polishing (*Neriage*) and Presenting Individual Solution Methods "Please teach how you came up with the answer clearly to the other students in the classroom."		• During the time the teacher walks around the classroom to see how the students are doing (*kikanjunshi*) I will take some notes on how the students are thinking. And I would like to ask the students to present in the order of (b), (c), (d). (refer to the students' expected solution methods above in the column "Expected Student Reactions")	a. Did the students present their own ideas in a loud voice? a. Could the students listen to their friends' presentations carefully?
"Are there any other ways to find the answer?"	• Yes, yes, there are.		
("Why did you break 12 up into 10 and 2?") ("Why did you break 7 up into 2 and 5?")	• Why did you break 12 up into 10 and 2? • Why did you break 7 up into 2 and 5?	• Ask the students to ask questions when they don't understand what other students presented because of lack of explanation. If the students do not ask any questions, the teacher will ask questions (so the explanation will be clear).	b. Did the students understand there are many ways to solve subtraction problems that involve regrouping?

(continued on next page)

5. Summary and Announcement of the Next Lesson			
"Let's try to solve 12-5 using whatever method you like."	• I will do it the same way I did it before. • I wonder if the solution that K used is more convenient?" • I will try to do it the way that N did. • I won't know until I do it.	• When the problem is posed, the teacher tells the students whose case they are dealing with (to be consistent with the other problems). • Take notes on the students who are listening to their friends' presentations and trying to solve the problem in a different way than they did before. Try to incorporate these observations into the next lesson.	c. Could the students solve the problem using the method that they understood and agree with each other?
"What do you think is the best way to solve 12-9?" "Let's try to find out what method is the best in the next lesson."	• Well, I think method (b) is the best. • I think method (c) is faster. •I want to try to solve it.	• Try to help and lead the students who are still using the method of subtracting numbers one by one from 12 to the method of breaking up 12 into 10 and 2 and subtracting the numbers one by one from 10 and counting the remaining numbers (because this method will lead to the "Subtraction-Addition" method).	a. Will the students be motivated to learn the following lesson?

* Each heading alphabet (a, b, c, and d) in the column "Evaluation" corresponds to the four categories shown in section 8, the goal of this lesson

FIG. 7.1   *continued*

Third, the section "Things to Prepare," which had previously been left blank, was completed. In it the teachers noted that they would need to create 19 student manipulatives and handouts. They also noted that they would be making hint cards for the lesson.

Fourth, a note was added about student M., the child in Ms. Tsukuda's class who still could not subtract. In it, Ms. Tsukuda explained that she would be preparing a special activity for this child to work on. This note is a bit confusing because the lesson plan should have been focused on Ms. Nishi's class instead. As already mentioned, Ms. Nishi had not had a chance to tailor the plan to her class. This section technically should have provided notes about children with special needs in Ms. Nishi's class and how they would be handled.

Lastly, a number of modifications were made to the four-column chart entitled "Progression of the Lesson," which described the lesson itself. First, certain aspects of the lesson described were now different. For example, the review problems were now 10 minus 5 and 12 minus 2. Furthermore these problems would be based on the family trees made by Ms. Nishi and Ms. Tsukuda. In addition, the problem 12 minus 5 was now listed as a practice problem along with 12 minus 9. Moreover, the lesson was now to conclude without focusing children on the counting–subtraction method but rather by simply telling them that in the subsequent lesson they would think about which method works best in the case of 12 minus 9.

Second, the information provided throughout this chart was now much more detailed and complete. More of the questions and comments that the teacher would make were provided and a number of issues that the teacher needed to address were highlighted and addressed. For instance, attention was devoted to describing how to make the children realize that they were doing subtraction or to how to make sure that they understood the problem context.

Finally, the evaluation column, which had previously been left blank, was filled in. Each evaluation item listed in this column was marked with a letter, either a, b, c, or d. This was done to indicate which of the four categories of lesson goals mentioned in "The Goals of this Lesson" section were being targeted by the evaluation in question.

CREATING MATERIALS AND REHEARSING

A couple of days before the lesson, Ms. Nishi and Ms. Tsukuda got together to prepare the student manipulatives and handouts. Ms. Maejima joined them after she finished her work. She helped them cut the square tiles and put them into 20 small plastic bags that contained 12 tiles each. Although they were not supposed to stay after 6 p.m., these teachers stayed until 8:00 p.m. to finish preparing all the materials they needed to use for the lesson.

The packets that Ms. Nishi and Ms. Tsukuda made for all the observers contained copies of the lesson plan and the student worksheet that these two teachers had agreed to finish designing (see Fig. 7.2).

A student seating-chart was also included so that the observers could record the solution strategies employed by each child (see Fig. 7.3).

All the teachers at Tsuta were given these packets a day prior to the study lesson so that they could familiarize themselves both with the design of the lesson and the focal points it was meant to target.

A day before the lesson, Ms. Tsukuda and Ms. Nishi met one last time in Ms. Nishi's classroom from 6 to 7 p.m. They rehearsed the lesson by going over the four-column chart describing the lesson process, that appeared in their lesson plan. They also carefully went over the use of the blackboard, which they wanted to be both neat and well organized. They pasted the story problem on the board and discussed how much space would be

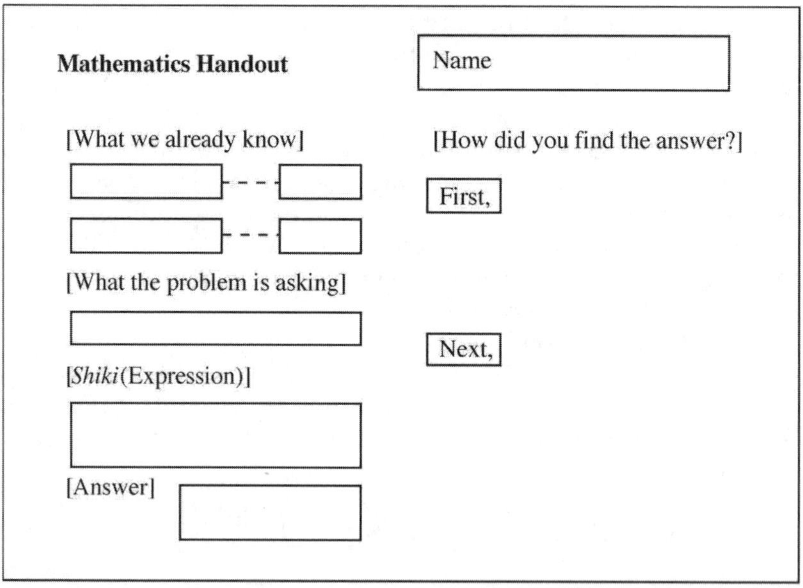

Mathematics Handout

Name

[What we already know]

[How did you find the answer?]

First,

[What the problem is asking]

Next,

[*Shiki*(Expression)]

[Answer]

$10 \times 14 \frac{1}{4}$ inch paper

FIG. 7.2   Handout for the first study lesson. The only change made from the previous version of this handout is that the sentence "what we already know" was changed to "something you already know."

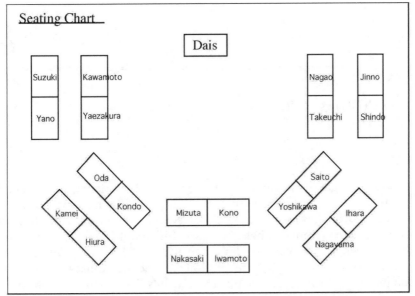

FIG. 7.3 Student seating chart to be used during the lesson observation.

needed for the teacher to write when she went over the handout. They considered how much space they should reserve for pasting the students' work on the blackboard. Finally, they checked one last time that they had all the instructional materials that Ms. Nishi would need and then went home to get a good night's sleep.

8

Teaching the Study Lesson

Ms. Nishi taught the study lesson to her class of 20 students (11 boys and 9 girls) during the third period, from 10:35 a.m. to 11:20 a.m., on Monday, November 15. This was the first time for Ms. Nishi, a first-year teacher, to teach a study lesson in front of other teachers at this school. She later recalled that she had been very nervous the day before this public teaching. Five minutes before the lesson began all the teachers at the school, as well as the principal and the vice-principal, showed up at Ms. Nishi's classroom with their copies of the lesson plan in hand. Many of the teachers recorded their observations directly onto this lesson plan, which they had attached to a clipboard to make writing while standing in the classroom more manageable.

All students at the school were left alone with assignments for them to complete while their teachers observed the study lesson. Some of the teachers asked their students to complete worksheets or to do a few pages from privately published exercise books, and others had the students work on art projects. In all cases, a class president and vice-president (*gakkyuiin* and *kyucho*) or two students on day duty (*nicchoku*) were assigned to monitor their classmates. Not one of these teachers had to leave Ms. Nishi's class to check on his or her students. In fact, during the 10 study lessons that Yoshida observed in the 1993–1994 school year, no teacher ever left the classroom and in only two cases did a student come to the classroom to consult with a teacher about how to manage his or her classmates. In both instances the student wanted to know what to do with classmates who had finished all the assigned work they were given.

Ms. Nishi's classroom (see Fig. 8.1) was typical of elementary school classrooms in Japan and resembled both those Yoshida visited in the Hiroshima area as a researcher and the ones he had attended as a child almost 30 years prior.

The only noteworthy difference was that the students' desks in Ms. Nishi's class were arranged in a U-shape, which is relatively unusual for a Japanese elementary school. According to Ms. Furumoto, this desk arrangement was adopted in the 1992–1993 school year in order to try to pro-

FIG. 8.1   Ms. Nishi's classroom.

mote students' ability to learn from each other, an objective that was an integral part of the school's *konaikenshu* goal.

In the rest of this chapter we describe how the study lesson actually unfolded when Ms. Nishi taught it to her students. Our description is organized using the same sectional headings that Ms. Nishi and Ms. Tsukuda used to describe the progression of the lesson in the four-column chart of their lesson plan (see chap. 6). This organization will allow the reader to refer to the lesson plan while reading what actually transpired in Ms. Nishi's classroom.

GRASPING THE PROBLEM SETTING

The lesson started about 5 minutes after the bell rang. It began with the two students who were assigned as day-duty monitors joining the teacher at the front of the classroom. These monitors turned toward the other students in the classroom and called to attention those who were distracted or talking. Once the whole class settled down, the day-duty students said in unison, "The mathematics lesson will begin," followed by, "Please bow." The teacher, the students, and all observers bowed. This is a very common ritual for beginning lessons in Japan, which probably explains why it was not described in the lesson plan.

Ms. Nishi began by reminding the class of the leaf collecting activity they had done a couple of days prior during Daily Living (seikatsu-ka) class. She said, "A couple of days ago we went to Hazu Hill, didn't we?" Many students nodded. Then Ms. Nishi continued by asking, "What kind of leaves were there?" The students enthusiastically called out the names of the leaves they had collected. One student said ginkgo leaves. Other students excitedly mentioned, maple leaves, persimmon leaves, ordinary leaves, acorn leaves, dead leaves, and the like. After the students settled down a bit, Ms. Nishi said, "Yes, we collected many leaves and we made many objects with them." Then she said: "We also went to the Shinto shrine and collected leaves. What did we collect there?" The students immediately answered, "Ginkgo leaves." Ms. Nishi then said, "I remember somebody said an interesting thing about the fallen ginkgo leaves." One of the students responded: "Chisa said it was like a yellow carpet." Ms. Nishi continued by asking, "How many leaves did I ask you to collect?," and many of the students responded "Twelve leaves." Then Ms. Nishi reminded the students of the family collages they had done after the field trip. She pointed to these collages, which were all pasted on one of the walls of the classroom (see Fig. 8.2) and asked the students how many faces they had drawn. Students responded according to the number of people in their family.

Ms. Nishi next mentioned to the students that she had made a collage as well. She took it out and showed it to the class (see Fig. 8.3).

She asked the students, "How many family members do I have?" Some students answered "Five people." Then Ms. Nishi started to talk about her situation. She said she collected 12 leaves but a student asked to have some of her leaves because he accidentally tore 2 of his leaves when he was making his collage. She said she gave 2 leaves to this student and so she ended up with 10 leaves. Then she explained that she had used 5 leaves to draw her family members and asked, "Can you understand how many leaves were left?" The students confidently responded by saying "Five leaves." Ms. Nishi said, "Is that right? How did you figure it out?" One of the students responded by explaining, "Ten minus 5 is 5." Ms. Nishi said, "I see."

PRESENTATION OF THE PROBLEM FORMAT

(1) Present the Problem Format and Use It on Previously Learned Subtraction Situations

Ms. Nishi started this segment of the lesson by pasting on the board the template for the ginkgo leaf story problem with its three blanks left unfilled (see Fig. 8.4).

FIG. 8.2   Students' collages on the upper part of the window.

FIG. 8.3   Ms. Nishi with her collage.

FIG. 8.4   Problem format on the blackboard. The small magnetic cards pasted in a vertical line on the left of the problem format are students' name cards.

She then asked the students, "Can you figure out what to put in the blanks?" One student immediately said "yes" in a loud voice and a couple of other students raised their hands quietly. Ms. Nishi called on the student who had said yes. The student answered "12, … 12 collected, … 2 ginkgo leaves.…" He was clearly confused about what he needed to put in the first blank. Ms. Nishi asked if there was anybody who could help him; however, the students in general seemed confused. In fact, at least one other student tried to fill in the first blank with the number 12. Ms. Nishi reminded them that she had 12 leaves but she gave 2 leaves to a student. The students now agreed that Ms. Nishi had 10 leaves so Ms. Nishi put a card with the number 10 in the second blank. She realized that the students were still having a hard time figuring out what would be in the first blank so she instead asked the students what she should put in the third blank. One of the students responded that the third blank would be 5 leaves, and Ms. Nishi pasted a card there with the number 5 written on it. After some struggle, Ms. Nishi finally got the students to come up with the idea that her name would go in the first blank and she completed the problem by placing a card with her name on the first blank.

Ms. Nishi next asked all the students to read the problem out loud and then asked them how they could write down the expression (*shiki*) that represented this problem. One of the students answered by saying 10 minus 5 equals 5. Ms. Nishi commented by saying, "It looks good," thus completing the first warm-up problem.

Ms. Nishi moved on to the second warm-up problem by asking Ms. Tsukuda how many faces of family members she had drawn on the leaves. Ms. Tsukuda, who was standing in the back of the classroom, smiled at the students and said that her family consisted of only two people, herself and her husband. Ms. Nishi showed Ms. Tsukuda's collage (see Fig. 8.5) and told the students that Ms. Tsukuda collected 12 leaves just like everybody else and did not lose any leaves because none of her students made mistakes. Then Ms. Nishi asked the students if they could make a story problem by using the template on the blackboard. About a half of the students enthusiastically raised their hands. One of the students read the problem by filling out the blanks correctly and Ms. Nishi pasted cards in the three blanks to represent Ms. Tsukuda's situation.

Next, Ms. Nishi asked the students if they could tell her an expression (*shiki*) for this problem. One of the students described the expression as 12

FIG. 8.5   Ms. Nishida with Ms. Tsukuda's collage.

minus 2, and another student provided the answer 10. Ms. Nishi asked the student how he got the answer 10. The student replied: "I subtracted 2 from 12." Then she asked him again how he had subtracted it. The student answered again "I subtracted 2 from 12." Ms. Nishi insisted, "Can you explain it in more in detail?," but she got no further response. It seemed as if it was not clear to the student what else the teacher wanted to hear. Ms. Nishi looked a little bit frustrated with the difficulty she was having getting the student to answer her question. Finally, one of the students provided an answer by saying, "Taking two of them one by one and it became 10." However, this answer did not seem to fully satisfy Ms. Nishi who decided to write down the expression, 12 – 2, on the blackboard and ask the student who provided the answer, "From where should we subtract? Which 2 are you subtracting?" The student pointed to the number 2 in the ones place of the number 12 on the blackboard and said "This 2." Finally, it looked as if Ms. Nishi had gotten the answer she wanted from the students. She went over what the student had said by explaining that he subtracted 2 from the 2 of 12's ones place.

(2) Using the Format to Set Up the Main Problem of the Lesson

Ms. Nishi began this segment by telling the students that they were now going to think about how many leaves would be left over in the case of Akira, one of their classmates. She called on Akira and asked him to tell the class how many leaves he used, to which he responded, seven leaves. Ms. Nishi then asked the students how they would complete the story problem in this case. A couple of students enthusiastically said "Yes!" and raised their hands. Mr. Nishi asked one of the students to read the problem for the class. The student said, "Akira collected 12 ginkgo leaves. Then, he drew 7 pictures of his family on the leaves. How many leaves are left over?"

Ms. Nishi told the students, "Today, I would like you to think about Akira's case." Then she passed out the lesson handout to the students. After students received the handout, Ms. Nishi said, "Okay, we are always doing this, aren't we? Let's find out what we already know and what the problem is asking." She said to the students that the answers were hiding in the story problem and instructed them to write down their responses to these two questions in the space provided on the handout. Ms. Nishi walked around the classroom and observed how her students were doing. From time to time she made suggestions to those who were having a hard time working on the handout. When she came back to the front of the class she asked the students to put their pencils down and she said that she noticed that many of them were having trouble. She asked the students what numbers they already knew. Students responded with the numbers 12 and 7. So Ms. Nishi wrote the words "12 leaves" and "7 leaves" on the blackboard. Next she asked the students to describe what the numbers 12 and 7 represented. It took a while to get the answer that Ms. Nishi wanted, but eventually students came up with the words "the number he collected" and "the number he drew." She wrote these words next to the two numbers 12 and 7 on the blackboard. Then she asked the students "What is the problem asking?" and she encouraged students who had not done so to participate. A student explained that the problem was asking: "How many leaves are left over?"

SOLVING THE PROBLEM

(1) Thinking About Writing an Expression (*Shiki*)

Ms. Nishi next asked, how to write an expression (*shiki*) to represent this problem. Many students raised their hands this time and one of them provided the answer 12 minus 7.

(2) Grasping the Topic

Ms. Nishi next asked the students if they could do the calculation for 12 minus 7. Some students immediately said: "Yes I can do it." The majority of the students, however, remained silent. So Ms. Nishi asked them which one was bigger, 12 or 7. Many students said that 12 was bigger. Finally, Ms. Nishi asked the students, "If 12 is bigger, then can you subtract 7 from it?" Many of the students said yes.

(3) Solving the Problem Individually

Ms. Nishi said to the students, "Today I would like you to think about how to find the answer for 12 minus 7." She instructed them to take out of their desks the manipulative, which she and Ms. Tsukuda had placed there before the lesson. Then she directed the students to take out all the tiles from the bags that came with the manipulative. As soon as the majority of the students had done this, Ms. Nishi asked everyone to look at the blackboard. She told the students that because all the ginkgo leaves had been used up for the collages, for this lesson they would use the tiles instead. Ms. Nishi pasted on the board a paper cut ginkgo leaf and a tile and drew an arrow in between them (see Fig. 8.6).

She asked the students to pay careful attention and said:

> Please think that these tiles are the ginkgo leaves. Use the tiles for the ginkgo leaves and think about how to find the answer. Attention, this drawing paper is sticky so the tiles will stay on it. You may paste the tiles any way you like and you can do whatever you want.

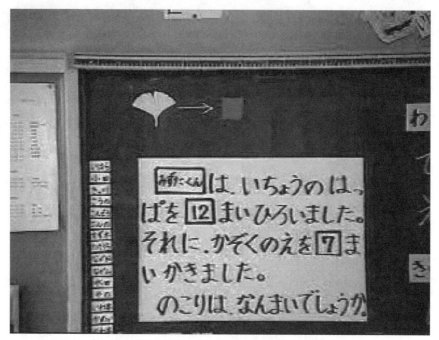

FIG. 8.6   Showing the relationship between a gingko leaf and a tile. This relationship is represented above the problem by a leaf and a tile joined by an arrow.

She also explained that after solving the problem students should write down in words on their handout what they had done. She then said, "Please start."

Ms. Nishi began to walk around the classroom but soon realized that she had not given complete instructions on how to use the tiles. She returned to the front of the classroom and told the students, "When you subtract tiles, please flip them over and put them back on the drawing paper." She borrowed a manipulative from one of the students and demonstrated what she meant by flipping over a tile (see Fig. 8.7).

She emphasized that to subtract they should not take the tiles and move them to the other side of the drawing paper, but that instead they should flip them over and leave them where they were. She instructed the students to resume working on the problem.

Ms. Nishi again started to walk around the classroom to observe how the students were doing. Soon after she started to do this the other teachers also began to walk around the classroom (see Figs. 8.8, and 8.9).

FIG. 8.7 Ms. Nishi explaining how to use the manipulative.

FIG. 8.8 The teachers observing and taking notes on their lesson plans.

FIG. 8.9   Students working on the problem.

The lower grade level teachers seemed particularly active in taking notes on the student seating chart and the lesson plan. Some even talked to each other in a soft voice and seemed to be discussing how the students were doing and their use of the manipulative. In addition, it was interesting to see their facial expressions. Some of them were serious and trying to figure out what particular students were trying to do. Others were nodding or smiling, indicating that they had found a student solving the problem in an interesting way. Teachers from other grade levels were also busy taking notes, walking around, and talking with each other about what they were seeing. None of them were coaching or tutoring the students who were having difficulty. They only interacted with the students when they were trying to understand how they were solving the problem; however, they never tried to teach the students.

POLISHING AND PRESENTING INDIVIDUAL SOLUTION METHODS (*NERIAGE*)

After the students had worked on their own for a while, Ms. Nishi eventually asked them to stop and commented, "It looks like you thought a lot and found various ways to solve the problem." She told the class that she would now call on students for them to explain how they found the answer that they came up with. Ms. Nishi called on a girl named Sachiko to present her idea in front of the class using her manipulative.

Sachiko's Solution

Although Sachiko came to the front of the classroom, she was somewhat apprehensive. It took some time for Ms. Nishi to convince her to speak up in front of everyone. Eventually she explained: "I pasted all 12 tiles face up. And I flipped over 7 of them. Then it became 5." Ms. Nishi asked Sachiko if she could explain how she counted the 5 tiles. She said that she counted the tiles 1, 2, 3, 4, and 5, from the left to right (see Fig. 8.10).

Ms. Nishi asked if other students understood her explanation. It looked like everybody understood, so she decided to restate Sachiko's solution herself. She said that Sachiko "lined the tiles up in one straight line. Then, she flipped over 7 from the left side." It looked like none of the students had

FIG. 8.10 Sachiko presenting her idea. The diagram in the box at the lower left corner depicts what was shown on Sachiko's manipulative on the blackboard.

questions about this solution so she asked the class if there was anybody who had had the same idea. She identified all the students who solved the problem in the same way and pasted their names next to Sachiko's work on the board. Ms. Nishi also took out a card that said, "Take one by one from 12 and count the leftovers," which she pasted above Sachiko's manipulative on the blackboard (see Fig. 8:11).

Ms. Nishi read the card and again described Sachiko's work by saying that she "took tiles out one by one from 12, then the remaining number is 5." Finally, she decided to ask other students to present their ideas for solving this problem.

Ken's Solution

Ms. Nishi next called to the board a boy named Ken, who explained his solution as follows: "I took out 2 from 12. Then, I took 5 from the remaining 10. And it became 5" (see Fig. 8.12).

Ms. Nishi asked this student to use his manipulative to show how he solved this problem. First, he put the 12 tiles back into one straight line. Second, he said that he had moved two of the tiles. He flipped over 2 tiles and

FIG. 8.11   Ms. Nishi pasting a card with a summary explanation.

FIG. 8.12   Ken presenting his idea at the blackboard. The diagram in the box at the lower left corner depicts what was shown on Ken's manipulative on the blackboard.

moved them under the first line to form two lines. Third, he flipped over 5 more tiles (see Fig. 8.13).

Then he tried to move the 5 tiles to the second line, where the other 2 tiles were located. However, Ms. Nishi asked him to keep the 5 tiles where they were. Ken looked at his classmates and asked, "Is it okay?" Many students responded by saying "yes." Then he asked if there were any questions. The students said "no." However, Ms. Nishi said that she had a question. She wanted to know why he took 2 tiles away from the 12 tiles and what he had done with the number 7. The student struggled to express himself but finally explained that he took out the 2 of the 7 and subtracted the 2 from the 12. Ms. Nishi seemed to think that this was not a convincing answer so she pressed him further by asking, "Why did you come up with the 2 from the 7?" However, Ken could not explain this, so Ms. Nishi decided to ask if he divided the number into two numbers. He said "yes" and after some further struggle he finally explained that he had divided the number 7 into 2 and 5. Ms. Nishi asked if others understood what Ken had done. Because

Step One

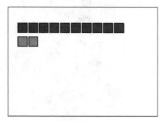

Step Two

Step Three

FIG. 8.13   Steps in Ken's explanation.

Ms. Nishi did not get a response from anyone, she took out a card that explained Ken's solution and pasted it above his manipulative (see Fig. 8.14).

Then she explained his method using her own words. She said that "he broke up 7 into 2 and 5" and then she added, "he decomposed the number 7 and carried out the subtraction." She continued her explanation as follows: "He subtracted 2 from 12 first, then subtracted 5 from 10." After her explanation she asked the class if anybody had solved the problem in the same way. There were only a few students who raised their hands to indicate that their solutions were similar.

Akira's Solution

Mr. Nishi asked a third student, a boy named Akira, to present his solution to the problem. Akira came up to the blackboard and explained his strat-

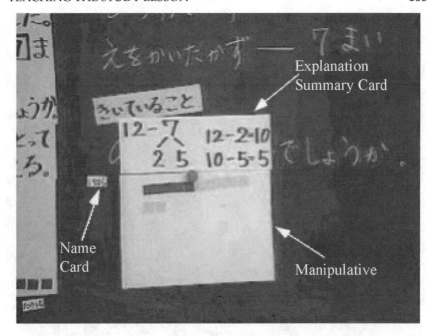

FIG. 8.14   The explanation summary card Ms. Nishi pasted on the black-board. Ms. Nishi pasted an explanation summary card above Ken's ma-nipulative. She also pasted Ken's name card next to his manipulative. The card you see right above the explanation summary card (it actually said "what the problem is asking" was pasted when the class was working on the handout. Also the explanation summary card is covering the writing.

egy as follows: "First, I flipped 7 tiles and added the remaining 3 and 2 and got 5. It became 5 all together" (see Fig. 8.15).

Then he asked other students if they understood his solution. A number of students responded with a "yes." Ms. Nishi, who did not seem con-vinced, asked the other students if they really understood. The class was si-lent but Ms. Nishi decided to continue. She explained that Akira had pasted the tiles in two lines, 10 tiles and 2 tiles. Then he had subtracted 7 from 10. He had next added the remaining 3 and 2 to get 5.

Although the bell had rung a few minutes before, she wanted the stu-dents to understand this method so she tried very hard to get their attention as she once again summarized Akira's work and pasted a card that ex-plained his solution. At first she pasted a card that said "Break 12 into 10 and 2, and take one by one from 10 and count the remaining tiles." As she tried to again summarize the solution, she realized the she had pasted the wrong card. So she replaced it with the correct one, about which she said, "This one is also decomposition of a number [see Fig. 8.16].

FIG. 8.15   Akira presenting his idea at the blackboard. The diagram in
the box at the upper left corner depicts what was shown on Akira's manipulative on the blackboard.

He broke up 12 into 10 and 2. Then, he took 7 from 10. Finally, he added
3 and 2." Ms. Nishi asked the class if there was anybody who had solved
the problem in the same way as Akira, but no students reported having
used this method.

Ms. Nishi wondered out loud about students who said that their solutions
were not represented by any of the three on the board. She asked these students if they had done something different. There was silence. It looked like
these students either could not come up with a solution or they could not tell
how what they did was similar to or different from the ideas presented.

SUMMARY AND ANNOUNCEMENT
FOR THE NEXT LESSON

Although the bell had rung a while back, Ms. Nishi did not forget to summarize the lesson. She started by saying, "Although we worked on the
same subtraction problem, there were various ways to solve it." The students nodded. Ms. Nishi said that it looked like there were more solution

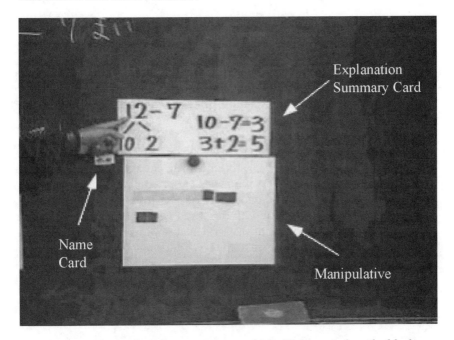

FIG. 8.16 The explanation summary card Ms. Nishi pasted on the black-board.

strategies for solving this problem but that it was time to find out the answer. The students enthusiastically raised their hands. She called on one of the students who said that the answer was five leaves. Ms. Nishi asked if all of the students' manipulatives on the board were showing five tiles remaining face up. The class confirmed this.

Ms. Nishi went on to say, "Today we thought about Akira's case." Then she added, "There are other cases like five people in the family, or four, and even other numbers." She said that they would be dealing with the case of 12 minus 5 for the next problem. She asked the students if they could tell which one of the strategies presented would be the easiest way to solve that problem. Different students pointed to various methods. Some claimed that their solution was the best. Ms. Nishi said that they did not have time to discuss which was the best, but that they would think about this during the next lesson. Ms. Nishi also asked the students to remember the three strategies presented during the lesson for solving the problem 12 minus 7. Thus the lesson ended with Ms. Nishi alluding to the practice problem 12 minus 5 rather than having the kids work on it. In addition, she did not follow the lesson plan's intent of discussing the merits of various methods presented. She simply ended the lesson by pointing out that there were various ways to find the answer.

The last thing she did was to instruct the class on how she wanted them to put away the manipulative. Then she asked the students on day-duty to end the lesson. The two students came up to the front. They made sure that all students were sitting nicely and quietly before they said, "The third period will now end" and "Bow." Everybody in the room bowed.

Overall the lesson felt smooth and Ms. Nishi looked confident teaching in front of the other teachers. The students were engaged and did not seem distracted by the many teachers who were observing them, but rather they seemed to enjoy having other people in the classroom seeing them work. Ms. Nishi proved to be patient with the students as she pressed for clearer explanations and tried to emphasize important points necessary to understand each solution. We now turn to the observers' reactions to this lesson.

9

Discussing How to Improve the Study Lesson

The lower grade teachers held two meetings to discuss their observations of the study lesson taught by Ms. Nishi and their ideas for revisions that should be made to it (see Figs. 9.1 and 9.2).

The first of these meetings was called for 3 p.m. on November 15, the same day that Ms. Nishi had taught the lesson. This meeting, which lasted 1 hour, was held in the principal's office. All the lower grade teachers attended, as did the principal of the school. The second meeting was held the following day. It too started at 3 p.m. and lasted 1 hour and 20 minutes. Although the first meeting had been scheduled in advance, the second one was added after the fact because the teachers thought that they needed more time to discuss the lesson. Unfortunately, Ms. Nishi was not available for the second meeting because of conflicting obligations. No schoolwide meeting was held to discuss this first implementation of the lesson, but the lower grade teachers did solicit and receive informal comments from their colleagues.

Discussion & Revising	11/15	On the same day as the study lesson, lower grade teachers reflected on the lesson and started revising it. (1.5 hours)
	11/16	Lower grade teachers continued to revise the lesson. (1 hour)
	11/16-17	Two first grade teachers finalized the lesson plan and prepared to teach the second lesson.

FIG. 9.1 Working on the lower grade subtraction lesson: Discussion and revising.

FIG. 9.2   Lower grade teachers discussing the study lesson. The papers in front of the teachers are the lesson plans and the seating chart, on which they took notes during their observations.

The first debriefing began with everyone praising Ms. Nishi. For example, Mr. Yamasaki, the principal of the school, commended her for her efforts in conducting the study lesson and thanked her for the opportunity to observe a good lesson. The other teachers also thanked Ms. Nishi. Ms. Maejima commented that she was impressed to see Ms. Nishi's first-grade students respond so quickly to their teacher. Ms. Tsukuda mentioned that, although Ms. Nishi spoke very fast, she was surprised to see how well her students responded to her. Ms. Furumoto jokingly pointed out to Ms. Tsukuda that she tended to speak so slowly that it would be quite different if she taught the lesson. Ms. Tsukuda recognized this and said, "I speak very slowly and repeat sentences." Everybody had a good laugh.

Aside from these polite comments, the remainder of this meeting and the one held on the following day were devoted to discussing in detail the lesson that Ms. Nishi had taught. In what follows we provide a summary of the key conversations that transpired over these 2 days of conversations.

IMPROVING THE USE OF TIME IN THE LESSON

One of the first issues raised by the teachers was that the lesson had run over. Ms. Maejima, who had been officially assigned to keep track of time in Ms. Nishi's classroom,[1] began by reporting that the total length of the lesson had been about fifty-seven minutes. This was 12 minutes longer than the 45-minute lesson that had been planned. One of the teachers wondered what had caused the lesson to be longer than anticipated. The teachers decided to go through the segments planned for this lesson one by one and to compare how long they had actually taken relative to the time that had been allotted for them. Figure 9.3 is a chart that summarizes the time discrepancies that they uncovered.

The teachers next decided to identify places in the lesson where they felt time could be saved, of which they found several. They began by discussing how they could reduce the time spent on the warm-up problem "12 minus 2." Ms. Tsukuda commented that Ms. Nishi's lesson had gone very smoothly until the class started to talk about this problem. She suspected that this was linked to a note to the teacher on the lesson plan that stated, "Remind them [students] of subtraction of two-digit numbers without regrouping and confirm that in this case they subtracted the numbers in the ones position from each other to find the answer." Ms. Tsukuda thought that Ms. Nishi had been prompted by this note to be too persistent in asking students to produce a good explanation for how they solved the problem. Ms. Maejima added that she thought that the students could not understand clearly the phrase that Ms. Nishi used at this point in the lesson, "Explain it in more detail." She said that because the calculation was very simple and the students already knew the answer, they did not know what else to "explain in detail." Ms. Maejima, for example, had noticed that the student who said "I subtracted 2 from 12 and it became 10" seemed confused when asked to explain further. Ms. Furumoto agreed with Ms. Maejima that it might be a little difficult to get a better explanation because the calculation was so easy for the students. At the end of the conversation, all the teachers agreed that in order to conserve time, it was not necessary to ask for further explanations about the warm-up problems as long as students got the right answers. They felt comfortable with this decision because these problems were not the main topic of the lesson.

The next segment that teachers talked about was when Ms. Nishi posed the story problem to the class. Ms. Maejima recalled that many of the students had trouble figuring out that they needed to complete the first blank

---

[1]Although the task of keeping track of time was assigned to Ms. Maejima, all the observing teachers seemed very aware of how time was spent during the lesson and many of them had made records of this on their copy of the lesson plan.

1. Grasping the Problem Setting (5 minutes) [1:40]

2. Presentation of the Problem Format (10 minutes) [17:39]:
    (1) Presenting the format and using it on previously learned
        subtraction situations (no borrowing situation) (5
        minutes) [10:14]
        • Problem 10 minus 5 [4:46]
        • Problem 12 minus 2 [5:28]
    (2) Using this format to set up the main problem of the
        lesson (5 minutes) [8:00]
        • Setting up the problem 12 minus 7 [1:56]
        • Students to filling the blanks in the handout [1:23]
        • Confirmation of the answers of the handout [4:06]

3. Solving the Main Problem (13 minutes) [18:59]:
    (1) Thinking about formulating an expression [0:35]
    (2) Understanding what the problem is asking [1:50]
    (3) Solving the problem individually [16:34]

4. Polishing and Reporting Individual Solution Methods (12
    minutes) [14:18]
5. Summary and Announcement for Next Lesson (5 minutes)
    [4:40]

FIG. 9.3   A comparison of allotted and actual teaching time for the first
study lesson. The times indicated in the parentheses show the allotted
time for each segment of the study lesson. The times indicated in the
brackets show the actual length of each of these segments.

with the name of a person. She recommended that the teacher simply fill in
the first blank after the class decided to use a particular person's case and
that students only be asked to fill in the two remaining blanks with the
quantities involved in the problem. Ms. Furumoto agreed with Ms.
Maejima that the name of the person was not really important for solving
this problem, as did Ms. Tsukuda. Ms. Tsukuda also mentioned that Ms.
Nishi and the class only read the problem after the three blanks were filled
in, but not when she first posted the problem on the blackboard. She felt
that holding back on reading the problem confused a number of students.
She suggested that had the class read the problem earlier on, perhaps filling

in the first blank may not have been as much of a hurdle. Ms. Chijiiwa and Ms. Maejima both agreed with this interpretation. Ms. Tsukuda added that she felt that it was quite taxing to ask such young students to recall the two quantities involved in the problem. She thought that this meant that there was too much going on in their heads and that as a result, they were rushing to fill in the numbers that they remembered in the first blank where they needed to write a person's name. Ms. Chijiiwa agreed with this and added, "Although the problem consists of only four sentences, it is quite a lot for first-grade students to read and understand." Ms. Furumoto agreed whole-heartedly. At the end of this discussion, the teachers came to the consensus that the class should read the problem out loud in unison when it first appeared, and that the teacher should fill in the first blank of the problem. The teachers felt that both of these modifications would reduce the time spent on this segment while also helping the students better understand the problem.

Next, the teachers commented that Ms. Nishi did not explain well how to use the manipulative. This made the students hesitant and as a result slowed down the pace of the lesson. Ms. Furumoto said that Ms. Nishi should have given clear instructions on how to use the manipulative when she first introduced it, particularly with respect to what to do with the tiles when subtracting—turning them over instead of pulling them aside. Ms. Tsukuda emphasized that because it was the first time for the students to use this particular manipulative, a clear and concise explanation on how to use it was all the more important. Ms. Furumoto suggested that Ms. Nishi could have demonstrated how to use this tool by solving a problem like 3 minus 2. However, other of the teachers thought that because the problem 3 minus 2 was not directly related to this lesson, this would be a bad choice.

Ms. Tsukuda added that lack of clear instructions on how to use the manipulative was not the only cause for the students' slow responses. She was concerned that perhaps they had not understood the relationship between the ginkgo leaves and the tiles. She thought that replacing real (or concrete) objects (*gutaibutsu*) (e.g., ginkgo leaves or paper cutouts of ginkgo leaves) with a more abstract representation (*han-gutaibutsu*) (e.g., tiles and blocks) was confusing to some students because they had not yet developed good association skills. She reminded everyone that although making these links was easy for an adult, this was not the case for first graders. She said that the students had become confused because Ms. Nishi explained the relationship between the leaves and the tiles at the same time that she gave instructions for how to use the manipulative. Ms. Furumoto agreed and suggested that the explanation for replacing the ginkgo leaves with tiles should be provided when the class worked on the problem 12 minus 2. The teacher could say, "Because we used up all the ginkgo leaves for the drawings, we do not have them any more. So let's replace them with tiles and think about the problem." Ms. Furumoto added that only the teacher should use the tiles at this point. Giving children these tiles should be held off until the main problem of the lesson was introduced. In this way, Ms. Furumoto thought that not only would the students understand the relationship between the tiles and the leaves, but they would also understand how to use the manipulative because they would receive a clear demonstration by the teacher when she explained the example problem 12 minus 2. Everyone agreed with these ideas, which they thought in the long run would make the lesson run more time efficiently and would lead to better student learning.

The teachers also felt that the students were confused and slowed down by the handout they were given. Ms. Furumoto pointed out that in particular too much time had been spent on the part of the handout where students were asked what they already knew and what the problem was asking them. Ms. Nishi had provided students 1½ minutes to fill in this information and spent about 4 minutes going over their answers. In addition, she spent about 2 minutes setting up the problem 12 minus 7. All in all, she had lost about 3 minutes during this segment, relative to the time that had been allotted for it. Several of the teachers also reported observing that many students struggled to provide answers to the two questions posed on the handout and that even when they were able to write something, it tended to be incorrect. Ms. Furumoto speculated that things would have gone more smoothly if the teacher had started by having the class discuss what they knew and needed to find out, and had let the children simply complete this information on their handouts.

REDESIGNING THE HANDOUT

This last interchange prompted the teachers to go on to discussing other modifications that could have been made to the handout. Ms. Maejima suggested that the story problem with the three blanks should have been reproduced on this sheet. She pointed out that by asking students to fill in the blanks in this problem, in essence one would be asking them to answer the question "What do you know?" but in a format that might be easier for them. She said that they could then ask students to underline in red what the problem was asking, a technique that she reported worked well with the second graders at the school. She felt that this would also be an easier way to ask students for information rather than having them write an answer to a question. Ms. Furumoto added that they could also ask the students to underline in blue what they already knew. Then the only thing the teacher would need to do would be to confirm the answers orally. Ms. Tsukuda, however, felt that her students would have been able to answer directly the questions asked in the handout used with Ms. Nishi's students. She explained:

Tsukuda:	My students have been doing this type of handout for a while.
Furumoto:	I see, I see ...
Tsukuda:	My students did something like that in the first quarter when they learned addition and subtraction. Then we did it in the beginning of the second quarter when they learned addition.
Maejima:	I see.
Furumoto:	If that is the case then the students should be able to do it. Maybe the students in Ms. Nishi's class could not do it for some other reason ...
Tsukuda:	But Ms. Nishi's class has been doing the same thing as what my class has been doing ...
Everybody:	Ha, ha, ha, ha ... [everybody laughed]
Furumoto:	I see ... you [Ms. Nishi] were doing the same thing ... Well, I am not saying that you were not doing a good job ... You were doing it the same way as Ms. Tsukuda, but for some reason ...

This conversation led the teachers to agree that generally asking first-grade students to write out sentences in answer to questions posed on a handout was a difficult task that required a lot of practice. Although Ms. Tsukuda told the teachers that her students had had practice with this type of handout, the teachers thought that it was not realistic to think that her students could fill in the blanks any more quickly than Ms. Nishi's students. In addition, Ms. Chijiiwa pointed out that working on a story problem containing blanks was already a challenge for first graders, as evidenced in Ms. Nishi's class. She felt it was too much to ask them as well to write explanations on the handout. All the teachers recognized that they were asking too much of the first-grade students. Although Ms. Maejima, Ms. Furumoto, and Ms. Chijiiwa applauded the effort of the first-grade teachers to promote their students' language development by encouraging writing during mathematics lessons, they were in favor of cutting back on the writing required to complete the handout. They felt that the focal point of the lesson was for students to think about the problem in various ways, not having them write. The teachers thought that it was very important to limit the scope of the students' tasks in order to maximize the quality of their thinking about the problem.

In the end, the teachers decided that first they would ask the students to talk as a whole class about what should be in the blanks in the story problem. The students would then be asked to fill in the blanks on the handout on their own. Second, the teachers also decided to fill in the first blank of the story problem, the one requiring the name of the person. They were convinced that having three blanks in the story problem was too difficult for first graders and took away from their ability to think about the problem.

CLARIFYING THE FOCUS ON SUBTRACTION

The teachers also discussed the fact that numerous students had difficulty realizing that the lesson dealt with subtraction, particularly in the beginning of the lesson. Ms. Maejima mentioned that she observed one student answering 14 to the problem, 12 minus 2. In response, Ms. Chijiiwa pointed out that Ms. Nishi did not say "this is a subtraction problem" until she was finished talking with the class about the second review problem, even though the lesson plan had specified doing this after the first review problem. The teachers all agreed that it was critical to help students realize early on in the lesson that they were learning about subtraction and they went on to discuss at length how best to do this.

Ms. Maejima said that because the story problem contained the term "left over," she thought that it was natural to talk about subtraction after reading the story problem for the first time. Ms. Furumoto added that each time Ms. Nishi had worked on a warm-up problem with the class she should have pasted on the board the corresponding collage and written next to it the subtraction problem it represented. She explained her reason for suggesting this in the following terms:

Furumoto: I think that if the teacher does not leave what the students did on the blackboard, the students cannot clearly understand what is going on, particularly the slow learners. The slow learners may just repeat what the other students say without really thinking and involving themselves in the lesson. For this reason I think the teacher should emphasize the concept of subtraction by leaving what they are doing on the blackboard. Pasting the drawings and writing the expressions ... and going through them very carefully ...

Maejima: I see, I see ...

Furumoto: So, we have to leave a strong impression with the students that "We are working on subtraction problems. We are doing subtraction calculations."

In other words, Ms. Furumoto believed that the students would understand that they were working on a subtraction problem if the explicit information about this was available to them on the blackboard.

The teachers seemed to like Ms. Furumoto's suggestions. In response, Ms. Tsukuda explained that she and Ms. Nishi had discussed pasting all the collages on the blackboard but had decided that there was not enough space. Ms. Furumoto, however, disagreed. She argued that because each collage was only about half the size of a typical sheet of drawing paper, there would be enough room. The teachers confirmed that she was right by drawing her suggestion out on a piece of scratch paper (see Fig. 9.4).

Ms. Tsukuda, who was now convinced that there was room for this proposed layout, said that she would incorporate it into the version of the study lesson that she would teach.

REFINING THE MANIPULATIVE FOR THE LESSON

The teachers also talked at length about the design of their lesson manipulative, with which they were still not satisfied. First, they felt that the paper on which they had had students paste their tiles was too big for the limited desk space available to students.[2] This made it hard for the stu-

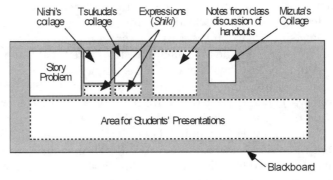

FIG. 9.4   Ms. Furumoto's idea for how to organize the blackboard.

---

[2]The size of the students' desktop space was 23¾ inches (width) by 15¾ inches (length).

dents to write their explanations on the handout while looking at what they had done with their manipulative. In addition, when children tried to keep both of these things on their desk, the handout kept getting stuck on the glue-sprayed drawing paper. Moreover, because pasting and peeling the tiles was fun, some of the students played with the manipulative instead of focusing on their work. Ms. Chijiiwa reported observing a number of students make patterns with the tiles instead of using them to think about the problem.

Ms. Maejima voiced a deeper concern about this tool. She recalled the difficulty she had had inferring from it the solution methods that Ms. Nishi's students had used. In particular, it was hard to figure out what the students were thinking if one had not seen how they moved their tiles. In other words, the manipulative failed to leave a record of the students' thinking process. All the teachers reported that they had felt the same way when they observed the lesson. Although this potential problem had been mentioned when the teachers were planning the lesson, the teachers were very disappointed to see their predictions pan out. Ms. Maejima added that this lack of clarity also affected students' ability to learn from each other's ideas. She thought that students were judging whether their solutions were similar to those presented on the board based on how the tiles were pasted, instead of carefully listening to the explanations provided. As a result, students were likely to identify a drawing paper with five tiles remaining on the left side and seven tiles on the right as identical to their work even if their solution strategy had actually been different.

A second problem highlighted by Ms. Tsukuda was the discrepancy between what the students did using the manipulative and what they wrote on the handout, which made it very confusing for an observer to figure out how students had actually tackled the problem. All the other teachers reported being similarly confused during their observations of students' individual work. Ms. Tsukuda recalled that she noticed that some students composed good written explanations. For example, she remembered a student who had written: "First I divided 12 into two and 10. Then I subtracted two (from two) and subtracted five from 10. And the answer was five." However, when she looked at his tiles he had two straight lines consisting of six tiles each. She was disappointed that she could not invite this student to present his work at the board because the discrepancies in his work would have confused the other students. Ms. Furumoto linked this inconsistent behavior to students' difficulty in understanding how to use the manipulative, which she thought was evident from her observation of a number of students who kept changing their minds about how to paste the tiles. Moreover, Ms. Furumoto said that she noticed that many students tried to move the tiles to represent what they had written on the handout, instead of using the manipulative to think about the problem and then recording their solution strategy on the handout.

Ms. Maejima and Ms. Furumoto therefore suggested that perhaps the manipulative might not be necessary for all the students. They thought that students who could solve the problem in their heads could express their solutions well in words and asking them to use the manipulative simply confused them. The other teachers agreed and reiterated that it seemed as if these students were moving the tiles in order to show what they thought in their head instead of moving the tiles to help them solve the problem. Ms. Maejima perceived those students as not seriously thinking about the solution while moving the tiles around; instead, they were using the manipulative because they had been asked to. Ms. Furumoto saw this as double work for the fast learners. They needed to think about the same problem twice, even though they already knew how to do it in their head. For these students their attention level with the manipulative would be even less than what might be expected from those who were simply playing with the manipulative. Ms. Furumoto pointed out that she noticed that some students had written down the decomposition of the numbers on their handout. Ms. Chijiiwa said that fast learners like these did not need a manipulative because they had already grasped the concept of regrouping. Ms. Tsukuda added that in fact none of the students had used manipulatives when they did addition with carrying over, a topic covered right before this subtraction lesson. For example, she said, in the case of 7 plus 8, the students could decompose the number 7 into 2 and 5, or the number 8 into 3 and 5, in order to make 10 (2 plus 8 or 3 plus 7), and get the answer, 15. Therefore, she felt that some students already knew a lot about how to solve the subtraction problem and did not need to use the manipulative. Despite all this, Ms. Tsukuda had difficulty abandoning the idea of using a standardized manipulative for all students and the teachers were unable to reach a consensus about how to settle this debate. They therefore decided to instead move on to talking about how to improve the manipulative, and to come back later to the issue of whether they should give the students the option of using the manipulative or not.

Ms. Furumoto launched the discussion about how to redesign the manipulative by mentioning that having 12 individual tiles encouraged students to use the counting–subtraction method, a strategy that she and other teachers had observed the majority of the students using. Moreover, Ms. Tsukuda reported that Mr. Nishimura, one of the sixth-grade teachers, commented to her after the lesson that a lot of the students had lined up the tiles in two rows consisting of 10 and 2. Similarly, she had noticed only a few students lining up the tiles up into a row of 5 and one of 7. These observations conflicted with the teachers' hypothesis that the students would demonstrate different conceptions of the number 12.

Just as the teachers were becoming discouraged by their conversation about the manipulative, Mr. Yamasaki, the principal of the school, came up with an idea. He thought that the current manipulative was not suited for encouraging the students to think about regrouping. He suggested that the teachers instead represent the number 12 with a strip of paper consisting of 10 linked tiles and 2 individual tiles.[3] In response to this suggestion, Ms. Tsukuda wondered if maybe she should use the 10-strip and focus on teaching regrouping since this was the first lesson to deal with this concept. However, Ms. Furumoto and Ms. Maejima were not convinced that using the 10-strip would change students' ways of thinking about this problem. They still thought that many students would do it in their heads and would simply use the manipulative to illustrate, rather than support, their thinking.

With this last comment the teachers found themselves again talking about using the manipulative as a supplemental material for only those students who were having difficulty solving the problem. At this point Mr. Yamasaki weighed in and said that he was not in favor of this idea because they were talking about the first lesson in the unit. Moreover, he thought there would be some benefit to using a manipulative even for those students who could solve the subtraction with regrouping problem in their heads. He felt using a manipulative would solidify their understanding. Before further explaining why he felt this way, he asked Ms. Tsukuda to estimate how many students in her class already could solve subtraction with regrouping prior to this lesson. Ms. Tsukuda said that three students in her class would be able to do such calculations in their heads. The principal responded in these terms:

> For example, in the upper grades students learn multiplication of fractions. They learn something like: When you do the multiplication of two fractions you multiply the denominator by the denominator and the numerator by the numerator to get an answer. They learn the pattern of how to do the calculation. If the students master only the calculation pattern without the reasons behind why they are doing it in such a way, they are incapable of solving this type of problem when they are stuck or face a mental block. I think the Ministry of Education and other educators recognize this problem and they are

---

[3]For some reason this suggestion seemed somehow to annoy the teachers. Ms. Tsukuda later explained that the teachers were reacting in this way because they felt that he had no appreciation for how hard they had already worked on the design of the manipulative. Moreover, the teachers felt that they already knew that the manipulative was key to understanding students' thinking, and they were very disappointed to realize that their attempt at designing a good manipulative had failed. She said it was the teachers' egos that were at first preventing them from listening to his comments. However, Ms. Tsukuda felt that these comments had marked a turning point in the meeting. An honest opinion from an outsider forced them to clear their thoughts and pointed them in a productive direction.

pointing it out as one of the necessary areas of improvement. In the case of this subtraction problem, 12 minus 7, Ms. Tsukuda mentioned that there are three students who can already solve this problem. Maybe there are more students who can. However, although these students can solve the problem we don't know how much they understand about the reasons behind the calculations that they are performing. So it is dangerous for us to think that we should not give them the manipulative at all. These students may have had a lot of practice calculating this type of subtraction so they can solve the problem; however, their foundation may not be strong.

All the teachers seemed to have been swayed by what Mr. Yamasaki was saying. After much debate, however, Ms. Chijiiwa suggested that it would be better to include strips representing the number 5 and the number 10. She thought, first, the teacher could give students one 10-tile strip and 2 individual tiles to represent the number 12. Then, when the students tried to subtract 7 from 12, they could exchange the tiles either for two strips of five tiles or 10 individual tiles. Ms. Tsukuda suggested that the teacher could say to students: "These tiles represent the number 12. Can you subtract 7 from them?" She and others agreed that by having a strip representing a group of 10, the students would not be able to simply subtract 7 by using the counting–subtraction method. Instead, they would have to say something like: "We have to break the tile representing the number 10 into pieces in order to solve the problem." The teachers thought this idea had potential; however, as discussed during earlier planning meetings, they also worried that the students might place more than 12 tiles on the drawing paper when they exchanged tiles. Ms. Chijiiwa was sure that at least a couple of students would make this type of mistake. Ms. Tsukuda and Ms. Furumoto were very concerned by this. They thought that if they gave too many tiles to the first-grade students, these children would lose their sense of the number 12 and the lesson would end up being a disaster.

Fortunately, Ms. Tsukuda eventually came up with an idea for a redesign of the manipulative that addressed a number of the concerns the teachers had voiced (see Fig. 9.5).

She suggested having an outline of 10 and 2 tiles drawn with dotted lines on the drawing paper that children would receive as part of their manipulative. At first a long strip representing the number 10 and 2 individual tiles representing the number 2, would be pasted on top of this outline. Ms. Tsukuda reflected that if the lesson's focus was for students to learn about regrouping, then children's concept of the number 12 was less critical for this particular lesson. Therefore she felt that it was okay to predetermine how students first saw the number 12 represented with tiles on their drawing board. The advantage of this strategy was that it would help prevent students from having more than 12 tiles on their drawing paper after they exchanged tiles in the process of solving the problem. She also suggested

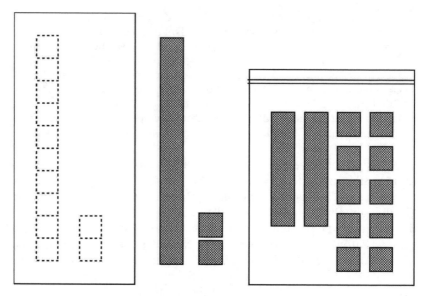

FIG. 9.5   The new *ohajiki-ban* suggested by Ms. Tsukuda.

that in order to address the problem of the limited desktop space available to children, that they should use a drawing paper about half the size of the one that had been used in Ms. Nishi's lesson. She proposed that this paper should be a little longer than the strip with 10 tiles and its width should be large enough to accommodate two rows of tiles. The front of the drawing paper would be sprayed with glue just like before. In addition, there would be a plastic bag available to students containing 10 individual tiles and 2 tiles representing the number 5.

Ms. Tsukuda explained to the group how she envisioned using this new manipulative. At first, the teacher would provide it to students and ask them: "How many tiles are there?" The students would say "Twelve." Then the teacher would tell them, "Let's subtract seven tiles from them." In response to the teacher's comment, one of the students would say, "We have to break up the long strip into pieces otherwise we can't just take away some of the tiles." At this point the teacher would tell the students, "There are some other tiles prepared for you to replace the ten-strip." The students would take out the plastic bag and replace the 10-strip either using individual tiles and/or a strip representing the number five. Finally, the students would take away seven tiles from the 12 tiles in order to get the answer. By looking at what type of tiles the students used and what part of the 12 tiles they took away the teachers could understand the subtraction method each student used.

Ms. Chijiiwa felt that this proposal addressed the difficulty she noticed Ms. Nishi's students had, placing 12 individual tiles in a straight line. She said that she saw some students trying to line up 12 tiles but because they left too much space in between the tiles, they ended up with 9 or 8 tiles in one line and the leftover tiles in a second line. For this reason she thought that preparing the outline of the tiles on the drawing board might be helpful. In addition, Ms. Chijiiwa agreed that because finding out how the students conceptualize the number 12 was of secondary interest to them, it would not be a bad idea to focus instead on studying how students decomposed the number 10 to do the subtraction problem. She explained her reasoning as follows:

> If we make the manipulative too complicated, it is too much for the first-grade students to handle. If they were third or fourth graders, it would be good to give them the freedom to explore various solutions, including how they place the 12 tiles. If we give too much freedom to the first-grade students, we will stray too far from the main focus of the lesson. The focus of the lesson is solving the problem 12 minus 7. I think how they conceptualize the number 12 is not the focus of the lesson so it is OK to show them how the 12 tiles should be placed on the drawing paper. We also have to think how the low achievers handle the situation. I think the manipulative should be easy to use and it should not be so advanced.

Ms. Chijiiwa also reminded everyone that the students had been in school for a little over one and a half quarters. Even though they were finally getting close to mastering addition with carrying over, quite a few of them could not add very quickly in their heads. Moreover, although they had already been studying subtraction without regrouping, it was important not to overestimate what they actually understood about subtraction and place unrealistic demands on them. At this point, all the teachers recognized that they had been trying to do too much and that the students probably had been burdened and distracted with deciding where and how they should paste the tiles on their drawing paper. The teachers were therefore unanimously in favor of using the new manipulative proposed by Ms. Tsukuda because it diminished the demands placed on students and focused their attention on the critical issue of regrouping.

In the course of subsequent discussions, however, some shortcomings of the new manipulative emerged. During their second debriefing meeting Ms. Furumoto reported that she had actually made the manipulative to help her think concretely about the kind of responses one might get from students. She predicted that not many students would use the strip representing the number

5 because it would be easier for them to count individual tiles instead. She also felt that the students who would replace the 10-strip with two 5-strips would be those students who already could solve the problem and knew how to explain their solutions well. Ms. Tsukuda took advantage of this opportunity to mention that she was still worried that many students would end up with more than 12 tiles on their drawing board. She anticipated having to ask the students to stop working and instructing them to check if they had exactly 12 tiles on their drawing paper. There were usually a couple of students who could not understand directions quickly and therefore she expected that using this new manipulative would be quite time-consuming.

The teachers were now a bit disappointed with the new manipulative and at a loss about how to improve it. After a few discussions that seemed to go nowhere, Ms. Tsukuda suddenly came up with the idea of giving children scissors rather than extra tiles (see Fig. 9.6).

She proposed preserving the idea of distributing a drawing board with a 10-strip and two individual tiles prepasted on it. However, she suggested two critical modifications. First, there would be lines drawn on the 10-strip to show the 10 individual tiles it represents. Second, children would be provided with a pair of scissors in order to cut the 10-strip wherever they wanted to so that they could subtract tiles.

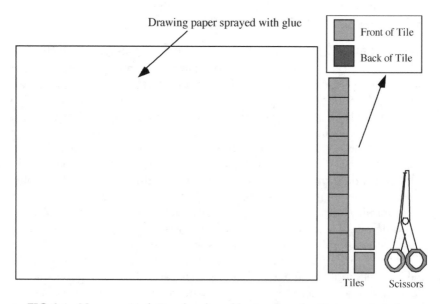

FIG. 9.6 New manipulative developed by teachers for the second study lesson.

The teachers were immediately excited by this idea and they began to think about how students might use this new version of the manipulative. An extract from this discussion is presented here:

Tsukuda:	So, there might be a student who will cut it into two pieces, each five tiles in length. Or, there might be a student who will cut it into 10 individual tiles. Or, they will have two individual tiles, so they might cut the 10-strip into a three-strip and a seven-strip, and put the two individual tiles together with the three-strip ...
Chijiiwa:	I see, that's a great idea. Yes, yes, yes ...
Maejima:	Yes, yes, yes ...
Tsukuda:	What do you all think?
Chijiiwa:	Yes, it is good.
Furumoto:	Yes.
Chijiiwa:	This idea is really good, isn't it?
Maejima:	Yes.
Tsukuda:	I'm a little bit concerned about letting the students use scissors.
Furumoto:	I see ...
Tsukuda:	I'm concerned ...
Furumoto:	Yes ...
Maejima:	A student might say "I cut in the wrong place."
All Teachers:	Hmm ...
Chijiiwa:	We have to have some extra tiles.
Tsukuda:	That's right.
Chijiiwa:	I can see them saying "I made a mistake ..."
Maejima:	They might say, "I didn't cut exactly on the dotted line" and "Teacher! Teacher! Well, I guess I don't need it anymore ..."
Chijiiwa:	Yes ... We'll have to tell them, "Use Scotch tape."
Tsukuda:	Well, I guess so ...
Chijiiwa:	Yes ...
Maejima:	Should we go with this?
Chijiiwa:	This is good.
Tsukuda:	What do you all think?
Maejima:	Yes.
Tsukuda:	How about the number 12?

All Teachers: Yes, good, good.

The teachers continued to talk about how children might use this new version of the manipulative, and became quite excited because they realized that with this design they could tell, based on how the children cut the 10-strip, which solution strategy was being employed. They still seemed worried about whether the children would actually come up with all the varied solution strategies they were hoping to see, but at the same time they were enthusiastic about implementing their new manipulative in a real lesson.

SPECIFYING WORDING AND QUESTIONS (*HATSUMON*)

Another topic that the teachers talked about was the use of *hatsumon* (key questions) during the lesson. Generally the teachers liked the clear and easy to understand questions that Ms. Nishi had posed. However, Ms. Furumoto had a concern about asking students in the story problem, "How many leaves are left over?" To her this sounded as if students were being asked to just provide an answer, not a description of their thinking. She felt that this way of asking the question did not fit in with their *konaikenshu* goal of understanding the process by which students reach their solutions. Ms. Furumoto mentioned that Mr. Saeki had also at one point suggested that teachers needed to give careful consideration to whether or not the wording of their story problems was in line with the school's *konaikenshu* goal.

The teachers discussed several possibilities for dealing with this issue. Ms. Tsukuda thought that instead of changing the wording of the problem the teacher should make sure to follow up with a good *hatsumon*. She said that if a student provided an answer right away, the teacher could respond by saying: "Well, that might be right, but please think about how you did it in today's lesson." However, Ms. Furumoto insisted that they should still think about the wording of the problem itself. She shared an idea that came out of a study lesson planned by the middle grade group. These teachers had used a story problem that was something like "S/he bought this and that. How much did s/he pay?" but they had realized that this phrasing led the students to immediately think of the answer. They therefore changed the phrasing to "S/he is buying this and that. How much should s/he pay?" They thought that using the present tense would prompt students to think more deeply about the answer because they would be able to easily relate to the situation and envision themselves standing at the register and taking money out of their wallets. Ms. Maejima suggested that they could change the wording from "How many leaves are left over?" to "Let's think about how many leaves will be left over." She also thought that the story problem could be divided into two parts, the background, and the question itself. The two parts could be written on two different colored pieces of paper in order to highlight the question. However, Ms. Tsukuda thought that such slight changes in wording would not be noticeable to first graders. Ms. Furumoto added that although teachers of older children often used sentences like, "Let's think about …," this type of wording was too vague for first graders to understand. Ms. Chijiiwa commented that the existing story problem already contained three blanks and consisted of three sentences; therefore, she thought that the teachers were already asking a lot from students. Plus, there were other areas that were new to the students. For example, the tiles and the handouts were novel. Thus, she thought that the story problem should stay the way it was.

The teachers, who at this point were pressed for time, decided to drop this issue and leave the phrasing of the problem intact. They did agree that Ms. Tsukuda would make sure to follow up with a question that directly asked the students to think about their process for solving the problem. They also agreed to revisit this issue after Ms. Tsukuda taught the lesson.

At the end of their second meeting, the teachers seemed pleased with their results. They were most happy about their breakthrough in the design of the manipulative. Ms. Maejima in particular was quite satisfied with the results of their hard work and excited about seeing the lesson implemented in a real class. Ms. Tsukuda, on the other hand, was a little bit nervous about teaching the lesson. She jokingly told Ms. Maejima to teach the lesson herself since she seemed so pleased with the outcome of their discussions. Ms. Maejima said that because she did not know much about Ms. Tsukuda's students, she would decline her kind offer. All the teachers had a good laugh, and the meeting was adjourned.

10

The Revised Lesson Plan

On the evening of the day that the lower grade teachers had met to finish discussing Ms. Nishi's lesson, Ms. Tsukuda updated the lesson plan to reflect all the ideas that she and her group members had come up with. This revised lesson plan is presented in Fig. 10.1, with changes made to it relative to the previous version highlighted in gray.

Mathematics Learning Lesson Plan

Instructor: Keiko Tsukuda

1. Date & Time: November 18, 1993 (Thursday), Second Period
2. Grade: First grade. Ume Class: 11 boys, 8 girls, total of 19 students
3. Name of the Unit: Subtraction (2)
4. Reasons for Setting up the Unit:

Up to this point, the students have been studying the concept of subtraction in situations where regrouping is not necessary. Moreover, by composing and decomposing numbers, the students have been able to notice the different forms in which a number can be expressed. Also, by using the versatility of numbers, the students have been thinking about various ways to add numbers when carrying (advancing numbers to the next denomination) is involved.

In this lesson, the students will encounter subtraction problems (such as 10 to 19 minus 1 to 9) that cannot be solved without regrouping (i.e. by subtracting the number from the number in the ones position). Students will see that by using concepts learned in previous lessons, it is possible to solve these problems by taking the one from the ten's position to make ten (i.e. regrouping). The students will realize that once this step is taken, they can proceed to solve the problem by using strategies they have learned in past. In addition, this lesson hopes to deepen the students' un-

FIG. 10.1   Lesson plan used for Ms. Tsukuda's lesson.

derstanding of the 10 decimal system (place value). Furthermore, through this lesson, the students should be able to perform subtraction with regrouping by choosing the most efficient method given the numbers involved.

The students in this class, except for student M, understand the concept of subtraction without regrouping and can use manipulatives to solve this type of subtraction problem. In addition, they can find the correct answer to such problems. However, the time it takes to solve this type of problem varies greatly among the students, and a great number of them still immediately try to use their fingers rather than using the manipulatives provided to them, such as blocks. Moreover, there are large differences in the students' ability to process these calculations. There are students who can calculate the answers in their heads by using difficult methods such as composition and decomposition of numbers, which is considered the foundation of addition with carrying and subtraction with regrouping. Others can draw on the concept of supplementary numbers of 10 (*ju no hosu*); and the calculation of three (single digit) numbers (*3-kuchi no keisan*). In contrast, there are students who take a long time to obtain the answer, even when they use a concrete object to aid them in their calculations.

Even under these circumstances, the number of students who say "I like arithmetic" is comparatively high. When asked why they feel this way, students respond with comments like: "It's fun to do activities using manipulatives like blocks and tiles," or, "It is fun because it is like a quiz game," or, "It is fun because you get to report your answers (in front of the class)."

In this lesson I plan to use problems based on the children's everyday life in order to motivate them to tackle the subject. Moreover, when I use manipulatives to facilitate student learning in this lesson, I plan to devise materials that will leave a record of the children's thought processes. It is my hope that having students solve these types of problems (problems based on the children's everyday life) will help in achieving the goal of this unit.

As for the numbers to use in the problem for this lesson, I decided on [12 minus 7] because I believe it will elicit many different ideas for how to solve the problem. Not only do I expect the subtraction-addition method (genkaho), but also the subtraction-subtraction method (gengenho), the counting-subtraction method (kazoehiki), and the supplement-addition method (hokaho) to come up.

In the next lesson, while thinking about the most efficient calculation method, the students will attempt to master the subtraction-addition method and the subtraction-subtraction method. In order to do this, I will make the students repeatedly practice through such activities as reflexively finding the supplementary numbers of 10 (*ju no hosu*). I will also have them practice decomposing the number that is subtracted in order to match the number in the one's position with the number that is being subtracted from (in subtraction with regrouping).

(continued on next page)

5. The Goals of the Unit:
   (1) To deepen students' understanding of the situations where subtraction is used.
   (2) To deepen students' understanding of how to formulate and read subtraction expressions written in symbolic form.
   (3) To foster students' understanding of how to calculate subtraction with regrouping by using the opposite concept of addition with carrying of two single digit numbers. (i.e. 6+7=13 —> 13-7=6)
   (4) To foster students' ability to confidently and reliably calculate subtraction with regrouping by using the related concept of addition of two single-digit numbers involving carrying (i.e. 6+7=13 —> 13-7=6).
   (5) For students to be able to represent a number as the difference between various pairs of numbers. (i.e. 5=11-6, 5=12-7, 5=13-8, etc.).
6. Related Items:

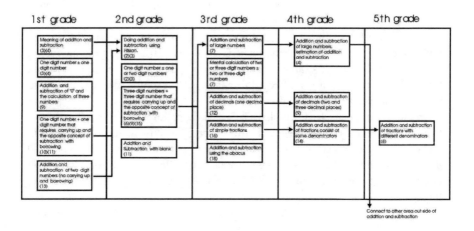

1st grade	2nd grade	3rd grade	4th grade	5th grade
Meaning of addition and subtraction (3)(4)	Doing addition and subtraction using Hissan. (2)(3)	Addition and subtraction of large numbers (7)	Addition and subtraction of large numbers, estimation of addition and subtraction (4)	
One digit number ± one digit number (3)(4)	One digit number ± one or two digit numbers (2)(3)	Mental calculation of two or three digit numbers ± two or three digit numbers (7)		
Addition and subtraction of '0' and the calculation of three numbers (9)	Three digit numbers + three digit number that requires carrying up and the opposite concept of subtraction with borrowing (6)(9)(15)	Addition and subtraction of decimals (one decimal place) (12)	Addition and subtraction of decimals (two and three decimal places) (9)	
One digit number + one digit number that requires carrying up and the opposite concept of subtraction with borrowing (10)(11)		Addition and subtraction of simple fractions (16)	Addition and subtraction of fractions consist of same denominator (14)	Addition and subtraction of fractions with different denominators (6)
Addition and subtraction of two-digit numbers (no carrying up and borrowing) (13)	Addition and Subtraction with blank (11)	Addition and subtraction using the abacus (18)		

Connect to other area out side of addition and subtraction

7. Plan for the unit (12 lessons)

   Section 1: To understand how to formulate an expression (*risshiki*) for subtraction when regrouping (*kurisagari*) is involved, and how to calculate this type of subtraction through the use of concrete manipulaitves —— (4 lessons)

      1st lesson: To think about calculation methods for subtraction when regrouping is involved (This period)

      2nd lesson: To foster a better understanding of the subtraction-addition method (*genkaho*) by calculating 12 minus 9 (12-9).

FIG. 10.1   *continued*

3rd lesson: To foster a better understanding of the subtraction-subtraction method (*gengenho*) by calculating 13 minus 4 (13-4).

4th lesson: To learn how to select the most efficient method of subtraction depending on the given numerical values.

Section 2: To apply subtraction with regrouping to different situations in problems —— (3 lessons)

1st - 3rd lessons: To increase proficiency in solving problems using subtraction with regrouping when you have differences and remainders.

Section 3: To make cards containing subtraction with regrouping problems and practice using the cards when calculating —— (3 lessons)

1st - 3rd lessons: To master the calculation process by enjoying playing games and using the calculation cards.

Section 4: Review —— (2 lessons)

1st - 2nd lessons: To review what the students have learned by doing exercises.

8. The Goal of This Lesson:

a. Interest • Attitude:

(How well do the students) attempt to progress in calculating subtraction while using concrete objects. (How well do the students) attempt to present their ideas.

b. Way of Thinking:

Ability to solve problems by using previously learned concepts and/or the idea of breaking numbers into tens.

c. Expression • Processing of Concepts:

Be able to do the calculation of "12-7"

e. Knowledge • Skills:

Understand the meaning and method of the calculation of "12-7"

9. Things to Prepare

A drawing paper coated with spray glue (19)

Tiles: 10-tile and two individual tiles (19)

Handouts (two kinds) (19)

A poster paper containing the story problem, various cards used for filling in the blanks of the story problem

Paper cutout Ginkgo leaves —— for a hint

Note: Student M., who is a mildly mentally retarded child, does not usually stay in the classroom with the other students during Arithmetic lessons because he receives individual lessons; however, during this lesson, he will stay in the classroom

(continued on next page)

so all the teachers can observe how he is doing. I would like to plan an activity that will help him learn one-to-one correspondence using Ginkgo leaves and the face of his family members during the time I'm walking around and observing the students to see how they are doing (*kikanjyunshi*).

10. Progression of the Lesson

Learning Activities and Questions [hatsumon]	Expected Student Reactions	Teacher Response to Student Reactions / Things to Remember	Evaluation*
1. Grasping the Problem Setting "The other day we went leaf collecting, didn't we? What kind of leaves did you get?" "That's right. You collected 12 leaves from the big Ginkgo tree at the Shinto shrine and drew the faces of the people in your family on the leaves.	• Red and brown leaves • There were miscanthuses and persimmon trees, too. • I collected chestnuts, too. • "The pictures turned out pretty funny." • "I collected so many leaves that I have some left over."	• Give praise to the students who did a great job reporting their answers and raising their hands at various points during the lesson. • Remind the students that they collected only 12 Ginkgo leaves after they changed the location. • Check out beforehand how many people are in each student's family.	a. Are the students positively trying to recall the event?
"How many leaves did you use for drawing faces, Student A?" "How many leaves did you use for drawing faces, Student B?" "How many leaves did Ms. Nishi use for drawing faces?" "Ms. Nishi collected 10 leaves and drew 5 faces."	A: 4 leaves. Oh, we had a new baby the other day, so 5 leaves. B: Because my family is 4 people, so 4 leaves. Ms. Nishi: 5 leaves.	• Make sure that all the students know that Ms. Nishi collected only 10 leaves.	

FIG. 10.1   *continued*

"How many leaves are left over?"	• 5 leaves • Well, (by using fingers) it is 5 leaves.	• Make students understand the problem setting and the teacher is looking for students to answer the questions by using subtraction. • Remind them of the supplementary numbers of 10.	b. Do the students understand they can solve these problems using subtraction? c. Were the students able to solve the problem 10-5?
"Did everyone have leaves left over?"	• (Yes) there were (leaves) left over. • I had a lot of leaves left over. • I had 8 leaves left over.		
2. <u>Presentation of the Problem Format</u> 1.) presenting the format and using it on previously learned subtraction situations (without regrouping)			
"Wow, you guys are great! You were studying math even during your Life Studies (a mixture of Social Studies and Science) lesson. What kinds of calculations (of the four: addition, subtraction, multiplication or division) were you doing?	• It's great, isn't it? • Well, what calculation do I need to use? • Subtraction.	• Point out to the students that they are using arithmetic not only during the arithmetic period, but in a lot of other situations too.	

(continued on next page)

"Were the problems you did in your head like this one?"			
******************** "Child _____ collected _____ ginkgo leaves. S/he drew _____ pictures of her/his family on the leaves. How many leaves are left over?" **********************		• Based on the conversations with the students, present some subtraction problems that they already know how to solve. By reviewing these problems, help students understand the situation of the subtraction problem.	
"What do you think?" "What should we write in the blanks?"	• I don't know what will be in the blanks. • I don't understand. • It must be the name of the person who collected the leaves. • They are the number of leaves collected and the picture drawn.	• When you present the problem, confirm what the necessary conditions are.	b. Did the students understand what would be in the blanks in order to complete the problem? b. Were the students able to fill in the blanks with appropriate numbers and think about the problem?
"What would you write in the blanks if it is Ms. Nishi's case?"	• It is "Ms. Nishi collected 10 Ginkgo leaves. And she drew 5 pictures of her family on the leaves. How many leaves are leftover?"		
"What is the expression (shiki) for this problem?" "What is the answer?"	• It is 10-5. • It's 5. • No, it's 5 leaves.		
"Now let's do Ms. Tsukuda's family. Ms. Tsukuda collected 12 leaves just like everybody did. Ms. Tsukuda's family has 2 members so she drew faces on 2 leaves."		• Change the numerical values in the problem little by little and confirm that you want them to use subtraction when they have a situation where they have to find the remainder.	

FIG. 10.1   *continued*

134

"Could you make a problem with Ms. Tsukuda's family?"

• It is "Ms. Tsukuda collected 12 Ginkgo leaves. And she drew 2 pictures of her family on the leaves. How many leaves are leftover?"

b. Were the students able to fill in the blanks with appropriate numbers and think about the problem?
c. Were the students able to do the calculation of 12-2?

"Do you understand? What expression did we use to get the answer?"
"What is the answer?"
"How did we find the answer?"

• It is 12 - 2.
• It is 10.
• I subtracted 2 from the 2 of 12.

• Remind them of subtraction of two digit numbers without regrouping and confirm that in this case they subtracted the numbers in the ones positions from each other to find the answer.

2.) Using this format to set up the main problem of the lesson "Now let's do Student C's family. How many faces did Student C draw on the leaves?"

• C: I drew 7 faces on the leaves.

"Let's make this the problem."

• It is "Student C collected 12 Ginkgo leaves. And then he drew 7 pictures of his family on the leaves. How many leaves are leftover?"

b. Were the students able to fill in the blanks with appropriate numbers and think about the problem?

"O.K. Now, please find out 'what you already know' and 'what the problem is asking'."

• The numbers we know are 12 and 7.
• The numbers we know are the number of leaves collected (12) and the number of faces drawn on the leaves (7).
• What the problem asking is "how many leaves are left over?"

(continued on next page)

3. <u>Solving the Main Problem</u> 1.) Thinking about writing an expression (*shiki*). "Think about making an expression from 'what we already know' and 'what the problem in asking'." 2.) Understanding what the problem is asking "That's right. But if you compare 12 and 7, which one is bigger?" "Well, then, it seems like you should be able to subtract it." "Today we're going to think about how to find the answer to 12-7."	• 7-12. • 12-7. • You can't subtract 7 from 2. • 12. • It seems hard. • That's easy.	• Ask students to write the expression on the handout. • Make the students notice that you can't subtract using these two one digit numbers (2-7), make them think about how to do this type of calculation.	d. Could the students construct the right expression?
3.) Solving the problem individually "Well, we already used the leaves for the drawing, let's think about the problem using these tiles today. We will be telling each other how each of you solved the problem so please write how you did it using words, too."	(a) It looks like I can do the subtraction, but what can I do? (b) Counting-Subtraction Method. • Take them one by one from 12 and find the remainder. • Break up 12 into 10 and 2, take them one by one from 10 and count the remaining numbers. • Since it's 12 minus 7, it's the same until 7, then you count on your fingers 8, 9, 10, 11, and 12. (Supplement-Addition Method)	• Give a tile representing the number 10 (long tile) and two individual tiles and let them cut the 10-tile freely in order to subtract 7. • Ask students to turn the tiles over and leave them on the drawing paper instead of taking them away when they subtract in order to understand where the numbers were subtracted. • Ask the students to write down their own solution using words on the handout.	a. Are the students positively trying to do the subtraction calculation using concrete objects? c. Did the students understand the meaning and the method when calculating 12-7

FIG. 10.1 *continued*

136

	(c) Subtraction-Addition Method	• Find out which students are the following 3 types when it comes to addition with carrying:	
	• Break 12 up into 10 and 2, then subtract 7 from 10. The answer to that (10 - 7) is 3, then you take the 2 you broke up and add that to get 5.	Type A: Composition and decomposition (breaking down) of numbers is simple for this type of student. Able to calculate it in his/her head.	c. Could the students do the calculation 12-7?
	(d) Subtraction-Subtraction Method		
	• Break 7 up into 2 and 5, and subtract 2 from 12. Then you take the answer 10 and subtract 5 from it to get the answer, 5.	Type B: Can find the answer by manipulating some sort of half concrete object. Type C: Finds it difficult to calculate unless he/she uses some sort of concrete object or his/her fingers. Give extra individual help especially to type C students when the teacher walks around to observe the students. Provide Ginkgo leaves if the type C students need them to think about the problem.	
4. Polishing (*Neriage*) and Presenting Individual Solution Methods "Please teach how you came up with the answer clearly to the other students in the classroom."		• During the time the teacher walks around the classroom to see how the students are doing (*kikanjunshi*) I will take some notes on how the students are thinking.	a. Could the students present their own ideas in a loud voice?

(continued on next page)

		And I would like to ask the students to present in the order of (b), (c), (d). (refer to the student's expected solution methods above in the column "Expected Student Reactions")	a. Could the students listen to their friends' presentations carefully?
"Are there any other ways to find the answer?" ("Why did you break 12 up into 10 and 2?") ("Why did you break 7 up into 2 and 5?")	• Yes, yes, there are. • Why did you break 12 up into 10 and 2? • Why did you break 7 up into 2 and 5?	• Ask the students to ask questions when they don't understand what other students presented because of lack of explanation. If the students do not ask any questions, the teacher will ask questions (so the explanation will be clear).	b. Did the students understand there are many ways to solve subtraction problems that involve regrouping?
5. Summary and Announcement of the Next Lesson "Let's try to solve 12-5 using whatever method you like."	• I will do it the same way I did it before. • I wonder if the solution that K used is more convenient?" • I will try to do it the way that N did.	• When the problem is posed, the teacher tells the students whose case they are dealing with (to be consistent with the other problems).	c. Could the students solve the problem using the method that they understood and agree with each other?

FIG. 10.1   *continued*

		• Take notes on the students who are listening to their friends' presentations and trying to solve the problem in a different way than they did before. Try to incorporate these observations into the next lesson.	
"What do you think the best way is to solve 12-9?" "Let's try to find out what method is the best in the next lesson."	• I won't know until I do it. • Well, I think method (b) is the best. • I think method (c) is faster. •I want to try to solve it.	(Ask the students to write the student's name whose solution method they liked, in order to solve the practice problem in the handout)	a. Will the students be motivated to learn the following lesson?* Each heading alphabet (a, b, c, and d) in the column "Evaluation" corresponds to the four categories shown in section 8, the goal of this lesson.
		• Try to help and lead the students who are still using the method of subtracting numbers one by one from 12 to the method of breaking up 12 into 10 and 2 and subtracting the numbers one by one from 10 and counting the remaining numbers (because this method will lead to the way of thinking on "Subtraction-Addition" method).	

* Each heading alphabet (a, b, c, and d) in the column "Evaluation" corresponds to the four categories in section 8, the goal of this lesson.

That same evening Ms. Tsukuda also created two handouts for the students to use during the lesson. The first handout was for the main problem 12 minus 7 (see Fig. 10.2).

As the teachers had agreed, this handout included the gingko story problem with three blanks to be filled in. The second handout was for the practice exercise 12 minus 5 (see Fig. 10.3).

Although the lower grade level teachers had argued that there would not be enough time left over to do a practice problem, Ms. Tsukuda decided to create a second handout because she wanted to have something available, just in case the lesson finished earlier than anticipated. Ms. Tsukuda added to this second handout a blank for the students to fill in the name of their classmate whose solution they liked the best. This was to be done after the students had listened to all the presentations made during the lesson. She also included on this second handout a drawing of 12 tiles to help the students think about the problem.

Ms. Tsukuda also drafted a seating chart of her classroom (see Fig. 10.4). This chart was different from the one used for Ms. Nishi's lesson in that it included schematic representations of the various solution strategies that the

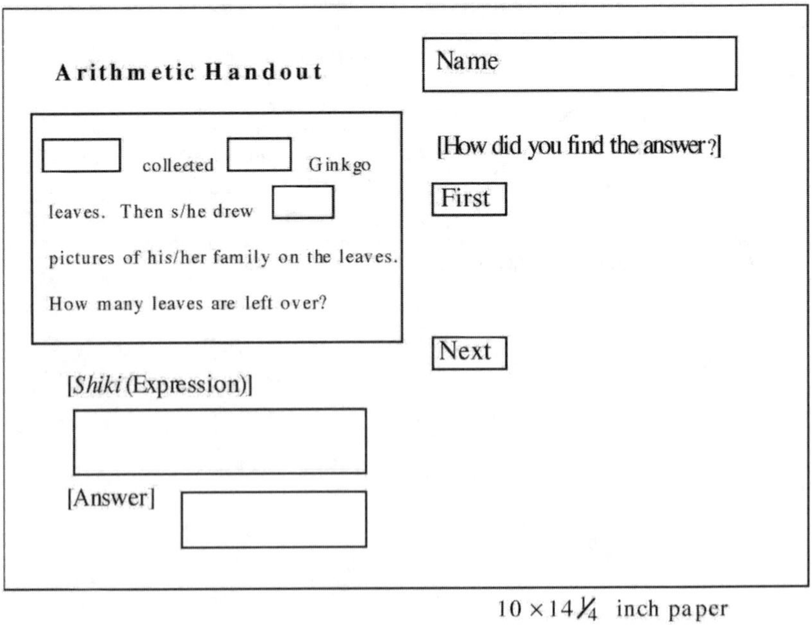

Arithmetic Handout

Name

[_____] collected [_____] Ginkgo leaves. Then s/he drew [_____] pictures of his/her family on the leaves. How many leaves are left over?

[How did you find the answer?]

First

Next

[*Shiki* (Expression)]

[Answer]

10 × 14 ¼ inch paper

FIG. 10.2   Handout for the second study lesson.

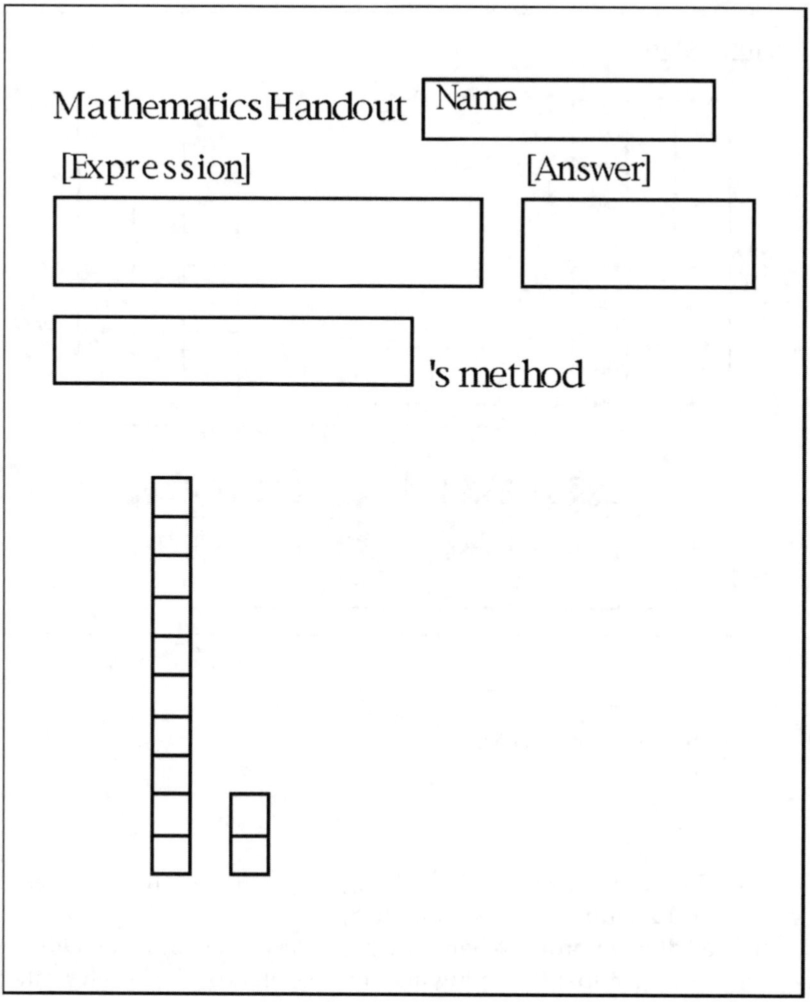

Mathematics Handout | Name

[Expression]   [Answer]

_____ 's method

FIG. 10.3   Handout for a practice problem.

10 x 7 inch paper

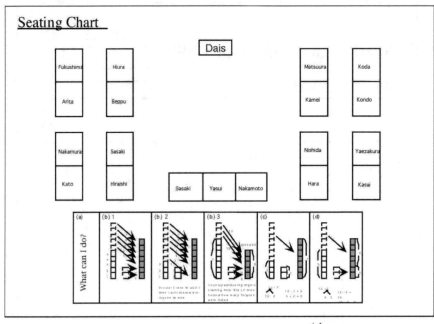

10 × 14 ¼ inch paper

FIG. 10.4   Student seating chart.

lower grade teachers had anticipated might come up as students tackled the problem 12 minus seven (see Fig. 10.5).

This was done in order to help observers keep track of what solutions they were seeing students employ, and for ease of recording, each strategy was labeled with a letter.

The next morning, Ms. Tsukuda and Ms. Nishi made enough copies of the lesson plan, student handouts, and seating chart to distribute to the teachers at the school, who all intended to observe the study lesson. After school on that same day, the members of the lower grade group (except for Ms. Furumoto) got together to make the new manipulatives that students would use during the lesson. A teacher who was not a member of the lower group also helped out with this task. At around 6 p.m., Ms. Tsukuda and Ms. Nishi went to Ms. Tsukuda's class to check that all the materials needed for the lesson were available. They also went over the organization of the blackboard, and left for the day at around 6:15 p.m.

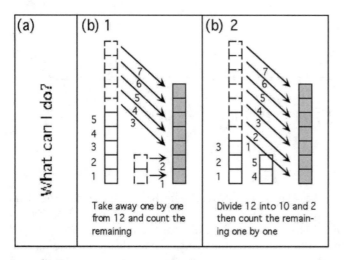

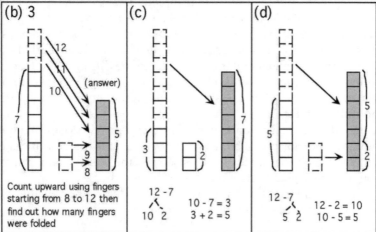

FIG. 10.5   Figure from the student seating chart.

11

Teaching the Revised Lesson

On the following day, Thursday, November 18, Ms. Tsukuda taught the subtraction study lesson to her class during the second period of the day, which was from 9:30 to 10:15 a.m. Just like for the first version of this lesson, all the teachers at the school came to observe while their students were left alone with assigned work to complete. The principal, the vice-principal, and the outside advisor, Mr. Saeki, were also in attendance.

There were 19 students in Ms. Tsukuda's classroom, 11 boys and 8 girls. A difference in atmosphere between this classroom and Ms. Nishi's could immediately be felt, perhaps due to the difference in teaching experience between these two teachers. Ms. Tsukuda's classroom had a warmer feeling than Ms. Nishi's because it had more decorations up on the walls (see Fig.11.1).

In addition, the students seemed calmer than Ms. Nishi's students, although some did seem a bit nervous having all the teachers and the video camera in their room. However, as soon as the lesson began they had no trouble focusing and seemed to forget all the adults.

The remainder of this chapter is devoted to describing how the study lesson unfolded in Ms. Tsukuda's classroom.

GRASPING THE PROBLEM SETTING

The lesson started on time with the students on day-duty calling the class to order and everyone in the room bowing. Like Ms. Nishi, Ms. Tsukuda began by reminding the students of the leaf collecting activity. She told them: "A couple of days ago, we went to Hazu Hill to collect fallen leaves, didn't we? Do you remember?" Many students replied by saying "yes." Then she asked the students what kinds of leaves they found on Hazu Hill. Several students enthusiastically called out the names of various types of leaves. Ms. Tsukuda then reminded her students that they had also gone to the Shinto shrine to collect leaves and asked them what kind of leaves they had collected there. A student answered "ginkgo leaves," and Ms.

FIG. 11.1   Ms. Tsukuda's classroom.

Tsukuda reminded the class that they had each collected 12 ginkgo leaves and done a collage of their families. She next asked the students how many leaves they each used for their collages. Students called out various numbers depending on their family configurations.

PRESENTATION OF THE PROBLEM FORMAT

(1) Presenting the Format and Using it on Previously Learned Subtraction Situations

Ms. Tsukuda next pasted Ms. Nishi's collage on the blackboard and asked the class how many family members Ms. Nishi had (see Fig. 11.2).

Many students answered in unison, "Five people." Ms. Tsukuda pointed to each face drawn on the ginkgo leaves and identified the family members as Ms. Nishi, her two older brothers, her father, and her mother. One student recognized that he had the same number and same configuration of family members and was very excited. Ms. Tsukuda next asked the students how many leaves they collected when they went on the field trip. The

FIG. 11.2   Ms. Tsukuda showing Ms. Nishi's collage on the blackboard.

class responded in unison, "Twelve leaves." Ms. Tsukuda pointed out to the
students that Ms. Nishi had actually only collected 10 leaves. Some students asked why this was the case, but Ms. Tsukuda did not provide them
with an explanation. Instead she asked the students how many leaves Ms.
Nishi had left over after she made her family tree. Immediately some students raised their hands and one of them answered, "Five leaves." Ms.
Tsukuda asked the class if the answer was right and many students responded that it was. One of the students said Ms. Nishi had collected 10
leaves and another pointed out that the number 10 was made of 5 and 5.

Ms. Tsukuda next asked the students how many leaves were left over after they drew pictures of their families. Some students were puzzled by this
question, but some started to answer based on their family configurations.
She praised her students by saying, "Well, although we were studying for
our Daily Living class, everybody was studying mathematics, too!" and
"That was terrific!" Then she asked the students what type of calculations
they had performed. Some of the students answered "subtraction" and
some "addition." Ms. Tsukuda smiled, but she went on without giving the
answer. Instead she pulled out a large paper with the story problem template written on it for all to see. She asked: "Was the problem you thought

about in your head like this?" The teacher asked the students to read the problem together, calling the blanks "rectangles" (see Fig. 11.3).

After the class finished reading the problem Ms. Tsukuda posed the following question: "Now that we have a mathematics problem, can we solve it?" Some students said "yes" and some other students said they could use addition to find the answer. Ms. Tsukuda asked one more time if the students felt they could solve this problem. A few other students said it was subtraction because the expression "left over" was used in the problem. Ms. Tsukuda neither agreed nor disagreed; she only said, "I see, it says left over in the problem." She again asked the students if they could solve the problem. Even though the blanks were not filled in, some students felt that they could solve it. Ms. Tsukuda asked the students if they had all the information they needed in order to solve the problem. Many said they didn't, so she asked them to think about the problem using Ms. Nishi's case and to complete the problem by filling in the blanks. Like Ms. Nishi's students, these students also had some difficulty filling in the first blank, which required the name of a person. In fact, the reader may recall that for this new version of the lesson the teachers had agreed that Ms. Tsukuda would com-

FIG. 11.3 Ms. Tsukuda pasting the problem format on the blackboard. Ms. Tsukuda and the students read the story problem in unison.

plete the first blank rather than having students do this task, which seemed to cause them difficulty. However, Ms. Tsukuda apparently forgot this decision. After some struggle the students finally figured out that the first blank should be "Ms. Nishi" and Ms. Tsukuda pasted a card that said "Ms. Nishi" in the first blank of the story problem. Next, one of the students was asked to fill in the other blanks and to read the story problem out loud. The student hesitated a little but in the end was able to fill in the blanks. As the student read the problem, Ms. Tsukuda pasted the corresponding cards in the problem blanks. She then asked the students if the problem now looked like a mathematics problem. The class responded with a resounding "Yes!"

Next Ms. Tsukuda asked the students how they would write an expression (*shiki*) for this problem, and she pasted a small yellow card on the board with the word expression written on it. One student answered, "Ten minus five." Ms. Tsukuda wrote "10 − 5 =" under the card she had just pasted. Many of the students agreed with this answer, but some thought it should instead be written as "5 − 10 =." Other students said it should not be 5 minus 10 because it is impossible to subtract 10 from 5. This explanation seemed to convince all students, so Ms. Tsukuda decided to move ahead and ask students the answer for how many were left over, which one of the students said was five. Ms. Tsukuda told the student to provide a complete answer, so he replied by saying, "Five leaves." The other students agreed with the answer, so Ms. Tsukuda pasted a card on the board that said "Answer" and wrote "5 leaves" next to it.

Ms. Tsukuda next moved on to the second review problem, 12 minus 2. She began by pulling out her collage and asking the students how many family members she had (see Fig. 11.4).

After the students correctly answered "Two people," she explained that she had collected 12 leaves just like everyone else and she asked the students to fill in the blanks in the story problem for her case. She took away all the cards that were pasted in the three blanks of the story problem template to represent Ms. Nishi's situation and pointed to the template. Many students enthusiastically raised their hands. Ms. Tsukuda asked one of the students to read the problem out loud. The student read the problem as "Ms. Tsukuda collected 12 ginkgo leaves. And then she drew two pictures of her family on the leaves. How many leaves are left over?" As the student read the story problem, Ms. Tsukuda pasted the three cards, "Ms. Tsukuda," "12," and "2," on the corresponding blanks in the problem. After the other students agreed that this was right, Ms. Tsukuda asked the class what expression (*shiki*) should be used for this problem. One of the students answered "12 minus 2 equals." The teacher pasted a card with the word "expression" on the blackboard and wrote "12 − 2 =" under it. Because the other students agreed with this, Ms. Tsukuda asked for the answer. One of the students answered 10. The other

FIG. 11.4   Ms. Tsukuda showing her collage.

students agreed but Ms. Tsukuda asked for the complete answer, to which the student responded, "Ten leaves."

Ms. Tsukuda wondered how they got the answer 10 for this problem. One of the students explained that since the number 12 is composed of 10 and 2 she took the 2 away and it became 10. Ms. Tsukuda asked the student to come to the blackboard to point to what 2 she was talking about. The student came up to the board and pointed to the 2 in the number 12.

Ms. Tsukuda told the class that she would have wanted to use real ginkgo leaves to show how the student had solved this problem, but that because she did not have any more real ginkgo leaves she would use tiles instead. She pulled out the manipulative for the lesson and demonstrated how to find 12 minus 2 with this manipulative (see Fig. 11.5).

She said that the tiles represented ginkgo leaves. The long strip had 10 tiles and represented the quantity 10, and the 2 individual tiles represented 2 more leaves. Using the manipulative, Ms. Tsukuda explained that the student took away two individual tiles. She suggested that they represent this by flipping those tiles over and pasting them on the right side of the drawing paper, which she did. She again explained to them that

FIG. 11.5   Ms. Tsukuda showing the manipulative to the students.

when they took something away they needed to make sure to turn over the corresponding tiles and move them to the right side of the drawing paper. She concluded by reiterating that if one moved the 2 tiles away, 10 tiles would be left over. Ms. Tsukuda asked the students if this was clear and she got an affirmative answer from the class.

(2) Using This Format to Set Up the Main Problem of the Lesson

Ms. Tsukuda next moved on to introducing the problem 12 minus 7 by referring to the collage made by one of the students in the class, Masao (see Fig. 11.6).

First, Ms. Tsukuda asked Masao how many family members he had. He answered that he had seven people in his family. Ms. Tsukuda mentioned that Masao had collected 12 leaves and asked the students to complete the blanks in the problem template using Masao's case. One of the students said Masao collected 12 ginkgo leaves. Ms. Tsukuda wrote Masao's name on a card and pasted it in the first blank. Then the student continued to read the problem and said, "And he drew seven pictures of his family on the

FIG. 11.6   Ms. Tsukuda showing Ms. Nishida's collage.

leaves. How many leaves were left over?" Ms. Tsukuda pasted the cards with 12 and 7 in the corresponding blanks of the problem template.

Next, Ms. Tsukuda passed out the first lesson handout and asked the students to complete the problem template on their handout to represent Masao's case. Some of the students were tempted to represent their own case, but Ms. Tsukuda reminded them that they should be working on Masao's case. Ms. Tsukuda walked around the classroom for about a minute to see if the students were completing the problem template correctly and then she asked the students what they knew about the problem. One of the students answered "Twelve leaves and seven leaves" and the other students agreed. Ms. Tsukuda circled with a red marker the numbers 12 and 7 in the problem. She asked what the number 12 represented. One of the students said it was the number of leaves he collected. Ms. Tsukuda said that was correct and she asked what the number 7 represented. Another student said the number of leaves Masao drew faces on. Ms. Tsukuda then asked what number the problem was asking for. Another students answered, "How many leaves are left over." Ms. Tsukuda underlined with her red marker the part in the problem that said, "How many leaves are left over?" (see Fig. 11.7).

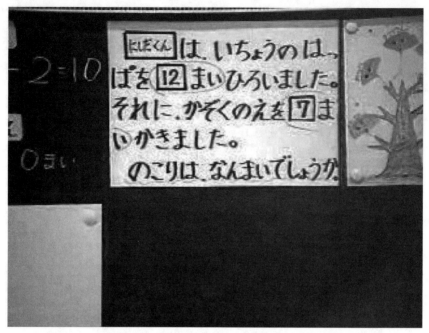

FIG. 11.7 Circles and an underline added to the story problem. Ms. Tsukuda circled "12 leaves" and "7 leaves" on the story problem with the marker. She also underlined the sentence "How many leaves are left over?" Blanks were filled in with a student's name and the number of leaves collected and used by this student.

SOLVING THE MAIN PROBLEM

(1) Thinking About Writing an Expression (*Shiki*)

Ms. Tsukuda next instructed the students to write an expression on their handouts to represent this problem. She walked around the classroom for about one minute and then asked one of the students to answer. The student said "Twelve minus seven" and he asked other students if they approved of his answer. Because the other students said it was correct, Ms. Tsukuda wrote "12 − 7 =" on the blackboard and pasted a card that said "expression" next to this.

(2) Understanding What the Problem Is Asking

Ms. Tsukuda continued by asking the students if they could subtract 7 from 12. Some students said they could and others said they already knew the answer. So Ms. Tsukuda asked one of the students to state the answer. The student said five. Some of the students agreed with this answer, but others disagreed and said the answer was seven instead. Ms. Tsukuda wrote both numbers on the blackboard and said that because both of the students were unsure of their answers, they would think together about how to find the answer to this problem.

(3) Solving the Problem Individually

Ms. Tsukuda explained to her class that after they worked on the problem, she was going have them present their solution strategies. She told them that they could write their solutions on the handout in words or using expressions, but that she wanted them all to use the manipulative she had shown them. Furthermore, because they did not have any real ginkgo leaves to work with, the manipulative would have tiles instead. She explained that each drawing paper had 12 tiles that consisted of a long strip with 10 tiles and 2 individual tiles (see Fig. 11.8).

FIG. 11.8   Ms. Tsukuda explaining how to use the manipulative to the students.

Ms. Tsukuda next asked the students if they thought it was possible to subtract 7 from 12. Some of the students said yes and some said no. She asked why some of them felt they could not take 7 away from 12 and queried them about which one of these two numbers they thought was bigger. Many students selected 12 as the bigger number, which prompted Ms. Tsukuda to again ask if they thought they could take 7 away from 12. This time only one student still said that one could not subtract 7 from 12. Ms. Tsukuda asked this student why he felt this way. The student said he could take away the two individual tiles but he would not be able to take the others away. Ms. Tsukuda responded by saying: "I see, it is difficult to take them away if the tiles are connected together like a strip." Then she asked the students what they should do about this problem. One student suggested they could cut the strip. Ms. Tsukuda said, "That is a good idea," and explained that they could use their scissors for doing this. She explained that they could cut along the lines drawn in to show the 10 tiles that made up this strip. Ms. Tsukuda also reminded the students one more time that if they took tiles away they would need to turn them over and paste them on the right side of the drawing paper. Finally, she passed out a copy of the manipulative to each student. Many students commented that the drawing paper was sticky and seemed excited about using it. After passing out the manipulative, Ms. Tsukuda explained one more time the procedure for using it. She also reminded the students that when they finished working, she would ask them to use the tiles to explain their ideas for how to solve the problem. She also again instructed them to write down in words on their handout how they had solved the problem.

During the 12½-minute period that followed, the children worked on the problem while Ms. Tsukuda walked around the classroom taking notes on her copy of the seating chart, which she had on a clipboard (see Figs. 11.9, 11.10, 11.11, and 11.12).

From time to time she made comments to the students. She said things to them like, "The tiles that you took away, please turn them over and put them down on the right side of drawing paper," or "When you finish with the tiles, please try to write in words how you solved it on the handout." Generally, however, she did not interact very much with the students as they worked. The other teachers, and in particular the lower grade teachers, also walked around the classroom and took notes on their copies of the seating chart of what the students were doing (see Fig. 11.13).

POLISHING AND REPORTING INDIVIDUAL SOLUTION METHODS

When Ms. Tsukuda called the class together and before selecting a first presenter, she told her students that she wanted all those who came to the board to do their best to explain their ideas.

FIG. 11.9   A student solving the problem using the manipulative. This student was cutting the 10-tile strip into individual pieces.

FIG. 11.10   Another student solving the problem using the manipulative. This student was cutting the 10-tile strip at the 5-tile length.

FIG. 11.11   An example of a student's work. It looked like this student cut the 10-tile strip into 3- and 7-tile lengths to find an answer; The 7-tile length strip is placed to the right and the 3-tile length strip and 2 individual tiles are put together on the left side of the drawing paper.

Kyoko's Solution

Ms. Tsukuda first selected a girl named Kyoko to come up to the board. She pasted Kyoko's manipulative on the blackboard and then asked her to read her ideas from her handout. Kyoko began by telling her classmates, "I am going to present my idea." She explained to them that she had pasted 12 tiles and had subtracted 7 tiles from these 12 tiles. Then she said because she subtracted 7 tiles, there were 5 tiles left over from the 12 tiles, and that was how she found the answer (see Fig. 11.14).

She asked the other students what they thought about her idea. Many students replied by saying that her solution was good. Ms. Tsukuda pointed to the five tiles on Kyoko's drawing paper and asked her how she had found the answer, five. Because the student did not respond, Ms. Tsukuda asked her if she counted the number of tiles to solve this problem. The student nodded. Ms. Tsukuda told the students that she would explain

FIG. 11.12   Another example of a student's work. It looked like this student cut the 10-tile strip into two 5-tile lengths to find an answer. A 5-tile length strip is pasted to the closer side of the drawing paper and another 5-tile length strip is pasted with 2 individual tiles side by side at the further side of the drawing paper.

Kyoko's solution to them. She said that she had cut the strip very carefully into individual tiles. Then she said there were 12 tiles and she turned over 7 of them one by one. Ms. Tsukuda pointed to the student's manipulative and pretended to move tiles by counting "1, 2, 3, 4, 5, 6, 7." Then she explained that Kyoko had counted the remaining tiles and had found the answer, five.

Ms. Tsukuda asked the students if any of them had come up with the same idea. While she was waiting for them to respond, she pasted a card above Kyoko's solution that read: "take away one by one from 12 and count the remainder" (see Fig. 11.15).

She also pasted above Kyoko's manipulative a small card with this student's name written on it. Because in the meantime the class remained silent, Ms. Tsukuda asked one more time if there was anybody who had solved the problem like Kyoko by taking away the tiles one by one. One of the students raised her hand and Ms. Tsukuda pasted her name card next to Kyoko's name card.

FIG. 11.13   Teachers observing the students' work.

FIG. 11.14   Kyoko presenting her idea at the blackboard. The diagram in
the box at the right corner shows Kyoko's manipulative on the blackboard.

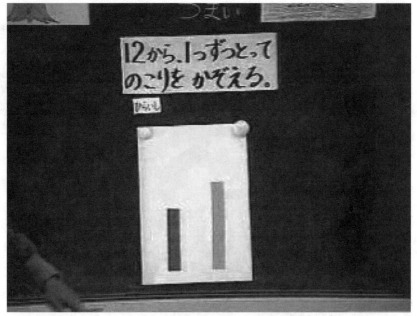

FIG. 11.15 Kyoko's manipulative and a card explaining her solution method. An explanation summary card was pasted above Kyoko's manipulative. A little card with Kyoko's name was also pasted there.

Ms. Tsukuda then asked the class if anybody had solved the problem differently and a few students raised their hands in response. She commented that there should be more people ready to present solutions because when she had walked around the classroom earlier she had seen many students writing solutions on their handouts, many of which were different from what Kyoko had presented. She allowed for a long pause after her comment and then asked a boy named Shigeru to come to the board to present his work.

Shigeru's Solution

On his way to the board Shigeru said that he hoped that he had done it correctly and that his solution might be similar to Kyoko's. Ms. Tsukuda reassured him about presenting his idea and pasted his manipulative on the blackboard. Shigeru began by saying, "Because the number twelve is made up of ten and two and seven is made of two and five so I took seven …" He continued to read what he had written on the handout but what he said was very confusing (see Fig. 11.16).

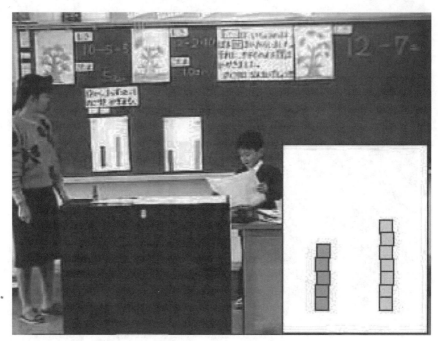

FIG. 11.16   Shigeru presenting his idea at the blackboard. The diagram in the box at the lower right corner shows Shigeru's manipulative on the blackboard. The view of the blackboard also shows how the blackboard was organized.

Ms. Tsukuda asked the other students if they had understood his explanation. Many of them said they had not, although there were a few students who claimed that they had understood. In order to help Shigeru, Ms. Tsukuda reminded the class that he had said that the number 12 was made up of 10 and 2 and that the number 7 was made up of 2 and 5. Then she asked Shigeru what he had done next but he remained silent. Ms. Tsukuda prompted him by asking if he had drawn a diagram similar to those she had had them use when they studied addition. The type of diagram she was referring to is called *edawakare* (branch off) and it shows how a number can be decomposed into two smaller numbers. Shigeru confirmed that he had used such a diagram to solve the problem. In response Ms. Tsukuda drew a branch-off diagram on the blackboard right above Shigeru's manipulative (see Fig. 11.17).

She then asked Shigeru what he had done next, but he again remained silent. Ms. Tsukuda seemed puzzled and asked if he did not know how to explain. Shigeru started again by saying that the number 7 is made up of 2 and

FIG. 11.17 Ms. Tsukuda's summary figure on the blackboard. Ms. Tsukuda summarized Shigeru's explanation with a figure. The diagram in the box at the upper right corner shows this figure.

5 but could not continue to explain further. Ms. Tsukuda asked him if he had taken away the number 2 that is part of the number 7 from the 2 that is in the ones place of the number 12. Shigeru nodded and said that he had taken the number 2 from the number 12 and then had taken 5 from the 10 of the number 12. Ms. Tsukuda asked other students if they understood this method. This time many students said that they had understood. Ms. Tsukuda told the class that she would explain the solution one more time. She said that Shigeru had cut the 10-strip into individual pieces and had lined up these 10 tiles in one row and 2 tiles in another row to show 12 tiles. Then she explained that because 7 is made of 2 and 5, first Shigeru took away the two 2s. She pointed to the 2 of the 12 and the 2 of the 7 in the diagram she had drawn. She explained that he had subtracted one 2 from the other 2 and she circled the two 2s on the diagram. Then she said that Shigeru still needed to take away the remaining 5 from the 10 of the 12 and she drew a line between the number 10 from the 12 and the number 5 from 7 on the diagram (see Fig. 11.18).

FIG. 11.18   Additional lines on Ms. Tsukuda's summary figure.

After this explanation Ms. Tsukuda asked Shigeru to ask the class if everyone had understood his method. He did so and many of his classmates
said that they had understood.

Ms. Tsukuda decided to ask the students one more time if Shigeru's solution method made sense to them, and one of the students admitted that it
did not. Ms. Tsukuda dropped her head and the other teachers who were
observing the lesson started to laugh. She then patiently began to explain
the solution again by pointing to the diagram. She said that 12 can be divided into 10 and 2, and 7 can be divided into 2 and 5. She made sure that
the confused student understood up to this point. Then she explained that
Shigeru had subtracted the 2 of the 7 from the 2 of the 12 and then subtracted the 5 of the 7 from the 10 of the 12. Then she said that 10 minus 5
equals 5 so the answer was 5. After her explanation, she asked the confused
student if he now understood better. This time he said that he thought that
he understood, as did many of the other students in the class. Ms. Tsukuda
next asked the class if there was anybody who had done the problem in the
same way as Shigeru. Nobody raised his or her hand, so she moved on to
ask a girl named Emi to present her work.

Emi's Solution

Ms. Tsukuda pasted Emi's manipulative on the board and asked her to speak up and present her idea (see Fig. 11.19).

Emi asked if she could write something on the blackboard to explain her idea. Ms. Tsukuda said "Yes" and asked her to write above her pasted manipulative. Emi wrote the expression "12 – 7 =" and then drew a branch-off diagram showing that the number 12 is made of 5, 5, and 2 (see Fig. 11.20).

She next circled the numbers 5 and 2 of the 12 and the number 7 (see Fig. 11.21).

Ms. Tsukuda pointed to the circled numbers in the diagram and asked Emi why she had circled them. Emi shyly whispered something to Ms. Tsukuda who in response asked her why the number 12 became 5, 5, and 2. Emi was silent for a while and then tried to speak to Ms. Tsukuda, who told her to speak loudly to the whole class, not to her. Emi again became silent. Ms. Tsukuda encouraged her by telling her that she should have confidence in herself. At first Emi remained silent, but after more encouragement from

FIG. 11.19   Emi presenting her idea at the blackboard. The diagram in the box at the lower left corner shows Emi's manipulative on the blackboard.

FIG. 11.20   Emi's diagram on the blackbard. Emi drew a diagram right above her manipulative. This diagram is shown in the box at the lower right corner.

FIG. 11.21   Emi added a circle in the diagram she drew. The diagram in the box at the upper left corner shows Emi's final diagram.

Ms. Tsukuda she finally looked at the class and said, "Because seven is five and two, I moved the five and two of the number twelve. Then I counted the remaining. I counted the five of the number twelve. Then it became five." She asked the class what they thought and many of the students said that her solution was good.

Ms. Tsukuda mentioned that Emi's solution method was a little bit similar to Shigeru's method. She then went over Emi's method and asked if anyone had solved the problem like Emi had. No one responded, so she only pasted Emi's name card by her drawing on the blackboard and moved on to ask for another idea to be presented.

Yasuko's Solution

This time a girl named Yasuko came up to the blackboard. Ms. Tsukuda had pasted her manipulative on the board and encouraged her to use her tiles to explain her method. She began by putting the tiles back in their original position and then she turned around and told all her classmates that she was going to present her idea. Yasuko explained that she had divided the 10 tile into 5 and 5 and then moved one of the sets of 5 to the right side along with the other 2 individual tiles. Next, she said that she had looked at what remained on the left side and saw five tiles. So she knew that the answer was 5 (see Fig. 11.22).

She then asked her classmates what they thought about her solution. Many of them approved of it. However, Ms. Tsukuda wanted to know where she had gotten the 10 from because originally she was dealing with 12, not 10. Yasuko decided to make a branch off diagram on the blackboard to answer this question. After some struggle, she drew a diagram that decomposed 12 into a 10 and a 2 and 10 into two 5s. She also drew a line between the 2 and one of the 5s (see Fig. 11.23).

Yasuko did not seem satisfied by what she had written, and after a while she decided to consult with Ms. Tsukuda. Ms. Tsukuda asked where, on her diagram, the number 7 was represented. In response, Yasuko erased her diagram and drew the correct one, this time with some help from her teacher (see Fig. 11.24).

After successfully completing this diagram, Yasuko again showed the class how she had moved her tiles (see Fig. 11.25).

She then asked everyone what they thought about her method. Many students again approved or agreed with her work by saying, "It's good."

Because in the middle of Yasuko's presentation the end-of-period bell had rung, Ms. Tsukuda told the class that she would hurry up a little bit to finish the lesson. Ms. Tsukuda reiterated Yasuko's solution one last time and then asked the class if any of them had solved the problem using this

FIG. 11.22 Yasuko presenting her idea at the blackboard. The diagram in the box at the upper left corner shows Yasuko's manipulative on the blackboard.

FIG. 11.23 Yasuko's diagram. Yasuko drew a diagram on top of her manipulative (manipulative on the left side). The diagram in the box at the upper left corner shows what she drew.

FIG. 11.24 Yasuko's new diagram. Yasuko erased her diagram and wrote another diagram. The diagram in the box at the upper left corner shows Yasuko's second diagram.

strategy. A couple of students raised their hands, so she pasted their name cards on the blackboard along with Yasuko's name card.

SUMMARY AND ANNOUNCEMENT OF THE NEXT LESSON

The lesson was supposed to end with the teacher having a discussion with the class about which solution method was better, and also Ms. Tsukuda had prepared a second handout with a practice problem on it. However, because time was running out, Ms. Tsukuda quickly ended the lesson without doing either of these things. She told her students that she regretted not being able to hear from more of them about how they had solved this problem, but that they would return to this in the next lesson. In summary, she told the class that during the lesson they had solved the problem 12 minus 7 in various ways and then she asked the students what answer they had found. Many students said "Five." Ms. Tsukuda requested a complete answer to the problem and the students answered, "Five leaves." She then pasted a card that said "Answer" on the blackboard and wrote "5

FIG. 11.25   The explanation summary card Ms. Tsukuda pasted for
Yasuko's solution. Ms. Tsukuda pasted a summary card right above
Yasuko's manipulative and diagram. The diagram in the box at the upper
left corner shows her card.

leaves" next to it. Ms. Tsukuda also asked the students to write their names
on the back of their manipulatives and to turn them in to her along with
their handouts. Finally, she announced that next time they would work on
the same ginkgo leaf problem using other students' collages and said that
the lesson was over. The students on day-duty came up to the front of the
class and said: "We are finished with our studies for the second period."
Everybody in the classroom bowed.

All the teachers then quickly migrated to another classroom to observe a
third-grade study lesson that had been prepared by the middle grade
group. This was followed by lunch, after which everyone participated in a
meeting to discuss the two study lessons taught on that day. That particular
day had been chosen for teaching these two lessons because it was a day on
which children were already scheduled to go home after lunch, thus freeing
up the teachers to meet peacefully in the afternoon to talk about the lessons.
In the next chapter we recount the parts of the afternoon discussion that focused on Ms. Tsukuda's lesson.

Sharing Reflections About the Study Lesson

Unlike when Ms. Nishi taught the subtraction study lesson, where only members of the lower grade group and the principal got together to share their observations, all the Tsuta teachers, the principal, the vice-principal, and Mr. Saeki attended the debriefing meeting that followed Ms. Tsukuda's lesson. This meeting, which was held in the staff room (see Fig. 12.1), began and ended with brief remarks from the school's principal.

The bulk of the meeting was devoted to discussing first Ms. Tsukuda's lesson and then a third-grade study lesson that was also taught on that day. Mr. Saeki was also asked to provide comments and suggestions. The conversations about each of these lessons were structured in the same way. They began with the teacher who had taught the lesson providing reactions, which were then followed by a whole-group discussion. The meeting lasted 2 hours and 20 minutes. The teachers spent about 50 minutes discussing each lesson. Mr. Saeki's remarks, plus the principal's opening and closing comments, lasted about 30 minutes. The head teacher, Mr. Mizuno, was in charge of facilitating the proceedings. We next provide an account of this entire meeting except for discussions and comments made specifically about the third-grade study lesson.

MR. YAMASAKI'S OPENING REMARKS

The principal's brief opening remarks began with him thanking all teachers for participating in the study lessons. He also thanked Mr. Saeki for coming to the school to observe the lessons and the lower and middle grade teachers for their efforts in developing these lessons. He next made a few brief comments about the two lessons taught that morning. In reference to Ms. Tsukuda's lesson, he said that he thought that the first-grade students were paying attention to what their teacher was saying during the lesson and that it looked to him as if they were learning every step of

FIG. 12.1   A view of the staff room. The teachers' desks are arranged in a U shape. The principal, the vice-principal, and the instructional superintendent sat at the front of the staff room. The far end of the picture shows where the lower grade level teachers sat. Other grade level teachers sat on the other side of these desks.

the lesson with confidence. He concluded by saying that he hoped that the meeting would be very meaningful for everyone.

MS. TSUKUDA'S SELF-EVALUATION OF THE LESSON

Ms. Tsukuda began by reflecting on her students' reactions to the study lesson (see Fig. 12.2).

She explained that right after the lesson had ended she had asked her students to write down their thoughts about what had transpired. She discovered that many of them reported feeling nervous because there were so many teachers in the classroom. Ms. Tsukuda remarked that in previous lessons a number of students had shown confidence and had wanted to stand out by presenting their ideas in front of the class. However, during this lesson even these students had been reluctant to speak up. She expressed her great disappointment in this and thought that she needed to help foster students' confidence to present their ideas in any situation.

Moreover, Ms. Tsukuda was very disappointed that she could not get a variety of student solutions on the board; in particular, she had hoped to see

FIG. 12.2   Ms. Tsukuda reflecting on her lesson during the all-staff meeting.

the subtraction–addition method presented. Moreover, contrary to her initial predictions, she had noticed that there were many students who used the subtraction–subtraction method. She explained that because her students were so used to finding supplements of 10 for addition problems requiring regrouping, she had predicted that it would be natural for them to instead use the subtraction–addition method. In retrospect, she now realized that in the case of 12 minus 7, it was natural for the students to focus on the quantity 10 that makes up the number 12. Ms. Tsukuda also suspected that the tendency to use the subtraction–subtraction method was linked to the numbers used in the review problems. Indeed, the numbers 2 and 5, into which they were decomposing 7, had appeared in the process of solving the two review problems (10 minus 5 and 12 minus 2). She commented that it is easy to divide 7 into 5 and 2 to begin with, and the review problems made this even easier. Ms. Tsukuda explained that the review problems had been chosen to help the slow learners in the class; however, perhaps this choice of problems had instead made the main problem too easy for many students and had focused them on the subtraction–subtraction method.

    Ms. Tsukuda also mentioned that in a number of instances what students did with the manipulative did not match their written explanations on their handouts. She reported that she had actually found a student who had used the subtraction–addition method and that she was looking forward to asking this student to present at the board. However, when Ms. Tsukuda checked what this student had written on his handout, she noticed that instead of accurately summarizing what he had done, he described dividing 12 into 10 and 2 and taking away 5 from 10. In general, Ms. Tsukuda was disappointed by the fact that her students could not write very well, even though they had been practicing this skill for quite some time during their daily mathematics lessons.

Ms. Tsukuda's reflections on the use of the manipulative were a mixture of good and bad. One the one hand, she was pleased that the new manipulative reduced the students' use of the counting-subtraction method and that it made it easier to understand the subtraction methods used by students. On the other hand, she felt that the students were reluctant to use this manipulative. In fact, some of the students had told her that it was difficult to think about the problem using the tiles. Indeed, Ms. Tsukuda noticed that her students were having particular trouble with flipping over and pasting the subtracted tiles on the other side of the paper. She felt that in order to build students' comfort level they needed to have more hands-on experience using this type of manipulative. She reported that she was thinking about consistently using one type of manipulative throughout the school year, which she felt would bolster student confidence.

Ms. Tsukuda acknowledged that perhaps the phrasing of the story problem focused students more on finding an answer than on their thinking process. She said that she and her colleagues were aware of this and had decided that after posing the problem, the teacher should follow with good process-oriented *hatsumon*, something that she had tried to do.

Lastly, Ms. Tsukuda reported that many of the students claimed, when she surveyed them after the lesson, that they had liked the lesson, particularly the part where they got to work with the manipulative. She thought that the reason the students responded positively was that they had enjoyed cutting tiles and pasting them on the drawing board. Despite this positive feedback, Ms. Tsukuda personally felt that the students did not truly enjoy the lesson because of the difficulty they experienced using the manipulative. She concluded by telling everyone that her rating of her lesson was a mixture of good and bad.

GROUP DISCUSSION OF THE LESSON

As the facilitator for the discussion, Mr. Mizuno began by inviting everyone to ask questions or simply voice their opinions. He also suggested they might start the discussion by talking about the two first segments of the lesson, which were described in the lesson plan under the headings "grasping the problem setting" and "presentation of the problem format."

Mr. Sato, a fifth-grade teacher, was the first to speak. He began by asking the lower grade teachers to describe how much time they had planned to devote to each segment of their lesson. In response, Ms. Tsukuda reviewed the time allocation plan she and her colleagues had drawn up (see Fig. 12.3).

Mr. Sato remarked that although he had not had much time to read the lesson plan carefully, he was able to follow the lesson very well and actu-

1. Grasping the Problem Setting (5 minutes) [1:37]

2. Presentation of the Problem Format (10 minutes) [15:02]:
   (1) Presenting the format and using it on previously learned subtraction situations (no borrowing situation) (5 minutes) [10:47]
     • Problem "10-5" [7:11]
       a. Setting up the problem (1:30)
       b. Introducing the story problem and filling in the blanks (5:41)
     • Problem "12-2" [3:37]
       a. Filling in the blanks and solving the problem (2:36)
   (2) Using this format to set up the main problem of the lesson (5 minutes)   [4:15]
     • Setting up the problem "12-7" [1:23]
     • Students to filling the blanks in the handout [1:1:39]
     • Confirmation of the answers of the handout [1:13]

3. Solving the Main Problem (13 minutes) [15:52]:
   (1) Thinking about formulating an expression [1:50]
   (2) Understanding what the problem is asking [12:18]
   (3) Solving the problem individually [12:44]

4. Polishing and Reporting Individual Solution Methods (12 minutes) [16:3]

5. Summary and Announcement of Next Lesson (5 minutes) [4:40] (1:13)

FIG. 12.3 A comparison of allotted and actual teaching time for the first study lesson. The times indicated in the parentheses show allotted time for each segment of the study lesson. The times indicated in the brackets show the actual length of each segment.

ally thought that it flowed very naturally. He also commented that the connection between the life study course (*seikatsu-ka*) and mathematics was very natural and engaging. In addition, he felt that the teacher had been skillful at engaging the students in conversations that were rich, yet easy to understand. However, Mr. Sato expressed concern that sections 1 and 2 of the lesson had taken too long, particularly in light of the fact that the central focus of the lesson was on the subsequent sections where the students were asked solve the problem and present their solutions. Mr. Sato pointed out that although about 15 minutes had been set aside for the two initial sections of the lesson, in reality 20 minutes had been devoted to these sections. He felt that instead more time needed to be reserved for later sections, particularly the *neriage* section. He added that although not all lessons need to be 45 minutes long, he believed that this was a good length for elementary school students because of their limited attention span. In his experience, successful elementary lessons tended to end right when the period bell rang. Thus for him, lengthening the lesson was not a good solution. Instead, he proposed that the review problem based on Ms. Nishi's family be cut out of the lesson.

Ms. Tsukuda responded that Ms. Nishi's case had been included in order to focus students on the number 10 because the teacher's manual and the textbook suggested that one of the concepts that the students need to understand when they are studying subtraction with regrouping is the subtraction–addition method. Ms. Tsukuda added that she had fully expected for the first two sections of the lesson to proceed faster than they actually had. In fact, her prediction had been that she would finish in 13 minutes instead of the 15 minutes set aside in the plan, or the 20 minutes it actually took her to get through this part of the lesson. According to her, these delays had to do with the students' difficulty switching gears from the previous addition lesson she had done with them, resulting in responses from them that were not as sharp as usual. She also admitted that she had been a little nervous at the beginning of the lesson, which also slowed things down.

Mr. Sato acknowledged that it was important in any lesson to spend time on the presentation of problems because this sets up students to work effectively on their own. The fact that he was able to understand very well the initial part of the first-grade study lesson gave him confidence that the students also had a clear understanding of what they needed to do when they were solving the problem on their own. According to Mr. Sato, where the lesson faltered was that achieving this clarity had been too time-consuming. However, he admitted that in his everyday lessons he often had a similar tendency of spending too much time at the beginning of lessons and less time for presentations and discussions. He wondered if there was any clever way out of this "catch 22," to which no one really responded, probably because they had nothing satisfying to contribute as an answer to this hard issue.

Mr. Sato next questioned the idea of having three blanks in the story problem. He said that it was too much for first-grade students to come up with all three blanks and it looked as if it was affecting their comprehension of the problem. He thought that if Ms. Tsukuda had filled in the first blank for the students, they would not have been confused about completing the problem and the lesson would have gone much more smoothly.

Ms. Chijiiwa mentioned that for the same reasons suggested by Mr. Sato, the lower grade level teachers had agreed that Ms. Tsukuda would complete the first blank of the problem. However, she said that Ms. Tsukuda was a little nervous at the beginning of the lesson and forgot what she was supposed to do. Ms. Tsukuda admitted that she had forgotten that point and she apologized to the other lower grade level teachers. Everybody laughed.

At this point there was a lull in the discussion, so Mr. Mizuno encouraged further comments by asking if anyone wanted to add anything to the discussion that had just taken place. Mr. Yamasaki, the principal, was the next to speak. He wondered if the subtraction–addition method had not come up perhaps because the children lacked knowledge of certain number facts. He asked Ms. Tsukuda to estimate how many of her students were good at finding supplements of 10. In particular, he wanted to know how many of her students could solve problems like 10 minus 5 and 10 minus 4. Ms. Tsukuda responded that she knew that many of the students in her class could easily do these calculations. She estimated that if she were to ask her students to find the supplements of numbers 1 through 9, four or five of them could complete this task in 10 seconds and even the slow learners in the class could do this in about 1 minute. She explained that she had in fact had her class do this task by creating a gamelike setting where she told the students "Ready, set, go" and used a stopwatch to measure their speed. As a result, Ms. Tsukuda was confident in her students' knowledge of these number facts and was quite surprised that only one student used the subtraction–addition method.

At this point Mr. Mizuno suggested that they move on to discussing the part of the lesson where the students solved the problem on their own, which he mentioned was section 3 in the lesson plan. He was very encouraging in soliciting comments, feedback, or questions. Mr. Yamasaki took advantage of this invitation to suggest that if the students had used coins instead of tiles, perhaps different solution strategies would have emerged. He explained that if the children had used one 10-yen coin and two 1-yen coins to make 12 yen, they probably would have immediately subtracted 7 yen from the 10-yen coin. His rationale was that one cannot actually see 10 coins in a 10-yen coin like one can see 10 tiles in a strip consisting of 10 tiles. Mr. Yamasaki argued that in particular coins would have been effective for the lower achieving students. He thought that these students might naturally want to subtract a number from the 10 first and then add or count the remaining coins to find an answer. In response, Ms. Tsukuda repeated the argument that she had presented in her opening remarks. She thought that the review problems had focused her students on the numbers 2 and 5, and that as a result the students decomposed the number 7 into 2 and 5 in order to subtract it from the 12. Although her planning group had prepared those problems as a review of previously learned subtraction problems, they did not help the students to pay attention to the number 10.

Ms. Furumoto added that she felt that the way the tiles were pasted on the drawing boards when these were handed out to the students caused the students not to be able to do the problem using the subtraction–addition method. According to her, pasting the 10-strip and the 2 individual tiles in two rows focused the students' attention on the 2 individual tiles first. She speculated that if all 12 tiles had been lined up in one straight line, the students might have cut the 10-strip into 7 and 3 to use the subtraction-addition method.

Mr. Mizuno added that if the numbers used in the problem had been numbers other than 12 and 7, students' solutions strategies would have been different. According to him, had the problem been 12 minus 8, the students would not have focused in on the 2 of the number 12 because the number 8 would most likely be seen by children as consisting of a 3 and 5.

Ms. Furumoto responded by recounting how at one point in their discussions the lower grade teachers had thought about making the problem 12 minus 8 or 12 minus 9. However, they had worried that the numbers 8 and 9 were so close to the number 10 that most of the students would use the subtraction–addition method. Ms. Tsukuda added that although most of the textbooks used problems like 12 minus 9, in her experience these numbers tended to lead students to the subtraction–addition method. She explained that the teachers in the lower grade group had worried that their lesson would be uninteresting if students did not utilize various solution methods. For this reason, they had decided to use 12 minus 7.

Mr. Saeki joined in by recalling a study lesson held at one of the schools that he visited, in which the teachers used 12 individual tiles and asked the students to paste their solutions on a board. He said some students pasted all their tiles in one row, some did it in two rows (one of 10 tiles and one of 2 tiles) and others did it with three rows (5 tiles, 5 tiles, and 2 tiles). Although this allowed the teachers to learn about each individual student's representation of the number 12, it did not support the teachers in learning about their students' thought processes as they moved on to subtract a quantity from 12. Mr. Saeki thought that compared to using individual tiles, using the 10-strip and 2 individual tiles was much more effective to help teachers understand student thinking about how to subtract 7 from 12. However, Mr. Saeki agreed with Mr. Mizuno's comment that the numbers used in the problem might have caused the students to focus on the number 2, instead of the number 10.

Mr. Saeki's comments prompted Ms. Tsukuda to add that the teachers in the lower grade group had also talked at length about students' conception of the number 12. She confirmed that in fact, in the first implementation of the lesson, they used individual tiles. However, as just suggested by Mr. Saeki, they learned that it was very hard to uncover students' thought processes.

Mr. Saeki continued by saying that he also felt that using individual tiles would prompt students to use a counting method. He then returned to the idea that the selection of the numbers 12 and 7 for the main problem of the lesson had not been an ideal choice. He proposed that had 12 minus 8, or 13 minus 7, been used instead, the outcome of the lesson might have been quite different. He argued that the selection of the review problems was at the root of only a small number of students using subtraction–addition method.

Mr. Mizuno chose this juncture to mention how important it was to revise and reteach a study lesson. He thought that the teachers in the lower grade level group had learned a tremendous amount from the first implementation of their lesson, which they applied to the design of their second version of this lesson. He felt that both the handout and the manipulative were improved and that the second lesson was smooth and easy to understand. In addition, the hands-on activities, particularly cutting the strip of tiles, helped the students stay interested in the lesson because it was easy for them to understand how to use the tiles. Thus, the survey results that Ms. Tsukuda reported on, which documented that the students truly enjoyed the lesson, did not surprise him. Ms. Tsukuda interjected that in fact there were some students who reported enjoying working on the manipulative because it was easy to paste and peel. She recalled that one of the students even said, "It was fun that the tiles stuck to the drawing paper."

Ms. Furumoto next shifted the conversation to the handout used for the lesson. She reminded everyone that in order for the students to write their explanations for how they solved the problem, they had been asked to write their solution in two steps using the words "first" and "next." However, Ms. Furumoto thought that this was confusing because she had noticed that many students wrote their entire explanation under the heading "first" and then wondered what they needed to write under the heading "next." She proposed that instead students should be asked to write their explanations freely. She acknowledged that this practice of using the terms "first" and "next" was being employed during the everyday lessons that Ms. Tsukuda's students took part in. However, her observations led her to conclude that students were having difficulty with this format. In addition, Ms. Furumoto mentioned that there were some discrepancies between what the students did using the manipulative and what they wrote on the handout.

She wondered how to solve this problem. Ms. Tsukuda did not respond to the second comment. With respect to the first, Ms. Tsukuda explained that when she was teaching addition lessons she decided to use this two-step explanation method because students tended to provide explanations like "I did it in my head." She had noticed that this improved the quality of her students' explanations. Ms. Tsukuda thought that the same practice should be extended to subtraction lessons.

Mr. Mizuno next mentioned that he had noticed the supplement–addition method listed among student anticipated solutions in the lesson plan. He wondered if there were any students who had used this method to solve the problem. Ms. Tsukuda explained that she and the other lower teachers had predicted that it would be unlikely for students to use this method. They had thought that if two values were being compared, then perhaps they might see some students using this method. However in this case, a situation of taking a quantity away from another, they thought the chances of this method emerging were very small. Ms. Furumoto added that the lesson manipulative was not conducive to the use of this method, and Mr. Sato seconded this claim. Mr. Mizuno admitted that although he did not know much about first-grade students, he was surprised by what was being said. His intuition would have been that if the students had just learned addition, then the supplement–addition method would come very naturally to them because it just involves counting up to the answer. Mr. Saeki decided to respond to Mr. Mizuno. He did this by further developing the idea that Ms. Furumoto had just put forth that the manipulative used in the lesson was not suited for eliciting this method. He said that this manipulative did not show separately the number being subtracted so it would be difficult to use such a method. He explained that if students had been comparing two values by lining up two quantities of tiles, then it would be natural to see one-to-one correspondences and then count up from there.

Mr. Mizuno, who seemed persuaded by these arguments, went back to his role of facilitator and asked the teachers if they had any comments to make about the next section of the lesson. Ms. Chijiiwa responded by sharing with everyone how hard their group had worked to come up with the idea of using scissors to solve the problem. She then returned to Mr. Yamasaki's earlier suggestion of using money and commented that she thought this would limit the lesson to shopping situations. Mr. Yamasaki said that using coins was simply an example and that the point he was trying to make was that using a bigger unit like 10 would be effective for teaching regrouping. Ms. Tsukuda commented that if she were to pose the same problem, but in a shopping context, the students with shopping experience could easily solve the problem. She thought that money was a very accessible mathematical tool for students to use.

Mr. Yamasaki next alluded to the importance of developing students' ability to write explanations of their work and its effectiveness in helping them to develop their own thinking. He said that it occurred to him as he observed the first-grade lesson that the issue of how to develop these writing skills in students might be a good topic to pursue for the next year's *konaikenshu*. He also commented that teachers want students to come up to the blackboard to explain their ideas. However, teachers generally know that as the number of student presentations increases, the students' interest in the lesson decreases. He reflected that there had to be a better way to structure the student presentations or an alternative approach altogether that the teachers might want to consider, and he encouraged everyone to think about this.

Ms. Sasaki, a third-grade teacher, thought that the lesson had improved a lot since the first implementation. She was also pleased to see that the new version of the manipulative made a significant difference in helping the teacher understand student solutions. She remarked that she understood that pasting tiles on the drawing paper with spray glue allowed students to easily bring their work to the blackboard. However she suggested that if an overhead or other media equipment were instead used during students' presentations, students could more easily demonstrate how they had moved their tiles. She argued that when students learn to use such equipment, they can explain their solutions, even when they are having difficulty finding the appropriate words.

Mr. Mizuno extended this point by asking if the students actually needed to write down their ideas on the handout in order present them. He thought that if the students were asked to present their ideas on the blackboard by simply saying "Move the tiles just like you did on your drawing board," it might be enough. Ms. Tsukuda countered that if students did not have a written document to refer to, they would tend to face the blackboard when presenting. She felt that many of them lacked the self-confidence needed to speak without an aid to help them organize their thoughts. Ms. Sasaki wondered if the second-grade students also evidenced similar behavior, and Ms. Maejima confirmed that they did indeed. Ms. Tsukuda added that the first-grade students could explain in general terms how they moved the tiles by saying things like "I moved this one this way." However, she thought that in order to get students to provide more detailed explanations, they would need more practice explaining their work. Mr. Mizuno suggested that maybe the presenting student did not need to explain in words what he or she did. Rather, the teacher could ask other students to look very carefully at how the presenting student moved the tiles on the board. Ms. Tsukuda added that she was convinced that if she could succeed in establishing a classroom environment where students felt comfortable talking to each other, then seeing a student demonstrate how he or she used the manipulative could easily lead to a dialogue. She thought that students would naturally want to ask questions like, "Why did you move the tile from here to over there?" "Because it became 10 by moving it like that." Mr. Mizuno asked her how well established such an environment was in her class. Ms. Tsukuda said that her students could do this sometimes, but not always. Ms. Furumoto thought that regularly exposing students to that style of presentation would help establish such a classroom environment. However, she felt unsure that all students in the first grade were capable of developing the skills needed to look at what other students were doing and understand what was going on. Ms. Furumoto argued that the teachers needed to consider the students' developmental stages when planning the presentation. Mr. Sato thought that the third-grade study lesson presented that morning demonstrated that the students at this later grade level could present their ideas by reading what they had written on handouts. He also felt that the presentations made by Ms. Tsukuda's students were quite good, given that these children were only first graders. He was also impressed that most of these young students had listened carefully to their classmates as they presented. He suggested setting guidelines for evaluating student presentations that took into account the developmental stage of the students involved and the style of presentation in question. In this way, the teachers could develop sound thinking about how to guide their attempts to improve their students' presentation abilities. He suggested that this topic could even be a goal for *konaikenshu* in the future. Many of the teachers nodded in agreement.

Ms. Tsukuda recognized that the first graders were limited developmentally in their abilities; however, she thought there were many things first-grade students could do. She expressed these thoughts as follows:

> I am not protecting my first-grade students but I've heard so many people telling me that first-grade students can't do things. When we look at the first-grade students, there are a lot of things they can do very well. I do think there are some areas in which we can train them to do better. I think, particularly today, they were a little bit nervous but they can do a lot of things. Therefore we cannot just think that they can't do certain things. Of course they cannot explain things in logical ways like the upper grade students do, but there are some students who can explain things well by saying, "I did it this way" or "I did it that way" using tiles to do some addition problems. So I think that if we can develop such skills in all the students, this would be good … I want all of my students to be able to present ideas. So I would like all the students to experience presenting their ideas.

Mr. Sato countered in the following manner:

> I think the first-grade students did very well today, even considering the fact that there were a lot of teachers in the classroom. I always tell my

fifth-grade students that it is important that they understand what they learn in a math lesson, but also the skills like speaking in public and explaining what they think in a logical manner are the important things that will help them when they grow up to be a member of society. These skills are the skills needed to do well beyond the subject of math. I think we need to foster these skills according to the students' developmental stages. I think it should apply not only to math lessons but also to Japanese language lessons and physical education lessons. In math lessons, these skills are acquired during *Neriage*.

Then Mr. Asada, one of the sixth-grade teachers, added:

I think one of the reasons that the first-grade students were able to provide such good explanations during the student presentations was because the lesson was associated with their real experiences in the Daily Living lesson. Because they had a clear memory of collecting ginkgo leaves, they were able to do such a good job. If the problem was not related to their real experiences and asked them to "explain how you did it," I think it would not have worked as well as it did in the lesson. I don't think all first graders need to be able to explain their thoughts logically starting in first grade ... Just like Mr. Sato said, I thought they were doing great. If we can foster the presentation skills little by little starting in the first grade I think they will be right on track by the time they are in sixth grade. In order to do this, I think we need to agree upon a certain lesson style for everybody to try in their classroom to allow the students to accumulate these experiences starting in first grade.

These remarks prompted Ms. Maejima, the second-grade teacher, to describe her own approach to coping with the students who were having difficulty writing down their solutions. She believed that these difficulties were often linked to lack of writing abilities rather than students' lack of understanding of their solution strategies. She explained that the first thing she usually did with these students was to ask them to describe what they wanted to say. In her experience, many of these students would try to explain their thinking in one sentence, but she tried to encourage them to explain their ideas one step at a time. Then she asked the students to write out the steps just like they had explained them to her in words. She had found that this helped tremendously in improving the quality of students' written explanations and that as these written explanations improved over the year, so did students' oral explanations.

It seemed as if teachers had more to discuss about how to develop guidelines for fostering student's presentation skills, but they were unfortunately out of time and needed to move on to talking about the third-grade lesson. Because we will not summarize the debriefing of this lesson, we instead turn to the comments Mr. Saeki made later that afternoon.

MR. SAEKI'S COMMENTS AND SUGGESTIONS

Mr. Saeki's remarks were a mixture of commenting directly on the study lessons he had observed on that day and providing broader information (see Fig.12.4).

In the first part of his remarks Mr. Saeki focused on the issue of what teachers should aim to teach in mathematics lessons. He urged teachers to think carefully about what were the most important "skills for living" (*ikiteikuchikara* or *ikiruchikara*) that students should be learning from their mathematics instruction. Mr. Saeki said that when the students are working on a problem, "The skills that help them change the problem into more basic forms and into forms that are already known to them are the skills that become useful and profitable to them when they grow up to be adults." For example, he explained that when teachers teach how to find the area of a trapezoid, they often emphasize teaching the formula of the trapezoid. However, according to him, teachers should instead put their energy into teaching children about the area of a rectangle and how to change the shape of a trapezoid (more complicated form) into a

FIG. 12.4   Mr. Saeki commenting on the study lesson.

rectangle (more simple form). He also suggested that teachers should help students realize that moving from complicated to more simple forms is a convenient and a clever thing to do. He concluded this first part of his remarks by stating that it is necessary for the teachers to study the curriculum more carefully and think about what their teaching should emphasize. He added that encouraging students to recognize the importance of changing things into their basic form should definitely be part of what teachers emphasize.

In the second part of his remarks, Mr. Saeki spoke about each of the two lessons he had seen that morning. He began his remarks about Ms. Tsukuda's lesson by saying that he felt that having a story problem with blanks was very effective because it allowed the class to look at several problems in the course of the lesson while using the same setting. He believed that keeping the problem setting consistent throughout the lesson and having it be connected to the activity of the ginkgo leaf project allowed the lesson to proceed very smoothly. He commented that often teachers are able to cover several calculation exercises in a lesson by doing away with providing a separate context for these problems. Moreover, Mr. Saeki thought that the approach taken by the lower grade teachers was more meaningful. Having the same setting throughout the lesson provided coherence to the work and encouraged students to use all the things that they learned during the lesson to solve subsequent problems they encountered as the instruction moved forward.

However, Mr. Saeki felt that teachers at Tsuta still needed to improve how they presented story problems to students. In particular, he suggested that they should focus on two key issues: the words and sentences used in the story problem, and the way they actually put forth the problems to students. For example, Mr. Saeki said that the sentence "How many leaves are left over?" used in Ms. Tsukuda's problem suggested that she was only interested in getting the students' answers, instead of finding out how they had solved the problem. Mr. Saeki acknowledged that he knew that the lower grade teachers had spent some time thinking about how to word the gingko leaf story problem, but that they had not come up with anything that particularly pleased them. Mr. Saeki also conceded that Ms. Tsukuda had followed up with a good *hatsumon* asking the students to focus on finding the solution instead of just the answer and he praised her for this. He believed that thanks to Ms. Tsukuda's good follow-up *hatsumon*, the lesson had gone smoothly and the students had focused on process despite the wording of the story problem. Nevertheless, Mr. Saeki felt that the sentence "How many leaves are left over?" was not suited to the school's *konaikenshu* goal, which he reminded everyone was aimed at having students come up with different strategies for solving problems and using these students' divergent ideas to promote learning. He thought that in order for other teachers to recognize Tsuta's *konaikenshu* efforts, they needed to pay attention to developing interesting ideas for how to present story problems.

Mr. Saeki made two concrete suggestions for how to improve the presentation of the story problem. First, he proposed dividing the story problem into two parts. The first part would contain the "conditions" (*jyoken*) of the problem. It would start from the beginning of the story problem and would end right before the question being asked of students, which instead would be included in the second part of the problem (see Fig. 12.5).

Mr. Saeki explained that the teacher would first paste the top part of the problem and discuss it with the students, and only then would the teacher present the second part. By having at first the problem not include a question to be answered, the students must use the information available to speculate about what they will be asked to solve, and this encourages them to read the problem carefully. He said that having students carefully read and analyze the problem would help them better understand the lesson.

Mr. Saeki's second suggestion related to how to discuss the problem with students. He mentioned that if a teacher used Ms. Tsukuda's story problem and immediately told the students that it was a subtraction problem because the words "left over" were part of the question posed, this would deter students from developing reading comprehension and understanding skills. To make his point clear, he shared a recent experience he had while observing a study lesson in another school. In this lesson the teachers presented a story problem to students using the method he described earlier of dividing the story problem into two parts. The story problem went something like, "It is said that there were 12 treasures on an island. And the pirates found seven treasures." The teacher provided a picture of the scene and talked about the situation with the students. Mr. Saeki thought that this was an interesting way to present a problem. However, he

> ☐ collected ☐ ginkgo leaves.
> Then s/he drew ☐ pictures of his/her family
> on the leaves.

> Please tell us how you think about how many
> leaves are left over?

FIG. 12.5   Mr. Saeki's idea for improving the story problem.

said that the students quickly said things like, "We need to solve it by adding" and "The answer is 19," but none of them thought the problem could be a subtraction problem. Surprised by these students' unexpected responses, he asked some of them why they didn't think of the problem as involving subtraction. The students explained to him that because there were no words like "left over" or "remaining" in the problem, they did not think that subtraction was involved. Mr. Saeki realized that because the teacher had been teaching the students to look for keywords to determine whether or not a problem involved subtraction, the students were not developing the analytical skills needed to understand problems more deeply. Mr. Saeki also regretfully reported that he had uncovered that his own child was also being taught to focus on keywords. He noticed that this was discouraging his son from developing the patience to read through story problems carefully and was causing him to make careless mistakes. He said that by seeing his own child's case, and in light of the lesson study experience described earlier, he thought that students' analytical and reading comprehension skills could not be fostered unless teachers thought carefully about their everyday approach to presenting story problems. Therefore, he thought that the teachers at Tsuta, particularly because they were studying problem solving, needed to put more thought into developing effective ways of presenting story problems to students.

Although Mr. Saeki thought that the idea of dividing the story problem into two parts had some advantages, he also conceded that this approach might not work with Ms. Tsukuda's story problem. He said that because the first part of the problem had three blanks, if no question was included, it would be difficult for students to understand it. An alternative strategy to consider was to make sure to have very good follow-up *hatsumon*. He again acknowledged that Ms. Tsukuda had worked on doing this, but he wanted to make sure that all the teachers in the room understood the critical importance of preparing good *hatsumon*. He closed this part of the talk by asking the teachers to work on further improving the presentation of story problems to encourage students to think about their actual solution process.

Mr. Saeki next mentioned that there are two basic ways to ask students to think about a problem and that each sets up the lesson *neriage* process differently. The first is to ask students to come up with a solution for the problem, and the second is to ask them to think about as many different solutions as possible. Mr. Saeki recognized that Ms. Tsukuda's lesson was a first-grade lesson and that what he was about to suggest might not apply when dealing with such young students. However, he thought that if each student did not experience for him- or herself several solution methods, he or she might have difficulty understanding which method was more convenient or efficient. He felt that this was particularly true for the numerous students who tended to think that their ideas were always the best. Mr. Saeki argued that in order for students to pit solution strategies against each other, they must be given the opportunity to make evaluations of these based on their own attempts to solve the problem. Mr. Saeki thought that Ms. Tsukuda had not heard comments like "Teacher, I found that this method is more convenient," or "This method is much faster," or "This method is better because it prevents me from making mistakes," because each student had experienced only one way to solve the problem.

Mr. Saeki's next comment pertained to how a teacher should react when the students are slow to respond to the main question of the story problem. He argued that in instances when students are responding slowly because they are having difficulty solving the problem, or getting the right answer, it might be a good idea to give them the answer to the problem sooner. He proposed that by doing this, many of the students feel relieved because they know what the right answer is, and then they can focus their attention on finding a solution strategy for getting this answer. In some cases, having an answer can point slow learners to a solution strategy, which in turn gives them a feeling of satisfaction with their achievements. Mr. Saeki illustrated his point with an example from the day's third-grade study lesson. In this lesson the problem had been, "A person bought 12 cookies that cost 23 yen each. How much did he/she pay?" He said that the students had had a hard time coming up with various solutions, and because the calculations they had to do were not easy, many children did not respond well to the lesson. He also mentioned that some students shared wrong answers with the class, which discouraged other students from presenting their solutions. Mr. Saeki said that if he encountered a situation like that, he would say to the students, "Actually, the answer to 23 times 12 is 276. Can you explain why it is 276? Or, why don't you think about how you can find 276?" By doing this, students could focus on the solution strategies instead of just thinking about what the right answer might be. Mr. Saeki reported that he had observed an actual implementation of this strategy during a study lesson taught at another school. He felt that it was quite successful and helped improve student responses during the lesson.

The last point that Mr. Saeki made was that the teachers at Tsuta could benefit from developing a list of *hatsumon* that could be used to facilitate the *neriage* process. He had actually prepared a handout with the following candidates for items that could go on this list:

1. "Please write down your solutions on the blackboard."
2. "Please explain each of the solutions written on the blackboard one by one."

3. "If you have anything that you would like to add to your friends' solutions, please tell us."
4. "Let's ask questions about your friends' solutions."
5. "Which solutions are similar to other ones?"
6. "Which of the explanations provided by your friends did you think were good?"
7. "Let's compare your own solution method with your friends' method."

Mr. Saeki mentioned that the teachers would not need to use all the questions on this list all the time but that they could choose among them to encourage rich student discussions.

Mr. Saeki concluded by making one final comment about Ms. Tsukuda's lesson. He believed that if Ms. Tsukuda had not written on the board "12 – 7 =" under the heading "expression," the students might have produced more varied solution methods. He thought that by having the expression on the blackboard, the students focused on what to do with the numbers appearing in it instead of using the manipulative to think about how to solve the story problem. As a result, the students were more focused on decomposing or branching out the numbers instead of actively using the manipulative to find a solution.

CLOSING REMARKS FROM MR. YAMASAKI

Mr. Yamasaki began by saying that during the two study lessons he had observed that many of the students were paying attention to the instructions and listening to each other. He also was happy to see some of the slow learners actually presenting their ideas, which he thought was critical for them to build self-confidence. Mr. Yamasaki mentioned that these positive aspects had been fostered in advance of the study lessons and that these lessons simply provided an exciting opportunity to learn about the accumulated accomplishment of everyday practice at the school. He added that although there were some differences in ability among the students, he felt that each student was getting something out of the lessons. Lastly, Mr. Yamasaki said he was impressed that the discussions in the lesson study meetings had gone beyond just talking about what to teach in the lesson to something much deeper, actually discussing how to teach and carefully analyzing the lesson. Mr. Yamasaki thanked Mr. Saeki for visiting the school, and Ms. Tsukuda and the third-grade teacher for teaching the study lessons. Then the meeting was adjourned.

Although the lower grade teachers held no other official meeting to continue discussing their lesson, in the days that followed they had many informal conversations about it. A common theme in these exchanges was how difficult it was to develop a perfect lesson. The teachers realized that despite their extensive planning, the numbers that they chose for the review and the main problems had turned out to be too similar to elicit a variety of solutions from the students. Often during their conversations the teachers bemoaned the fact that none of the students had presented the subtraction–addition method. Despite their disappointments and concerns, the teachers also expressed a true sense of accomplishment, camaraderie, and enjoyment of their work together.

Follow-Up Activities:
Sharing and Reflecting

Although the lower grade teachers completed work on their subtraction lesson on November 18, major lesson study work still lay ahead of them for the remainder of the 1993–1994 academic year. In particular, these teachers still had to help with a lesson study open house and they would also take part in a schoolwide end of year reflection about the *konaikenshu* work carried out at the school that year. In this chapter we first describe the planning and conduct of the open house in order to give the reader a better understanding of what this type of event entails and its function in the lesson study process. Next we provide an account of how the teachers went about reflecting on their work.

TSUTA HOSTS A LESSON STUDY OPEN HOUSE

The reader may recall that the school had scheduled a lesson study open house (*kokaijyugyo*) for February 17 and that the lower level grade group had committed to teaching one of the three study lessons that would be presented on that day. For this event the lower grade teachers worked on a second-grade lesson entitled "Addition of Three Numbers That Add Up to 100." The middle grade teachers presented a fourth-grade lesson called "Fractions: Improper and Mixed," and the upper grade teachers worked on a fifth-grade lesson entitled "Ratio and Graph: How Crowded is the Bus?"

Each of these lessons was planned, tried out, and refined before the open house, during which revised versions of these lessons were taught. All 3 lessons were designed with an eye to presenting a comprehensive view of Tsuta's past 2 years of work under its chosen *konaikenshu* theme.

Preparing for the Event

In addition to actually planning three study lessons, the teachers at Tsuta had to accomplish a number of other tasks to get ready for the open house.

Toward the end of December 1993 they held a facultywide meeting to discuss the results of their *konaikenshu* to date and to plan how these results might be presented at the open house. At this meeting the Tsuta teachers generated the following list of results they felt they had achieved and of issues they felt they were still facing.

Results of the Lesson Study and Other Issues

Results:

1. Because we [the teachers at Tsuta] have been encouraging the students to have their own ideas when they work individually, many students who previously were conscious of not being good at mathematics and who were passive learners have started to show a more positive attitude toward learning mathematics.

2. In order to strengthen students' ability to express their ideas in front of others we have provided increased opportunities for them do so. As a result, students' activities in a small group setting have become more active. In addition, these efforts have produced a positive impact on learning about other subjects.

3. Pursuing *konaikenshu* under the theme of "problem-solving-based learning" has led teachers to become aware of using teaching methods that foster students to respect each others' ideas. This change in teaching methods has helped students show a more positive attitude toward learning during the lesson. The students seem to enjoy lessons more, and to be paying attention more autonomously and enthusiastically.

4. By having all the teachers at the school (all grade level teachers) observe a lesson under the focus of one theme, the teachers have become aware of the basic flow (or progression) of a lesson that focuses on "problem-solving-based learning."

5. The teachers have been able to develop a unified format for their lesson plans and the contents of these plans have become more organized, detailed, and clear.

6. Using a story problem containing blanks has become an established practice for carrying out lessons that focus on "problem-solving-based learning." Teachers' techniques for introducing story problems during lessons have improved.

7. Because the relationship between the three grade level teacher groups and the teaching staff as a whole has been very good and teachers' roles and responsibilities have been clear and comprehensive, the teachers have been able to carry out *konaikenshu* efficiently and at a deep level.

Issues:

(A) Teachers need to conduct further research on how best to conduct *neriage*.

- Fostering the students' ability to express their own ideas by themselves.
- Improving teachers' interactions with the students. Using hint cards to support individual students. Paying attention to how time is allocated across the lesson and especially during *neriage*.

(B) Teachers need to conduct more surveys in order to understand more fully students' thinking.

(C) Teachers need to think about ideas for how to evaluate student learning more effectively.

(D) Teachers need to focus on a few important issues to discuss during the postlesson meetings because the time is limited and the depth of the discussion is key to having a productive experience.

(E) Teachers need to communicate and exchange ideas even further. In particular, they need to discuss how to teach the students who have difficulty with mathematics.

In the end, this list of results and issues was incorporated into the "research bulletin" that the Tsuta teachers wrote about their work and distributed at the open house (Tsuta Elementary School, 1994). We remind the reader that in order to keep a record of their *konaikenshu* work, schools generally produce a research bulletin every year. However, these reports tend to be much more extensive when they are to be distributed at an open house. For example, Tsuta's report was 75 pages long. It was composed of six main sections written by the Tsuta teachers and a brief preface written by the principal.

The first section of Tsuta's report (pages 1–4) described the mission statement of the school and outlined the broader educational goals that the school was committed to working toward. It also presented the school's organizational chart and basic information about the management of the school.

The second section (pages 5–11) provided a summary of the schools' *konaikenshu* work. This part had eight subsections. The first stated the *konaikenshu* goal that Tsuta was pursuing. The second contained an explanation for why the school had selected this goal. The third articulated specific hypotheses that the teachers were exploring vis-à-vis their lesson study goal. The fourth outlined the focal points that the school had chosen to look at in exploring its goal (e.g., carefully examining the *neriage* process).

The fifth subsection explained some of the techniques that Tsuta teachers had instituted for conducting their lesson study (e.g., engaging in the careful analysis of student handouts and videotaping certain lessons). The sixth subsection provided an organizational chart for the conduct of lesson study at Tsuta. The seventh outlined strategies the school had used to promote lesson study. The final subsection contained a calendar for the lesson study work carried out at the school in 1992–1993 and in 1993–1994.

The third section of this report (pages 12–60) included copies of all the final lesson plans for all of the 14 mathematics study lessons conducted at the school between 1992 and 1994. Each plan was accompanied by a summary of the discussions that took place about the lesson in question.

The fourth section (pages 61–62) first explained what the teachers at Tsuta saw as the major results of their work and then laid out implications of these findings for future work to be conducted at Tsuta. This section closely mirrored the results and issues list described earlier.

The fifth section of this report (pages 63–74) included two resources that the teachers had made. The first was a proposed model for how best to structure problem-based lessons (see Appendix C). The second was a curricular plan for how to sequence, across Grades 1 through 6, instruction related to numbers and basic operations.[1]

The last section of this report (page 75) provided a list of all the teachers who had been involved in lesson study work at Tsuta between 1992 and 1994. Thus, teachers who were no longer at this school were acknowledged for the role they had played in this work.

Two other booklets were also created for distribution at the open house (see Fig. 13.1).

The first one contained the agenda for the open house, a map of the school, and copies of the three lesson plans needed for the day of observations. The other was a list all the participants and their school affiliations. This list indicated which one of the three study lessons each person would be observing.

In addition to these three booklets, a survey was also prepared for distribution to all participants. Participants were asked to provide their comments and opinions about the open house study lessons, the operation of open house itself, and the school.

In addition to preparing these materials, the Tsuta teachers also had to get ready for actually hosting the open house. This process was highly organized. In fact, the teachers created for themselves a chart of tasks and point

---

[1]The reader may recall that the teachers at Tsuta had decided that all their lessons would focus on topics related to numbers and calculations. Choosing this focus allowed them to step back and reflect on how they were sequencing teaching in this area across all grades.

FIG. 13.1 Handouts prepared by Tsuta teachers. Three booklets were included in the package for visitors to the open house—from left to right, study lesson procedure, list of participants, and study bulletin.

people. The list of duties to be filled, with the help of the fifth- and sixth-grade students at the school, included putting up directional signs to the school around its vicinity and arranging for parking spaces. Individuals were also assigned to organize and clean up classrooms, meeting areas, the lunchroom, the bathrooms, and any other space that guests might be visiting.

Hosting the Event

Registration

Two Tsuta teachers were assigned to manage the registration process, which took place between 9:30 and 10:00 a.m. on the morning of this event. The written materials already described were passed out to all participants and money to cover lunch expenses was collected. In early September the school had sent out invitations to all the schools in the western region of Hiroshima prefecture. As a result, 60 teachers from 25 schools attended this event. In addition, a number of the 21 other education officials and dignitaries invited to this event actually came to the open house. Among them were the head of the Hiroshima Education Office and its mathematics instructional superintendent, as well as a number of elementary school principals. The Mayor of Saeki City, the Chairman of Saeki City Assembly, and the Chairman of the General Affairs and Educational Committee of Saeki City Assembly were also in attendance, as were the head of the Saeki City Board of Education and the chairperson of the PTA. This turned out to be one of the larger open houses conducted in the region during the 1993–1994 school year.

Presenting the Study Lessons

The three study lessons planned for the day were all taught from 10:00 to 10:45 a.m. and observed by different groups of visitors. All three of the classrooms were very crowded, with teachers filling up all available space in the back and two sides of the classroom (see Figs. 13.2, 13.3, and 13.4).

One classroom was so crowded that the observers had to spill out into the hallway, along which there were windows that allowed them to see and hear what was going on in the classroom (see Fig. 13.5).

FIG. 13.2   A scene from the second-grade lesson.

FIG. 13.3   A scene from the sixth-grade lesson.

FIG. 13.4   Visitors observing the sixth-grade lesson.

FIG. 13.5   Another scene from the fourth-grade lesson. Some visitors watched the fourth-grade lesson from the hallway because the classroom was too crowded.

Only the students who were involved in these lessons attended school on this day. These children left the school at 10:45 a.m., right after the study lessons ended.

Postlesson Conference

Next, between 11:10 a.m. and 12:10 p.m., separate postlesson conferences (*bunnkakai*) were held for each lesson. The teachers moved to classrooms where the desks had been arranged in advance for these discussions. In each room, four teachers (the teacher who taught the lesson, two other members of the same grade-level group, who filled the role of chairperson and record keeper, and a reactor from outside the group) sat at the front, facing rows of desks where all others were seated (see Fig. 13.6).

All three post-lesson conferences progressed in a similar fashion. First, the teacher who taught the lesson provided his or her reflections. Next there was a question and answer session that everyone in the room was invited to join. Finally the outside reactor provided thoughts and suggestions about the lesson. The outside reactors on that day were two principals who were

FIG. 13.6   A scene from the sixth-grade postlesson conference.

well known as mathematics educators in the western region of Hiroshima prefecture,[2] and Mr. Saeki, the school's outside advisor.

Lunch Break

Next all the visitors moved to the school's lunchroom where they were served a meal similar to what students would receive except for one addition. The City of Saeki had donated some Matsutake mushrooms, a very special and expensive mushroom, which was added to the Japanese miso soup. This gesture was both in celebration of the open house and to show gratitude to the teachers for their ongoing efforts to improve their teaching. During this lunch the teachers mingled and talked about the lessons they had observed. Many of the teachers from different schools knew each other and were happy to be reunited.

---

[2]It is interesting to note that these principals had once been teachers at Itsukaichi Elementary School where lesson study in the area of mathematics was first initiated in the western region of Japan (see chap. 3).

All Teacher Meeting

After the lunch break, an all-teacher meeting (*zentaikai*) was held from 1:10 to 3:20 p.m. (see Fig. 13.7).

Five agenda items were covered during this meeting. First, several VIPs greeted everyone and gave congratulatory speeches (see Fig. 13.8).[3]

Each of these speakers made sure to thank the Tsuta teachers for their hard work, the teachers from other schools for their participation, and all the teachers for their everyday efforts to promote student learning in their own classrooms.

Second, Mr. Mizuno, Tsuta's head teacher reported on the school's *konaikenshu* progress. During his remarks he often referred to the research bulletin that Tsuta teachers had distributed to all their guests. Mr. Mizuno explained that about 2 years prior to the 1993–1994 school year, the teachers at Tsuta had realized that their instruction was not sufficiently aimed at de-

FIG. 13.7   A scene from the all-teacher meeting.

---

[3]The Head of Saeki City Board of Education, the Head of Hiroshima Education Office, and the Mayor of Saeki City were some of the invited VIPs who gave congratulatory speeches.

FIG. 13.8   A guest giving greetings and congratulatory speech.

veloping students thinking and desire to learn. He described how for the next 2 years (1992–1994) the teachers at the school focused their attention on developing students who could think on their own autonomously, invent, and learn from each other. He explained that during these 2 years the teachers at Tsuta had paid careful attention to two key components of lessons. During the 1992–1993 school year they worked on the step where the students work on a problem on their own, and during the 1993–1994 school year, they focused on the part during which the students go through the *neriage* process.

These remarks were followed by a question and answer session during which the visitors asked questions of the teachers at Tsuta (see Fig. 13.9).

Some of them wanted clarifications about certain of the words used during *konaikenshu* at Tsuta. Questions were asked about, for example, *"ko no yosa* (merit of individual)" and *"sansu no yosa* (merit of mathematics)." Although these words were briefly explained in the teacher's manual, some of the participants were interested in finding out how the teachers at Tsuta interpreted them. Other guests wanted to know about the approach to *neriage* that the teachers at Tsuta had developed and how that model had been illustrated in the actual study lessons.

FIG. 13.9   A visitor asking a question.

Next, as Tsuta's outside advisor, Mr. Saeki gave a brief talk (see Fig. 13.10).

He began by reading from a letter he had gotten from a first-grade teacher whom he had recently observed at a different school teaching a study lesson. He explained that he had made some harsh comments after this study lesson and then he read the following passage from the letter:

> I don't usually brood over anything that people say about my lessons but the day you were here was very difficult for me. On the next day when I came to school, my first graders greeted me very cheerfully with: "We are going to study large numbers today in math class! Yes, we will. Yeah! Teacher! Let's count tiddlywinks again!" The voices of these children helped cheer up my spirit. This is my first year as a first-grade homeroom teacher. When I started to teach this grade, most of the students said things like "I don't dislike any subjects" or "I like to study." I was very surprised by this. It made me realize that children enter school as first graders with the belief that studying and learning is interesting. And I thought to myself: "I am the one making children dislike learning." This made me feel very disappointed in myself and very sad.

FIG. 13.10   Mr. Saeki speaking to the participants.

Mr. Saeki saw this letter as a reminder that teachers are the ones who make the students dislike learning or have difficulties understanding. Teachers often say that students are not active, do not want to share their ideas, or are afraid of making mistakes. However, in the words of Mr. Saeki, "These phenomena are results of what we teachers are doing in the classroom."

Mr. Saeki went on to explain that in the new "course of study" the ministry of education had recently introduced a novel way of thinking about academic ability (*atarashii gakuryokukan*). In this document, developing students' academic ability meant to foster in them: (a) interest and healthy attitudes toward learning, (b) sound ways of thinking, (c) the ability to express ideas and argue about difficult concepts, and finally (d) basic content knowledge and skills. Mr. Saeki said that although he had taught for 19 years, he had never thought of students' academic ability in this way. He remembered that he generally evaluated students based simply on pencil-and-paper test scores. He also pointed out that part of the challenge was that when teachers had themselves been students, they were not educated and evaluated in this way. He said that therefore these new ideas represented fundamentally different ways of thinking about teaching and learning. Mr. Saeki reminded everyone how in past efforts to develop better instruction, teachers had been asked to shift from teacher-led instruction to a more student-centered style of teaching. In order to genuinely make this shift, teachers had had to look carefully at themselves and their teaching. Mr. Saeki emphasized that improving students' learning always begins by teachers carefully examining what they themselves do and how they think. He mentioned that there were a number of other new concepts in the course of study, such as "merit of individual" (*ko no yosa*) and "skills for living" (*ikiteiku chikara*), which described dispositions teachers should try to develop in their students. However, what teachers needed to realize was that these concepts in essence outlined directions along which teachers themselves needed to change.

Mr. Saeki next spoke a bit about Tsuta's *konaikenshu* efforts. He mentioned that this school had decided to study how problem-solving skills are developed in students. He reminded everyone how the idea of problem solving had emerged when child-centered instruction was introduced in Japan. However, he pointed out that because this expression was used widely and in many different contexts, it was critical to identify what problem solving meant in the context of a classroom. He described how, in their efforts to grapple with this question, the teachers at Tsuta had explored how to structure lessons around having students work on problem solving. In order to do this, they had experimented with designing lessons that had four major parts: (a) presenting the problem and making sure students grasp it, (b) letting students solve the problem on their own, (c) *neriage* (presenting and discussing ideas), and (d) expansion (practice what was learned). He referred everyone to the Tsuta research bulletin for further detail and said that he would highlight what he felt were important insights gained from these 2 years of work at Tsuta.

He began by talking about the issue of how to present a lesson problem and make sure students have grasped it. Mr. Saeki commended the teachers at Tsuta for paying attention to connecting lessons to students' prior knowledge, which he said did not have to be exclusively classroom based but could also relate to student's experiences in their lives. He said that, for every lesson, teachers must have clarity in their minds about the previous knowledge that they will want students to draw on. In addition, lessons need to be launched by having some conversation or activity that motivates children to take part in the lesson. A lesson cannot just start with giving students a problem on a sheet of paper.

By way of illustration, Mr. Saeki asked everyone to look at the lesson plan for Ms. Tsukuda's subtraction lesson taught in November, which was included in the research bulletin. He pointed out that Ms. Tsukuda had engaged her students by relating her mathematics lesson to a daily living lesson. In addition, by using a story problem that contained blanks that could be filled in according to each student's family situation, children were drawn into the lesson by their desire to think about their own family. Mr. Saeki took advantage of this opportunity to comment that this thoughtful lesson was not developed by a single teacher but by a team of teachers, and he reminded everyone about the importance of collaboration for carrying out successful lesson study. Mr. Saeki next read a passage from a letter Ms. Tsukuda had sent him after teaching this lesson. In it she described how in subsequent lessons she continued to draw on students' excitement about solving problems based on their family trees. She narrated how in one lesson she had had the class make a giant ginkgo leaf collage that assembled everyone's individual collages. Mr. Saeki said this was a good example of how strong student engagement in one lesson can serve as the basis for developing students' further learning.

Mr. Saeki used the example of Ms. Tsukuda's lesson to explain how the Tsuta teachers had explored the effectiveness of using blanks in a story problem. He mentioned that not only had the teachers used the blanks for flexibly replacing numbers in a problem, but also they had sometimes used the blanks for hiding an important condition needed to solve the problem. He said this strategy helped students learn how to identify necessary information needed for tackling problems. It also helped them develop skills for creating their own problems.

Mr. Saeki next made some remarks about *neriage*. He said that in order to have a successful *neriage* during a lesson, it is important to develop a good relationship among all students. Students have to have in place the skills needed to understand and recognize the ideas and viewpoints of others. It is of critical importance to develop students' ability to influence each other through interaction and discussion. Children also need to come to appreciate that even a wrong answer can be a rich source of learning. Mr. Saeki next went over the list of useful *hatsumon* for establishing a healthy exchange of ideas in the classroom, which the teachers at Tsuta had generated through their conduct of lesson study. Mr. Saeki said that this list provided a very concrete way to think about the *neriage* process. He added that although this list came out of 2 years of lesson study at Tsuta, the teachers were just beginning to regularly use its content in their everyday lessons. Although time would have to pass before the school could assess the impact of these strategies, he was optimistic that they would lead to improved student learning.

One issue he felt the teachers at Tsuta still needed to think about carefully was how to make sure lessons exposed students to multiple ways of solving problems. He argued that it is hard for students to think about what are good, or best, solution strategies when they only hear about a single idea for how to tackle a problem. Children need to be placed in a situation where they have the opportunity to disagree, argue, and experience conflicting points of views. He referred teachers to the work of a researcher named Mr. Yoshimoto for more ideas about this important issue.

Ms. Saeki concluded by calling for all the teachers present to emphasize the type of collaboration among teachers that makes them feel joint ownership of the study lessons they create. He also compelled all the guests to follow-up the experiment (*tsuishi*) of Tsuta's study lessons with in their own study lessons in their classrooms.

Mr. Saeki's comments were followed by closing remarks from Tsuta's principal (see Fig.13.11).

First, Mr. Yamasaki thanked all the participants for coming to the school. Then, he made some humbling remarks in which he said that Tsuta's *konaikenshu* might not have seemed any different from any other school's *konaikenshu* and that the study lessons the participants had seen were imperfect and still had lots of room for improvement. He did acknowledge that an original approach taken by the teachers at his school was to try to convince each other that it was their fault if the students disliked or did poorly in mathematics, not the students' fault. Their surveys had shown them that the majority of their students liked mathematics. For this reason,

FIG. 13.11   Closing remarks by Mr. Yamasaki, the principal of Tsuta elementary school.

it was the teachers' responsibility to make the effort to improve their teaching. If they succeeded in improving their teaching, Mr. Yamasaki said, the students would follow suit by doing better in mathematics. He recounted how during meetings the teachers often shared student comments such as "I enjoyed the lesson" or "I started to understand." He thought that this exchange of student comments helped raise morale among teachers and sparked their desire to collaborate and improve their teaching. Lastly, Mr. Yamasaki thanked the participants for attending the open house and for their support and cooperation. He also thanked Mr. Saeki for all his help, and requested his support and instruction for the school's future *konaikenshu* activities.

Follow-Up Celebration

The evening of the open house the teachers, the principal, and the vice-principal all went out to a local restaurant to celebrate (see Fig. 13.12).

This type of celebration was not at all unusual for Tsuta teachers who tended to spend quite a bit of time socializing outside of school. For example, they held parties at local restaurants in order to say good-bye to teachers who

FIG. 13.12   A scene from a school event closing party.

were leaving the school and welcome new teachers to the school. Similarly, they gathered to celebrate such events as the end of a trimester, the completion of the annual sports day or the annual music day, or a school field trip. The Tsuta teachers also got to know each other well by organizing other "extracurricular" events such as, for example, a staff physical education day where they enjoyed playing sports together. This kind of socializing, which is common in most Japanese schools, is believed to help create bonds that are useful for the conduct of *konaikenshu* and a healthy school life in general.

Celebrations organized by the Tsuta teachers were often boisterous and included a fair amount of social drinking, which is also quite typical in Japan. In this setting teachers seemed more relaxed and willing to talk openly about their life at the school and each other's teaching. The party that followed the open house was no exception. For example, at one point a senior teacher candidly told a first-year teacher that he liked the way she talked during the study lesson because her voice was full of life. He noticed that her students were very lively because of that. However, he said that her pace of talking was too fast for first-grade students and that her handwriting and organization of the blackboard were careless. Despite the risk of being criticized more severely, the teachers at Tsuta seemed to enjoy these informal and candid conversations. In fact, one of them explained that he liked to go drinking with other teachers, particularly experienced ones, because he could learn a lot from them when they opened their hearts. He said that these outings provided him an occasion to hear the real opinions of his colleagues, which were not voiced as readily during *konaikenshu* meetings. He truly believed that honest opinions like these, even though they were sometimes severe and critical, helped him to seriously think about how to improve his teaching.

YEAR-END REFLECTION ON *KONAIKENSHU*

On February 21, about a month before the end of the school year and 4 days after the open house, the teachers at Tsuta held an all-staff meeting to reflect on their *konaikenshu* work in general and their open house in particular. The meeting, which was the last one to focus on *konaikenshu* for that school year, began with the record-keepers summarizing the notes that they had taken during each of the postlesson conferences at the open house. After these presentations, the teachers freely brought up comments, suggestions, and issues that they wanted to discuss and later consider as they planned and improved their future *konaikenshu* work together. We next summarize the gist of this discussion.

Mr. Yamasaki began by suggesting that in order for the experiences gained by the teachers through *konaikenshu* to have an impact on student learning, teachers needed to make a greater effort to apply their *konaikenshu* work to their everyday lessons. He also suggested that standardized tests might be used to evaluate the effect of the *konaikenshu* efforts at the school. Although many teachers agreed with Mr. Yamasaki's call for assessment, they were not sure that standardized tests would be appropriate. They argued that these tests were more focused on procedures and calculations and less on ideas for solving a problem, which was the focus of the *konaikenshu*. The vice-principal mentioned that the lower grade teachers had been experimenting with measuring students' attitudinal changes toward learning and that they had seen a shift in the second-grade students who were not good in mathematics. Compared to the beginning of the school year, many of these students were now starting to participate more often in student presentations. She said these kinds of changes could be indications of the impact of the *konaikenshu* and might represent a good way to evaluate student learning if combined with other methods. She also felt strongly about the need to develop new kinds of tests or methods for evaluating the effect of *konaikenshu* on student learning. For example, she thought that they needed to find a way of evaluating students' ideas and processes for solving a problem.

The teachers also spent a large amount of time discussing issues related to *neriage*. Mr. Sato pointed out three important conditions needed in order to carry out good *neriage*. First he explained that if students have not acquired the knowledge or concepts necessary to solve a problem, the whole process of *neriage* will not go smoothly and the students' discussion will never reach a deep level. Both Mr. Sato and Ms. Tsukuda mentioned that by extension this means that teachers need to study carefully their curriculum. In particular, Mr. Sato emphasized that in problem-based instruction teachers need to understand the relationship between the knowledge required to solve a problem and the new knowledge that students will acquire through solving this problem. Ms. Tsukuda added that this meant that teachers needed to study the curriculum at the beginning of the year and determine the most important concepts they would be teaching. She explained that by using these selected key concepts as a starting point, the teachers could next develop a map of how lessons would link to each other. When Ms. Tsukuda was asked about these comments during a follow-up interview she elaborated as follows:

> I think that Mr. Sato and I were trying to tell the other teachers about the importance of identifying the most critical topic or unit one needs to teach during a year. Because we are very busy every day we cannot teach every single lesson in a fully prepared manner. Also, many units are connected to each other and, as Mr. Sato mentioned, learning a new concept in mathematics often requires the use of previously learned knowledge. For example, I think decomposing two numbers to make a group of 10 in an addition with carrying over and subtraction with regrouping are very important concepts in the

first grade. So I think that the lessons that teach these concepts are the ones that I need to really think carefully about and prepare, and other calculation lessons in my mind are less critical. Mr. Saeki told us that when you teach the concept of how to find the area of shapes, the area of basic shapes is what needs to be emphasized ... We often forget about this and spend a lot of time teaching, for example, how to find the area of a trapezoid when we should be emphasizing the area of a rectangle. I think all the teachers already knew the importance of studying the curriculum but I wanted to make sure that we gave ourselves time to study curriculum at the beginning of the year.

The second important condition for good *neriage* mentioned by Mr. Sato was that teachers needed to develop good ways to encourage a class to function as a group (*gakkyu shudan zukuri* or *gakkyu zukuri*) or circle of friends (*nakama zukuri*). Many of the teachers nodded in agreement when Mr. Sato brought up this point and several of them followed up with related comments. Ms. Sasaki, a third-grade teacher, said that it was critical to find ways to create an environment where students felt comfortable presenting their ideas. She recalled how one of their study lessons had experimented with giving the answer to a story problem in the early stages of a lesson. This experiment had helped the students to focus on the process for solving the problem instead of getting the right answer. She said that developing and testing more teaching ideas like this one was the way to move toward more effective *neriage*. Mr. Yamasaki emphasized that the development of this type of supportive classroom environment, where students respect each other's opinions and ideas, must be cultivated during the teachers' everyday practice and requires ongoing efforts and cooperation among all teachers. Ms. Furumoto mentioned that *shudanzukuri* (developing a group) could be thought of as developing students who are willing to tell each other anything, or who are willing to help each other out. She said that these two aspects of group dynamics were also important for creating effective *neriage*.

Mr. Sato added that to learn how to have an effective neriage process, teachers would need to study not only their use of *hatsumon*, but also their *takuto* (teacher orchestration of a lesson).[4] He said that understanding how

---

[4]The origin of the word *takuto* is from the German word *taktstock*, which is a baton that a conductor uses for orchestrating a band or a symphony orchestra. According to Yoshimoto (1992), *takuto* includes not only what a teacher teaches, asks, and does during a lesson, but also the teacher's approaches to understanding and appealing to students' feelings both with words and body expressions. It also includes the teacher's actions to make students question their understanding. Yoshimoto also explains that in order to use *takuto* skillfully during a lesson, the teacher needs to prepare for the lesson by anticipating student solutions and reactions. The teacher also needs to plan for ways to react to student confusion, and ways to react to student agreement and disagreement with the teacher's ideas and that of their classmates. Moreover, in order for the teachers to prepare lessons in this way, they need to think about "how students understand something from a lesson" (p. 179).

to use students' conflicting or supportive ideas and their state of confusion to orchestrate the lesson in order to increase student interest and deep thinking was critical for effective *neriage*.

Time allocation during study lessons was also a topic of some discussion. Many of the teachers agreed that they needed to further study how to organize a lesson within the 45 minutes available to them. They felt that study lessons are the way to showcase a school's *konaikenshu* efforts and that these efforts will not come across clearly if the lessons are cut short or accelerated. In addition, students are generally expected to finish when the period bell rings; therefore, the teachers cannot expect to have their attention after that. Although these issues were brought up, no particular solutions were reached.

A few teachers also mentioned that the head teacher and the vice-principal had taken too much of the burden to make sure that the open house ran smoothly. One teacher felt that others could have taken more responsibility in order to balance the workload. Another mentioned that starting the preparations for this event earlier might have taken some of the burden off the head teacher and the vice-principal. In addition, Mr. Sato mentioned that there were some parents who hesitated to send their children to school on the day of the open house because they were concerned that they might behave badly. Mr. Sato thought that the teachers needed to make it clear to parents that the school was for all students, and that although an open house is an important day for the school, the parents need not be concerned about behavior-related distractions.

At the end of the meeting, Mr. Mizuno mentioned that the issues discussed would be revisited at the start of the new school year when planning for that year's *konaikenshu*. The meeting was then adjourned.

14

Strategies for Avoiding Isolation in Order to Enhance Lesson Study

The lesson study open house held at Tsuta illustrates one of the ways in which Japanese teachers connect with colleagues outside of their group in order to extend the learning opportunities that lesson study affords them. Open houses not only allow those organizing them to enrich their lesson study work, but they also provide many learning opportunities for those in attendance, and by extension, the respective lesson study groups that they represent. These benefits explain why some open houses can be quite large, particularly when they are hosted at schools with a good reputation. Most notably, national schools regularly hold open houses, which sometimes are attended by thousands of teachers from all over the country.[1]

In this chapter we describe the various other ways in which lesson study groups share their experiences with each other in order to mutually enrich their work. In our opinion it is this sharing that makes lesson study particularly powerful because it provides a means not just for small groups of teachers within a school to learn from each other, but more importantly for teachers from all over Japan to do so. We begin by reminding the reader of two common strategies for sharing lesson study work that we have already alluded to in our portrayal of the activities carried out at Tsuta: enlisting an outside advisor, and publishing a research bulletin. We then discuss a number of other sharing strategies, which are both prevalent and critical to mak-

---

[1]Similarly, designated research schools (*kenkyushiteiko*) also attract large numbers of teachers to their open houses. A designated research school is a school selected and supported financially by the Ministry of Education to do research on a particular topic, generally through conducting lesson study. These research topics tend to be linked to newly introduced or planned changes in the "course of study" that the Ministry of Education is interested in learning more about. Many schools apply to this program because the financial support made available is large (500,000 yen, which is about $3,600). It is also a popular program because teachers feel that they can have an influence on the government's decisions about changes in the "course of study."

ing the work of lesson study groups interconnected, but which we have not yet touched on in our description of the work carried out at Tsuta.

THE OUTSIDE ADVISOR SERVES TO CREATE LINKS ACROSS LESSON STUDY GROUPS

Undoubtedly, enlisting the help of an outside advisor provides a mechanism by which lesson study groups can learn about each other's work and more importantly can make sure to build from each others' successes and failures, rather than trying to reinvent the wheel. This learning is possible because the outside advisor provides a bridge between the various lesson study groups that he or she works with or knows about. The reader may recall that on a number of occasions Mr. Saeki made suggestions or comments that were based on recounting what he had observed in other schools doing lesson study. In fact, Mr. Saeki had ample experiences to draw from because he visited three to four schools per week. Thus, through their outside advisor the Tsuta teachers were privy to lesson study work being conducted elsewhere. Moreover, Mr. Saeki also helped the Tsuta teachers set standards for their work that were in line with those set by other groups. Indeed, there was a certain severity in Mr. Saeki's evaluation of Tsuta's *konaikenshu* work, in part because his role impinged upon him to challenge the teachers and in part because he was not evaluating this work on its own merits, but rather by comparing it to other schools' *konaikenshu* activities. Thus, he helped the Tsuta teachers gain a perspective on what they were doing and achieving that took into account the work of their peers.

RESEARCH BULLETINS—A VEHICLE FOR SHARING LESSON STUDY INSIGHTS AND STRATEGIES

Lesson study groups can also learn from each other by sharing written reports, like the one created by the Tsuta teachers. Open houses and other occasions when outsiders visit the school provide natural venues for the distribution of these reports. In addition, lesson study reports are also kept at the regional education offices in order for instructional superintendents like Mr. Saeki to be able to share them with the schools they visit and support.[2] They are sometimes also gathered at local education centers where teachers go to receive inservice training.[3]

---

[2]Having these reports handy allows regional education offices to monitor each school's achievements. Needless to say, gaining recognition from this entity for one's *konaikenshu* achievements is a good strategy for securing future funding.

[3]These reports serve as a source for innovative teaching materials and lesson plans to be used during the workshops and other activities conducted at these centers. Moreover, these centers use these materials to continually analyze the state of *konaikenshu* in order to think about future direction for their own teacher training.

Furthermore, innovative and motivated groups sometimes pursue publishing either a monograph or articles about their lesson study. These writings, which are similar to the reports described earlier, except that they tend to be more polished and detailed, are often distributed nationwide through major bookstores (see Fig. 14.1).

It is true that teachers from national schools or designated research schools produce a good number of these publications. However, it is not uncommon for teachers from regular schools like Tsuta to engage in this writing as well. As a result, teachers can easily gain access to an array of publications written by their colleagues about their lesson study experiences. For example, a mathematics teacher can read on what lesson study groups have learned about such diverse topics as how to improve students' presentations, how to promote rich mathematical thinking in students, how to improve teachers' use of questions during instruction, and how to use the blackboard effectively. In fact, according to Sato (1991), "Journal publications of research conducted by and for teachers outnumber those of university researchers in Japan: Of the total publications, about two thirds are written by teachers" (p. 133). Sato (1992) has also reported that the Na-

FIG. 14.1   Education section of a major bookstore.

tional Institute for Educational Research compiles every year over 4,000 research papers written by teachers. Together these writings provide an extensive repository of professional knowledge and ideas that teachers engaged in lesson study can learn and build from. Clearly, through this well-developed system of publications, teachers from all corners of Japan can learn from each other's lesson study activities.

LESSON STUDY GROUPS CONNECT THROUGH THE MEMBERS THEY SHARE

It is also common for individual teachers to belong to more than one lesson study group and thus serve as a link between the experiences of these groups. Indeed, teachers can conduct lesson study in a number of venues other than within their individual schools. The possibility of doing lesson study both within and across schools not only helps create an interconnected lesson study system, but also allows for a great wealth of lesson study work to be generated and shared.

There are a number of study groups that assemble teachers (and administrators) from different schools. We next describe the two most prevalent cross-school groups—regional study groups and teacher clubs—and we discuss their role in generating learning experiences, and in particular lesson study experiences, that other lesson study groups can build on.[4]

Regional Study Groups

Regional study groups bring together teachers from a handful of schools in a large city or several neighboring towns. The schools in the western region of Hiroshima, for example, had a highly organized system of regional study groups. The 40 elementary schools in this region were divided into six subregions, each with its own network of study groups. Tsuta's subregion assembled teachers from five schools, located in the town of Saeki and the village of Yoshiwa. There were 17 different study groups in this subregion that teachers could join. Nine of these groups studied subjects in the following curricular areas: Japanese language, mathematics, social studies, science, music, arts and crafts, health education, physical education, and life study (for first and second grade). The other cluster of eight groups focused on the following top-

---

[4]It is also important to keep in mind that in addition to these study groups a number of national educational organizations in Japan incorporate lesson study into their regular events. For example, when the national organization of mathematics teachers holds its regional and national meetings, a common practice is for conference attendees to spend their mornings taking part in open houses at local schools that have volunteered to host these events. Afternoons are spent at conference facilities in follow-up discussions, workshops, and presentations.

ics: instructional media, moral education, tree planting, library, special education, school meals and nutrition, extracurricular activities, and administrative affairs. On Thursday afternoons, usually from 2:00 to 5:00 p.m., the five schools in this subregion took turns hosting study group meetings, which for each group occurred on average every other month.

Although membership in regional groups is voluntary, teachers often perceive it as quasi-mandatory. For example, in the survey administered to teachers as part of this research they were asked to list study groups that they were involved in and to label each of them as either voluntary or mandatory. About half of the teachers were not sure what label to choose for regional study groups. One teacher at Tsuta made the following clarifying comment about membership in these groups:

> Teachers' participation in these study groups is voluntary. However, even if you don't have a good reason, you still participate in these study groups because that's the way it is, that's what all teachers do, and everybody thinks it is a good thing to do. Generally teachers are "*majimena*" (serious and earnest) people and therefore they can't say no to something as good and meaningful as these study groups.

In fact, at the beginning of every year, each teacher at Tsuta was encouraged to "volunteer" to join two regional study groups, one from each of the two clusters described earlier.[5] The school also tried to have a teacher representative in each of the seventeen groups in order to keep abreast of what was going on in the various areas of study. Even the principal and the vice-principal joined two regional study groups. For example, during the 1993–1994 academic year, the principal was both in the social studies and the instructional media study group, and the vice-principal was a member of the health education and moral education study groups.[6]

---

[5] Although each year teachers paid a flat fee of $10 to join these groups, the communities of Saeki and Yoshiwa provided supplementary financial assistance. For example, during the 1993–1994 academic year, the total amount of money provided by these two townships to the 17 groups was $2,600. This money was divided equally among all the study groups and was used mainly to invite lecturers, purchase materials, and photocopy documents.

[6] Administrators also attend their own study group (*gakkounei-kenkyukai*) meetings, which, it turns out, also provide support elements for *konaikenshu*. For example, all the vice-principals from the western region of Hiroshima would meet every year for 2 days during the summer. Ms. Furumoto explained that the main function of these meetings was to exchange ideas on conducting *konaikenshu*. Ms. Furumoto said that during this gathering all the vice-principals presented the *konaikenshu* goals that their schools were pursuing and discussed any problems they had come across carrying out *konaikenshu*. She said that learning about how other schools coped with problems, and in particular how they handled keeping teachers motivated and creating a feeling of togetherness was very useful. More broadly she found that learning about the work of other schools gave her reasons to push her teachers to do a better job.

It is quite common for regional study groups to organize themselves around doing lesson study, although this is by no means the only activity that these groups carry out.[7] For example, of the 17 study groups in the Saeki/Yoshiwa subregion, 9 chose to conduct lesson study during the 1993–1994 academic year. However, it should be noted that the conduct of lesson study in regional study groups varies a fair amount from what we have described for *konaikenshu*. For one thing, teachers in these groups will face limitations inherent in having group members spread across various schools. For example, in these groups, study lessons are generally prepared and taught by a single teacher, who then is observed by the rest of the group. Also, because the work of these groups is spread across long time spans, in most cases, a study lesson is only taught once. Moreover, goal selection for regional study groups is generally less involved than what we described for *konaikenshu*-based study groups, where teachers critically examine (and collect information about) who they are as a school and their achievements with students. In contrast, a regional science group, for example, might decide, without extended deliberations, to work on lessons that foster scientific inquiry in students simply because this is an objective being encouraged in the science education community (see Box 14.1 for an illustration of how a regional study group conducts lesson study).

Teacher Clubs

Clubs or circles represent a second category of outside school study groups, which teachers in Japan can join. Compared to the very systematically organized regional study groups already described, these clubs, which are run by teachers or local unions, are of a more informal nature. Teachers join these clubs solely on a voluntary basis with the purpose of pursuing their interests in an unconstrained manner with colleagues who are serious and committed.[8] According to Sato, Akita, and Iwakawa (1993), "These informal groups

---

[7]They might read and discuss articles, study curriculum material. Some groups make field trips to visit local museums, historical places, or private companies or industries to gather knowledge about the community, in addition to getting ideas for teaching topics and materials.

[8]The teacher survey administered as part of this research included a question about participation in these types of study groups. Out of the 101 teachers who responded to this question, 58 reported that they were part of these types of clubs during the 1993–1994 school year. The following are some of the groups mentioned by these teachers: Mathematics Study Club, Social Science Study Club, Human Rights Education Study Club, Drawing and Manual Arts Circle, Lesson Development Study Club, and Speech Club. Kamiyama and his colleagues (Kamiyama, Sakamato, Imazu, Sato, & Sato, 1983) surveyed 3,987 teachers, 53% of whom reported being active in one of these study groups

Box 14.1
The Saeki-Yoshiwa Mathematics Study Group

During the 1993–1994 school year this group was made up of eight teachers from five schools. During their first meeting in April these teachers made a schedule for their work and decided on the following study goal: "the development of a lesson progression that fosters students' desire to learn enthusiastically." During each of the group's next three meetings, which took place in different schools in May, June, and September, a study lesson was taught by a group member for others in the group to observe and discuss. Normally this group would have simply met a fifth time, most likely to reflect about their work and write a report. However, during this particular year the teachers in this group volunteered to hold a regional open house.* As a result, this group ended up holding six meetings in addition to a one-day open house. The fifth meeting was devoted to planning the open house, which was to be hosted by Tsuta on October 14, a day on which all the schools in the western region of Hiroshima were off. The schedule for this day was similar to the *konaikenshu* open house held at Tsuta in February and described in chapter 13. In the morning guests chose to attend and then discuss one of two study lessons, one of which was taught by a Tsuta teacher and another by a teacher from Asahara Elementary School. Special arrangements were made for the two teachers' regular class of students to come to Tsuta during the first morning period to take part in the lesson. After a lunch break, there was whole-group discussion and remarks by an invited reactor. This open house also served as an occasion for other regional groups to provide updates on their activities and to distribute reports of their work.

After this open house, the eight teachers in this study group met on one final occasion in February. This meeting was devoted to writing a report of their work. The teachers also composed a one-page summary of the activities they were planning for the following year. This document was to be included in a booklet that would assemble similar descriptions from all 17 regional groups and that would be used for recruiting group members for the coming year.

*Only one of the other nine groups in the region doing lesson study that year chose to hold an open house. This was the physical education study group.

of in-service teachers have played a very important role in guaranteeing high quality teaching and in developing teacher's autonomous professionalism within the bureaucratic school system and its traditional culture" (p. 101).

How these groups structure their work is in no way limited to lesson study, and in fact in any given year a single club or circle might engage in an array of activities, but it is not at all uncommon for lesson study to figure among these activities.[9] Similarly, the frequency with which these groups meet and the intensity of their work is variable and closely linked to the motivation of its members. In addition, compared to regional study groups, these clubs vary more broadly in terms of the range of schools from which they draw members. Indeed, these groups can often involve teachers from several regions within a given prefecture, who are willing to travel sometimes a long distance to attend meetings. Moreover, the regional study groups described above are elementary, middle and high school specific, whereas it is not uncommon for teachers from a wide range of grade levels to belong to the same study club (see Boxes 14.2 and 14.3 for a description of the activities of the two of these clubs).

As already alluded to, clearly these regional study groups and clubs provide a network through which lesson study groups can build on each other's work. Certainly, when teachers at Tsuta were asked why they participated in regional study groups and clubs, the general consensus was that this activity provided an excellent opportunity for professional growth, which enriched but also supplemented their *konaikenshu* activities. Several teachers mentioned that they often brought what they learned in these study groups to their *konaikenshu* work and vice versa. One teacher at Tsuta also explained: "In the case of *konaikenshu*, you sometimes have to study a subject that you don't want to study, but this system [the outside school study group] allows me to study a subject that I'm really interested in." In another teacher's words, "I like to go to these [the outside school study group] meetings because I can learn something from the teachers who have good knowledge and experience with the topic we are studying."

A SYSTEM OF REGULAR TEACHER ROTATIONS ALLOWS LESSON STUDY GROUPS TO LEARN FROM EACH OTHER

In Japan there is a system of regular teacher rotations, which guarantees that every few years, teachers are reassigned to a different school within

---

[9]There is some limited funding that these groups can apply for, but the application process is highly competitive. If chosen, the groups usually receive about 100,000 yen (about $700) a year. The groups in turn commit themselves to reporting on their activities to the Regional Board of Education at the end of the year. However, the vast majority of these autonomously run study groups are not funded in any way except that teachers have to pay between 5,000 to 10,000 yen (between $40 and $70) a year to become members.

Box 14.2
The Hiroshima City Mathematics Study Club—HCMSC
(*Hiroshima-shi Sansu Dokokai*)

In 1994 this club had about 25 members and was affiliated with four other mathematics clubs within the Hiroshima prefecture, which together counted 130 teachers. HCMSC meetings were usually held once a month on Saturday afternoons between 2 and 5 p.m. During these meetings, the teachers were divided into three groups, representing the upper, middle, and lower grade levels. The main activities for the meetings were studying teaching materials (e.g., textbooks or student manipulatives), discussing lesson ideas, and reporting on the results of implementing certain lessons. Teachers in this group did not collaboratively plan or jointly observe lessons but simply discussed their teaching. On occasion, however, a teacher would bring in a videotape of a lesson in order to be able to better discuss his/her teaching with group members. In addition, this group invited guest lecturers (e.g., college professors, instructional superintendents, and innovative and experienced teachers) in order to learn about recent changes in the "course of study," the teaching experiences of others, and innovative ideas about mathematical thinking and learning.

Furthermore, every February the HCMSC, in collaboration with its four affiliate clubs, organized an Annual Hiroshima Prefecture Mathematical Education Conference. In 1994, about 70 people from nine prefectures in western Japan participated in this event. In the morning there was a presentation of innovative lesson ideas by one of the members of the study group. This member presented a videotape of a sixth-grade lesson entitled "Instructional methods for developing student understanding—The case of a computer simulation aided lesson about symmetric figures and geometric transformations." A question-and-answer session followed this presentation. Next the group conducted a business meeting, during which an announcement was made about where the next annual conference would be held. In addition, the dates and other information for another two-day conference to be held in November were also discussed. After a lunch break, an invited teacher from a national elementary school affiliated with Hiroshima University* gave a talk about recent changes in the "course of study." The title of the talk was "Developing lessons that stand up to the new concept of academic ability (*atarashii gakuryokukan*)."

(continued on next page)

> At the end of the session, a booklet called *Sansu* (Mathematics), compiled by the HCMSC, in collaboration with its other four affiliate clubs, was made available for sale for 300 yen (about $3). It contained about 10 teacher-written research papers based on study lessons. The Hiroshima Prefectural Board of Education had provided around 100,000 yen (about $700) for printing this booklet.
>
> *National elementary schools have the mandate to test and generate cutting edge ideas in education, and in particular about the course of study. According to Lewis and Tsuchida (1997), there are 73 national elementary schools in Japan and most of them are affiliated with national universities. Furthermore, because of the close affiliation of these national schools with the national universities, they provide university professors with an outlet for contributing to education.

the same or nearby region.[10] Moreover, as part of this rotation system, enthusiastic teachers can apply or can be appointed to a teaching position at a national elementary school for a couple of years, after which time they return to their regular school to spread what they learned.

These rotations contribute greatly to interconnecting to the work of lesson study groups. By regularly reshuffling the membership of lesson study groups, the insights gained by one group become accessible to others. For example, the reader may recall that Ms. Tsukuda's ideas about how to use flip tiles in the classroom came from a colleague at her previous school.

The down side of these rotations is that sometimes effective groups can lose the wind in their sails as key members relocate. This is an outcome that in fact befell Tsuta when at the end of the 1993–1994 school year, vice-principal Furumoto was sent to another school, as were some of the more committed *konaikenshu* participants, including Ms. Tsukuda and Mr. Sato. Originally Tsuta had planned for the 1994–1995 school year to represent a culminating year for the *konaikenshu* work initiated back in 1991. In fact, the open house held at Tsuta had been planned for the third year of this intended 4-year cycle, so that the school could get lots of ideas to fuel its final year of work. As it turned out, lesson study in this final year was not nearly as focused or intense as it had been in the previous couple of years.

When this turn of events was discussed with Ms. Furumoto, she explained that a school needs to have a core group of enthusiastic teachers in order sustain lesson study work over an extended period of time. She was disappointed that Tsuta had no such group during the 1994–1995 school

---

[10]The teachers surveyed as part of this research reported that they were relocated from school to school on average every 4 years. These changes were based on teachers' own requests, as well as reviews of their performance and recommendations made by both their principals and the regional Board of Education.

Box 14.3
The Hatsukaichi Lesson Development Study Group—HLDSG
(*Hatsukaichi jugyozukuri kenkyukai*)

This club was established in 1990 and in 1993 it had 11 members, eight elementary school teachers, 1 high school teacher, and 2 prospective teachers from local universities. This study group met once a month on Saturday afternoons between 2 and 5 p.m. In addition, the group organized two overnight retreats each year, one in the summer and one in the winter.* The teachers in this small club were all lively participants and seemed to really enjoy getting together. One of the members even joked that their study group was an excuse for them to go out drinking and socializing, which the teachers in this group did quite often.

The HLDSG was not studying a particular content area but rather focused on a broad range of core academic subjects, (e.g., mathematics, Japanese language, and science). The main study goal of this group was to develop instruction that fostered students' autonomous learning. A secondary goal of this group was to exchange information that could help teachers with their classroom management. Group members were also committed to helping the two prospective teachers prepare for their first teaching job.

The teachers in this group had decided to come together to experiment with the use of video technology to support and anchor their discussions about instruction. This was an innovative idea because in Japan although teachers are used to being observed during lesson study, they tend to shy away from being videotaped. One of the teachers in this group explained that the reason for this "shyness" is that many teachers in Japan are afraid of leaving a permanent record of their teaching. This group's method of using videotapes was called "Stop Motion" and had been developed by a group of teachers and university researchers.† This lesson evaluation method consisted of first having teachers observe a study lesson in a classroom and then view it on tape. During this viewing teachers paused the tape at key points to discuss particular issues that they wanted to focus on. During one of their meetings in 1993–1994 this group viewed a mathematics lesson where they paused the tape to analyze the teachers' use of questions. At one point, for example, someone asked to stop the video right after the teacher on the tape had presented the students with the main problem that they would be working on during the lesson. This observer noticed that this problem contained two questions, which he felt was confusing to students and might encourage them to provide

(continued on next page)

ambiguous answers. The teacher who had taught the lesson recognized his mistake and he discussed with the group alternative formats for posing the problem to students.

The other interesting thing about this study group is that it was a part of a nationwide organization called Lesson Development Network (*jyugyouzukuri network*). This organization produces a well-known periodical called "Lesson Development Network," which many individual teachers and study groups contribute to. The purpose of this publication is to serve as a venue for the exchange of ideas about how to develop lessons. HLDSG organized its winter retreat in 1993 through this network. About 50 teachers, some college professors, and undergraduate and graduate students in education attended this event. One agenda item for this meeting was to do stop motion on an elementary science lesson. The second activity was to discuss how to incorporate debate methods into the classroom. A teacher gave a lecture on this topic and also provided a hands-on opportunity for participants to experience debate methods among themselves. During the remainder of the time various teachers gave short presentations on their lesson development ideas and practices. The main social event was a big dinner during which many of the teachers stayed up very late talking about their ideas and experiences in the classroom.

*The group received 100,000 yen ($700) from the Hiroshima Prefectural Board of Education and collected 6,000 yen (about $40) a year from the members in order to carry out their study activities.

†For more information about this method, refer to *Lesson Study by the Stop Motion Method* by Nobukatsu Fujioka (1991).

---

year and she regretted having been transferred because she would have liked to stay at Tsuta at least one more year to help the teachers there build on their past few years of lesson study achievements. Hopefully, she and the other teachers that Tsuta lost were able to infuse the new groups that they joined with their energy and enthusiasm.

In summary, it is important to realize that when teachers at a school do lesson study, this work is never conducted in a vacuum. It is both directly and indirectly influenced by the work of others and has outlets for influencing others. It is these connections that allow teachers to maximize what they can get out of engaging in lesson study. The critical issue that we have yet to discuss is what teachers actually gain from doing lesson study. This topic is the focus of the next and final chapter of this book.

15

Conclusion

In this concluding chapter we reflect about what Japanese lesson study can teach us here in the United States. We begin, however, by focusing on two related issues that need to be addressed first. First, we discuss why Japanese teachers engage in lesson study—why do they see it as a powerful and worthwhile activity? Second, we try to disentangle what is powerful about lesson study per se from what Japanese teachers do to make lesson study the rich activity that we have described in previous chapters.

WHAT DO TEACHERS STAND TO GAIN FROM ENGAGING IN LESSON STUDY?

Lesson study provides teachers with an opportunity to discuss the content that they are called on to teach and in so doing teachers can refine their understanding of this content. As illustrated by the work of the Tsuta teachers, there are many content-related issues for teachers to consider and come to understand more deeply, even when they are working on a study lesson that centers on a topic as basic as first-grade subtraction with regrouping. Certainly, in the course of working on their subtraction lesson, the lower grade teachers had many thought-provoking, and no doubt enriching, conversations about what it means to regroup and how this type of subtraction relates to addition, to subtraction without regrouping, and to place value.

In addition, through doing lesson study teachers can learn a great deal about how children tend to understand and approach the content that they study in school. According to one Hiroshima principal, "One of the purposes of conducting lesson study is to help teachers to recognize how interesting it is to find out how students think and learn new things. This feeling of enjoyment cannot be achieved easily in everyday teaching because teachers lack the time to think about student thinking in any detail."[1] The work of the Tsuta lower grade teachers illustrates this quite vividly. These teachers devoted an extraordinary amount of time to discussing how children think about situations involving regrouping and what this thinking implies for how to teach them about this type of subtraction. For example, their debates about the choice of numbers for the main problem of the lesson allowed them to grapple with subtle distinctions that are critical to developing students' understanding of subtraction with regrouping. In the course of these debates they recognized that, for instance, $12 - 7$ and $13 - 9$ are, in fact, significantly different problems for students, who might approach them in different ways and learn different things from them.

Notwithstanding this, in the course of the 1993–1994 school year the lower grade teachers at Tsuta worked on only two study lessons and their upper and middle grade colleagues worked on a total of five other study lessons, a typical scenario for a school carrying out lesson study. Given that during that school year the teachers at Tsuta were called upon to teach numerous lessons covering a wide range of areas in mathematics, how could they possibly justify working on a handful of lessons, despite what they might have learned about the content covered in these lessons? Was this a good use of their time? In what follows we discuss why the teachers at Tsuta, and their counterparts all over Japan, would argue that doing lesson study is a highly justified activity.

Japanese teachers value lesson study for a number of reasons. First of all, lesson study allows teachers to come together to develop their pedagogical knowledge and skills. Indeed, in the course of planning their subtraction lesson, the lower grade teachers were able to share and evaluate a number of ideas about classroom practice. For example, they spent time discussing the desirable qualities of a manipulative, the types of questions that encourage students to share work with each other, and productive formats for posing word problems. These conversations allowed them to think about principles that could guide their everyday teaching of mathematics, and which they could then continue to experiment with and refine in their own classrooms. In other words, although these teachers were focusing on a handful of lessons, they used these lessons as a testing ground for their thinking about what constitutes good practice more broadly defined. Ms. Furumoto and Ms. Tsukuda articulated this fact well during their interviews:

> I am not teaching in the classroom any more, but I still feel like I am learning a lot from the lesson study experience. And I sometimes feel that I wish I had my own students so that I could try out some of the things I've learned.

> Also, through these [lesson study] experiences, it's possible to produce some good instructional materials or teaching techniques that can become good tools for all of us to use.

---

[1]Interview, 11/27/93, with Mr. Harada, the principal of Itsukaichi Minami Elementary School in Hiroshima, Japan.

Furthermore, lesson study can help teachers establish meaningful goals for their students' learning and their teaching that reach well beyond the few study lessons that they work on together. For example, the Tsuta teachers used lesson study to examine their teaching goals in order to make sure that learning across the grades was a coherent and well-connected experience for students. The reader may recall that their lesson plan included a section where connections between the study lesson and instruction in other grades were articulated.[2] Moreover, section five of their report contained a plan developed by the Tsuta teachers for how to organize children's learning about numbers and calculations across the six grades of elementary school. Similarly, through their lesson study work, the Tsuta teachers discussed the kind of classroom environment they needed to create in order for students to engage in substantive discussions with each other. They also came to grips with the concerted schoolwide and long-term efforts that would be required to do this. Ms. Tsukuda described this process as follows:

> At our school, we [the teachers] talked about the development of these skills at the beginning of the year. As you know, we focused our goal of *konaikenshu* on improvement of *neriage*. So we talked about how much of these skills we could ask of students at each grade level. Because these skills can not be developed overnight, or even in a couple of months, we talked about it and decided that all the teachers at the school needed to recognize the importance of these skills and work in close cooperation in order to support the students' gradual growth.

In addition, the conduct of lesson study can greatly influence teachers' general attitudes about teaching, which in turn shape what happens in the classroom, day in and day out. By doing lesson study, teachers can develop a better understanding of what it takes to plan and teach a good lesson. In particular, lesson study can highlight for teachers the complexities of teaching, while also providing them with an opportunity to work together on how best to address these difficulties. In the words of Ms. Tsukuda and Ms. Furumoto:

---

[2]It is in fact very common for lesson plans created as part of lesson study and for lesson study reports to articulate cross-grade connections. This concern with vertical learning is no doubt enhanced by the fact that in Japan elementary teachers are regularly rotated through grade levels. Generally these rotations are planned so that the teacher gets to follow the same set of students for 2 years. By the end of the first decade of their careers most elementary teachers will have taught Grades 1 through 6 at least once. At the beginning of their careers, teachers teach many different grade levels. However, when they become more experienced, teachers often specialize in teaching certain grade levels. For example, some teachers become fifth- and sixth-grade specialists and rotate with their students between those two grade levels.

Every time I participate in lesson study I learn the difficulty of making a good lesson. I am often discouraged by these experiences, but at the end I always bounce back and gain energy from wanting to become better at teaching. I think realizing how difficult it really is to make a good lesson has been a plus for me.

I hope these teachers in the group learned the difficulty of developing a lesson ... Teaching a good lesson is a very difficult thing to do. Many well-thought-out preparations and anticipations are required. I think realization of the difficulty of making a good lesson and the importance of preparing students' anticipated reactions or behaviors is good medicine for all teachers because we often forget about these things because we are very busy everyday.

Lesson study can also help teachers see their own teaching from a realistic and grounded perspective, and this can help teachers set ambitious, yet realistic, goals for their professional growth. This aspect of lesson study is captured very poignantly in the following testimonial from Ms. Tsukuda:

I remember one time I did an awful [study] lesson ... As a result, I got a lot of severe criticism from the other teachers ... I got so upset I started to cry in front of the other teachers. I still remember the event and every time I recall it, I still feel shivers down my spine. I guess I started to cry because I was disgusted with myself and embarrassed about my teaching ability. I thought I was a good teacher, but my confidence and pride were destroyed ... Also, I remember I was thinking about my students when I was crying. I felt very sorry for my students, who had always admired me and were faithful to me. I thought I was pretending to be a good teacher but the truth was I was not as good as I thought ... Later on that day, some of the teachers took me out for a drink. And they told me that they were hard on me because I was a tough person and had the potential for becoming a good teacher ... I took the event as my own medicine and now I am very seriously thinking about improving my teaching ... I think that recognizing the reality of your teaching skills is very important to improve your teaching. It is a very hard thing to do because everybody has pride in his or her teaching. I know nobody likes to hear about their weaknesses ... But other teachers will help to measure your real teaching skills by looking at your lessons.

In sum, there is no doubt that teachers stand to gain a great deal from engaging in lesson study and that much of this learning transcends the study lessons that they work on. This explains why the lower grade teachers were positive about their lesson study experience despite their overall disappointment with how the subtraction lesson unfolded. In the words of Ms. Tsukuda and Ms. Nishi:

I have been teaching for about 10 years and I have done lesson studies during all those years. So I have taught many study lessons. However, I still have not succeeded in developing a perfect lesson. The lesson I taught yesterday was a good example. I thought, as did other teachers in the group, that it would be a good lesson. But it ended up leaving a bitter taste in our mouths because our predictions were not good enough to understand students' thinking ... It is possible that I will never be able to teach a perfect lesson ever in my career, but I believe that if we try hard to aim for the perfect [study] lesson, the experience of trying will result in improving everyday teaching practice.

I learned a lot from the lesson study. I learned a lot about what the other teachers are thinking when they are developing a lesson, observing the lesson, and evaluating the lesson. I learned how to organize the blackboard. I liked thinking about what I need to do in the classroom with other experienced teachers. And studying a lesson in the lesson study showed me how I can think about the school goal we talked about in the beginning of the year in a very realistic situation.

Looking at a concrete lesson and talking about our school goal with other teachers made me more clear about what I need to do in the classroom in order to achieve our school goal. I learned a lot.

THE ROLE OF TSUTA TEACHERS IN ENHANCING AND SHAPING THEIR LESSON STUDY EXPERIENCE

Although Japanese teachers tend to view lesson study as a rich learning experience, it is important that we do not take this learning for granted. Might there be certain important aspects of the way in which Japanese teachers approach lesson study that contribute to the power of lesson study? Would lesson study yield much less impressive work in the hands of teachers who did not bring what the Tsuta teachers brought to this activity? We now address this important question.

Treating Lesson Study as Directed and Systematic Inquiry

How did the Tsuta teachers make the most out of lesson study? For one thing, they were very careful to be directed and systematic in their use of lesson study to examine their practice. They set a clear research question that they wanted to answer by looking at their practice, and they made sure that this question figured prominently during every step of their work, including when they presented their lessons to each other and to the guests who attended their open house. In other words, their interest in figuring out how to get their students to think in autonomous and inventive ways and to be able to learn from each other's rich ideas served as a driving force behind their work.

They designed their lesson with this goal in mind, making sure that, for example, the problems presented, the questions posed, the manipulative employed, and the worksheet assigned allowed them to understand students' thinking and to have them share this thinking with each other. As a result, for instance, the two main guidelines they used to develop a manipulative for the lesson were, first, that the manipulative should promote variety in student thinking, and second, that it should help the teachers, and thus other students, understand each student's solution processes.

They also made sure to articulate what they would be looking for in the lesson to assess whether their planning efforts were well guided. They even created an observation tool to facilitate the collection of the data that they wanted to gather about student solution strategies and later made sure to carefully go over the solution strategies that they observed students employ during the lesson. They questioned why certain solutions had not come up during the lesson, and why there was a discrepancy between students' written answers and their use of the manipulative. The care with which they used their observations to develop insights about how to revise the lesson to better meet their goals was a tribute to them being very focused on the inquiry that they set out to conduct.

The Tsuta teachers' ability to maintain a clear focus and sense of purpose throughout their lesson study allowed them to have a targeted learning experience. Without this emphasis, their planning, observations, and discussions would have been more disjointed and the end result would have been a more haphazard, and therefore less powerful, learning experience.

The Tsuta Teachers Worked Toward Designing a Specific Type of Lesson

No doubt, the work of the Tsuta teachers was also greatly affected by the very specific vision of teaching that these teachers had in mind as they worked on their study lessons. Next, we first provide a broad outline of this vision of teaching, and then we describe why we think it was critical in how lesson study unfolded at this school.

The Tsuta teachers worked on designing a lesson that first had students struggle with a problem and then had them present and discuss their ideas as a whole class. This type of instruction is very common in Japanese elementary and middle schools and has been well documented elsewhere (Stigler, Fernandez, Yoshida, 1996; Hiebert & Stigler, 2000; Becker, Silver, Kantowski, Travers, & Willson, 1990; Stigler & Hiebert, 1998). This approach to teaching is based on the premise that hearing the ideas of other students is key to opening children's minds to new understandings and conceptualizations. As the author of one educational text put it:

> The intellectual confrontation that occurs during student discussions fosters students' motivation to learn. In addition, the learning that occurs is deeper. In the student discussions, the students see the different ideas that were pre-

sented by others, they evaluate and rethink their own ideas, and they think about strategies for convincing others of their ideas. This exercise cannot work if learners work individually. It is a well-known fact that learning about some classmates' mistakes deepens other students' learning of content. In addition, as one student's thinking evolves, this affects other students' learning. As other students see the changes in that one student's thinking, they will in turn change how they see that student and they will also start to change their own thinking. (Matsugaki, 1991, pp. 24–25).

Similarly, Ms. Furumoto echoed the ideas just expressed during one of her interviews:

Learning about other students' solutions will provide occasions for students to reflect on their own solutions. In this reflection process, the students compare their solutions to those presented by others and think about which one is better. [This process] ... can help further students' understanding of the concept that they are learning about during the lesson.[3]

This vision of teaching requires that student presentations and discussions be well managed, a process that Japanese teachers refer to as *shudanshiko no soshikika* (organizing collective thinking). According to one educator, *shudanshiko no soshikika* aims at "each student in the classroom developing abilities for understanding, thinking, and expression by going through the process of comparing between someone else's and his/her own opinion or understanding and interacting with these collectively" (Yoshimoto, 1992, p. 197). Japanese teachers see *shudanshiko no soshikika* as taking place most actively during the *neriage* part of lessons and requiring that teachers prepare good *hatsumon* to promote its success. Japanese teachers say that casually providing occasions for students to exchange ideas or to help each other in a small group setting does not achieve the goal of *shudanshiko no soshikika*.

This view of teaching of course assumes that students will produce multiple solutions to problems and that they will be able to explain their solutions to others. Moreover, seeing lessons as an exercise in encouraging deep conceptual understanding by orchestrating rich whole-class exchanges requires that teachers always think about their lessons from the perspective of students, both intellectually and emotionally, a stance that Japanese teachers often refer to as "trying to see lessons with students' eyes."

In retrospect, one can see that much of what the Tsuta teachers discussed during their lesson study work was either directly or indirectly related to the view of teaching just described. In fact, the decision to focus on under-

---

[3]Interview, 3/21/94, with Ms. Furumoto at Tsuta Elementary School in Hiroshima, Japan.

standing how to develop students' ability to express their ideas and listen to each other is a direct outgrowth of this view of teaching. So is the genuine concern that they had with making sure that students presented ideas, even if these were mathematically unsophisticated. Similarly, their deep disappointment with the small number of solutions that came up during the lesson and their lengthy discussions about how to foster good listening skills also make sense in light of the type of lesson they were trying to design.

It also makes sense that the Tsuta teachers spent a great deal of time putting themselves in the shoes of the students who would take part in their lesson. In thinking about the problem they would pose, they used what they knew about the children to design a problem that would challenge them, attract their attention, and help them develop a better understanding of regrouping. In particular, they made every effort to pick a problem that students would solve in multiple ways. They made sure to anticipate all the possible student responses and solutions that might come up and to use these responses as a resource for their lesson planning. In fact, several of the teachers at Tsuta explained during their interviews that carefully anticipating student responses is the key to understanding students' thinking processes. They were also of the opinion that the study of students' anticipated answers and possible counteranswers prepares a teacher to lead a well-organized discussion that builds from student ideas.[4]

The point that we are trying to make is that had the Tsuta teachers had a different view of teaching, the content and focus of their work would have been quite different. Realizing this is critical for a good understanding of lesson study, because much of what was impressive about the lesson study work of Tsuta teachers was what they chose to think about and discuss.

WHAT IMPORTANT LESSONS CAN WE DRAW FROM JAPANESE LESSON STUDY?

We have argued that Japanese lesson study is impressive in its own right as a powerful approach for teachers to come together to learn from their practice. However, we have also been careful to emphasize that Japanese lesson study is impressive because of the purposeful and powerful ways in which Japanese teachers, like those at Tsuta, engage in it. Therefore, there are lessons for us both in the Japanese practice of lesson study and in how Japanese teachers practice lesson study. The former provides us a vision for how to create a process whereby teachers can engage in collaborative, sustained, and grounded reflection about their practice from which they

---

[4]The anticipation of student responses and the inclusion of these in lesson plans is a common element of Japanese lesson planning, both everyday and in the course of lesson study.

stand to learn a great deal. The latter provides us a vision of what this reflection can be like when it is carried out in a powerful manner.

We also see Japanese lesson study as providing us with an inspiring vision of teaching as a profession. In the United States there is currently much talk about the need to professionalize teaching. In the context of these conversations one often hears calls to break the pervasive isolation of teachers that makes it difficult for them to learn from each other and develop a joint body of professional knowledge (Fullan, 2001; King, 2002; Lieberman, 1992; Little & McLaughlin, 1993; Web, Heck, & Tate, 1996; Wilson & Berne, 1999). Many decry the lack of meaningful and enriching professional development experiences available to teachers. Most teachers in the United States learn to teach in a sink-or-swim approach that ignores the fact that teaching is a highly complex and profound enterprise that cannot be mastered without giving teachers ample opportunities to think deeply about the work that they do in the classroom.

In contrast, the teachers at Tsuta, and their counterparts all over Japan, clearly have rich professional lives and there is no question that this is, at least in part, due to their involvement in lesson study. Lesson study provides a venue for teachers to come together to share ideas and pool their brainpower. It provides an opportunity for teachers both to reflect on everyday teaching and to think deeply about teaching in a non-everyday context. For example, Ms. Maejima and one of her colleagues explained:

> When I'm faced with the challenge of developing a lesson during lesson study, I often think about my students. I feel so sorry for my students when I think about how careless my everyday lessons can be. I think lesson study is a good way to keep reminding me to reflect on my everyday teaching.

> If you want the students to respond to a study lesson in a certain way, you need to think if you are doing similar things in your everyday lessons so that your students know what to do.

Similarly, Ms. Tsukuda referred to the experience of teaching a study lesson as "an opportunity to think about your teaching very seriously."

Moreover, lesson study allows teachers to feel connected to each other and to a body of knowledge that they generate, share, and continually refine because, in the words of Ms. Furumoto, "There is no end to improving teaching." This is probably why throughout their lesson study work the Tsuta teachers behaved with the conviction that they stood to learn a great deal from their own teaching, and that of others. In fact, a number of them mentioned that observing somebody's teaching combined with trying out similar lessons on their own was the best way to learn how to teach. One of them even quoted a common Japanese proverb, "Improve yourself by looking at others (*Hito no furi mite waga furi naose*)," and said that it would be impossible for him to think about progressing as a teacher without observing others. Ms. Chijiiwa also expressed this stance when she explained:

> Everybody teaches in the classroom so we have a lot of things that we can talk about. Even hearing somebody saying something like, "Today one of my students said 'I like mathematics,' but he is not a good student in the class" can give me a chance to think about my students.

Perhaps when all is said and done the most important take-home message for us in Japanese lesson study is about the huge disservice that we do to teachers when we deprive them of a professional life. How can we expect teachers to grow and develop if they do not have opportunities to do the kind of work that lesson study allows and to have this work be sanctioned and treated with utmost seriousness, as would the work of any professional?

References

Chokshi, S. M. (2002). *Impact of lesson study: Report for the NAS/National Research Council Board on International and Comparative Studies in Education.*

Cochran-Smith, M., & Lytle, S. L. (1999). The teacher research movement: A decade later. *Educational Researcher, 28*(7), 15–25.

Feiman-Nemser, S. (2001). From preparation to practice: Designing a continuum to strengthen and sustain teaching. *Teachers College Record, 103*(6), 1013–1055.

Fernandez, C. (2002). Learning from Japanese approaches to professional development: The case of lesson study. *Journal of Teacher Education, 53*(5), 395–405.

Fernandez, C., Cannon, J., & Choski, S. (2003). A U.S.-Japan lesson study collaboration reveals critical lenses for examining practice. *Teaching and Teacher Education, 19*(2), 171–185.

Fujioka, N. (1991). *Stoppu moshon-houshiki ni yoru jugyokenkyu no hoho [A method for lesson study: Using stop motion method].* Tokyo: Gakujishuppan Kabushikigaisha.

Fullan, M. (2001). *The new meaning of educational change* (3rd ed.). New York, NY: Teachers College Press.

Gakkotosho Kabushikigaisha Henshu-bu (Ed.). (1992). *The elementary school mathematics teacher's instructional manual.* Tokyo: Gakkotosho Kabushikigaisha.

Hiroshima Education Office. (1993). *Yoran [Handbook].* Hiroshima, Japan: Hiroshima Education Office.

Inagaki, T., Terasaki, M., & Matsudaira, N. (Eds.). (1988). *Kyoshi no life course [The life course of teachers].* Tokyo: Tokaidaigaku Shuppankai.

Kamiyama, M., Sakamoto, H., Imazu, K., Sato, H., & Sato, M. (1983). Kyoshoku nitaisuru kyoushi no taid [Teachers' attitudes to their profession]. *Mie University Educational Research Bulletin, 34.*

King, M. B. (2002). Professional development to promote schoolwide inquiry. *Teaching and Teacher Education, 18*, 243–257.

Kitayama, E., & Yamada, S. (1991). *Kyoin tokubetsu kenshu kenkyuin kenshu hokokusho: Konaikenshu [A report by teachers of special teacher training: Konaikenshu].* Hiroshima, Japan: Hiroshima City Education Center.

Lampert, M., & Ball, D. L. (1998). *Teaching, multimedia and mathematics: Investigations of real practice.* New York, NY: Teachers College Press.

Lewis, C. (1995). *Educating hearts and minds: Reflections on Japanese preschool and elementary education.* New York: Cambridge University Press.

Lewis, C. (2002). *Lesson study: A handbook of teacher-led instructional change.* Philadelphia: Research for Better Schools.

Lewis, C., & Tsuchida, I. (1997). Planned educational change in Japan: The case of elementary science instruction. *Journal of Educational Policy, 12*(5), 313–331.

Lewis, C., & Tsuchida, I. (1998). A lesson is like a swiftly flowing river: Research lessons and the improvement of Japanese education. *American Educator, Winter,* 14–17 & 50–52.

Lieberman, A. (1992). The meaning of scholarly activity and the building of community. *Educational Researcher, 21*(6), 5–12.

Little, J. W., & McLaughlin, M. (1993). *Teacher's work: Individuals, colleagues, and contexts.* New York, NY: Teachers College Press.

Maki, M. (Ed.). (1982). *Kyoin kenshu no sogoteki kenkyu [A comprehensive study of teacher training].* Tokyo: Gyosei.

Mathematical Sciences Education Board (2002). *Studying classroom teaching as a medium for professional development: Proceedings of a U.S.-Japan Workshop.* Washington, DC: National Academy Press.

Matsugaki, K. (1991). *Isseijugyo no gijutsu [An art of whole class instruction].* Tokyo: Meijitosho.

Monbusho [Ministry of Education, Science, and Culture, Government of Japan]. (1989a, March). *Shogakko gakushu shido yoryo [Elementary school course of study].* Tokyo: Ohkurasho Insatsukyoku.

Monbusho [Ministry of Education, Science, and Culture, Government of Japan]. (1989b, March). *Shogakko gakushu shidosho—Sansu-hen [Elementary school instructional manual—Mathematics edition].* Tokyo: Ohkurasho Insatsukyoku.

Nakamura, T., Takahashi, A., & Kurosawa, S. (1989). *Jugyookenkyuu no susumekata, fukamekata, norikirikata [The lesson study].* (Vol. 10). Tokyo: Tooyookan Shuppansha.

Nakatome, T. (1984). *Konaikenshu o tsukuru: Nihon no konaikenshu keiei no sogoteki kenkyu [Developing konaikenshu: A comprehensive study of management of Japanese konaikesnhu].* Tokyo: Eidell Kenkyusho.

Putnam, R. T., & Borko, H. (2000). What do new views of knowledge and thinking have to say about research on teacher learning? *Educational Researcher, 29*(1), 4–15.

Research for Better Schools. "What Is Lesson Study?" *Currents, 5*(2).

Sato, M. (1992). Japan. In H. B. Leavitt (Ed.), *Issues and problems in teacher education: An international handbook.* New York: Greenwood Press.

Sato, M., Akita, K., & Iwakawa, N. (1993, Summer). Practical thinking styles of teachers: A comparative study of expert and novice thought processes and its implications for rethinking teacher education in Japan. *Peabody Journal of Education, 68*(4), 100–110.

Schifter, D. (1998). Learning mathematics for teaching: From a teachers' seminar to the classroom: *Journal of Mathematics Teacher Education, 1*(1), 55–87.

Seago, N., & Mumme, J. (2002). The promises and challenges in designing video-based professional development curriculum. Paper presented at the annual meeting of the American Educational Research Association, New Orleans, LA.

Seidel, S. (1998). Learning from looking. In N. Lyon (Ed.), *With portfolio in hand.* New York, NY: Teachers College Press.

Shimahara, N. K. (1991). Teacher education in Japan. In E. R. Beauchamp (Ed.), *Windows on Japanese education* (pp. 259–280). New York: Greenwood Press.

Stevenson, H. W., & Stigler, J. W. (1992). *The learning gap: Why our schools are failing and what we can learn from Japanese and Chinese education.* New York: Summit Books.

Stigler, J., & Hiebert, J. (1998). Teaching is a cultural activity. *American Educator, Winter,* 1–10.

Stigler, J., & Hiebert, J. (1999). *The teaching gap: Best ideas from the world's teachers for improving education in the classroom.* New York: Free Press.

Tsuta Elementary School. (1994). *Kenkyukiyo: Mizukara kangae, kufu shi, tomo ni manabiaou chikara o sozosuru—Mondai-kaiketsu-teki-gakushu o kihontoshita sansu-ka no kenkyu o hashiratoshite [Bulletin of research: Promoting students' ability to think on their own, autonomously, invent, and learn from each other—Based on the study of problem-solving-like learning for mathematics].* Hiroshima, Japan: Tsuta Elementary School.

Webb, N. L., Heck, D. J., & Tate, W. F. (1996). The urban mathematics collaborative project: A study of teacher, community, and reform. In S. A. Raizen & E. D. Bitton (Eds.), *Bold ventures, volume 3: Case studies of U.S. innovations in mathematics education* (pp. 247–360). Dordrecht: Kluwer Academic Publishers.

Wilson, S. M., & Berne, J. (1999). Teacher learning and the acquisition of professional knowledge: An examination of research on contemporary professional development. *Review of Research in Education, 24,* 173–209.

Yoshida, M. (1999a). *Lesson study: A case study of a Japanese approach to improving instruction through school-based teacher development.* Unpublished doctoral dissertation, The University of Chicago, Chicago, IL.

Yoshida, M. (1999b). *Lesson study [Jugyokenkyu] in elementary school mathematics in Japan: A case study.* Paper presented at the American Educational Research Association (April, 1999 Annual Meeting), Montreal, Canada.

Yoshimoto, H. (1992). *Jugyo o tsukuru kyojugaku kii wado [teaching key words for developing lessons].* Tokyo: Meijitosho.

Appendix A
A Glossary of Japanese Education Terms Referred to in this Book

Through working together, particularly during lesson study, Japanese teachers have developed a large array of technical terms and expressions to help them communicate more effectively. This professional language is widespread and specific to teaching in that none of these terms or expressions can be found in a regular Japanese language dictionary. Instead, there are several technical dictionaries that educators use as reference tools.

In addition, many new education words (or ideas) are introduced by the Ministry of Education or by researchers (e.g., *ko no yosa* [merits of individuality], *mondaikaiketsu-gakushuu* [problem-solving learning]). As teachers try to make sense of these words, in the context of their practice and through the conduct of lesson study, they develop a grounded and shared understanding of these words. This allows for these terms to become more than just catch phrases or buzz words, but rather meaningful and useful to teachers.

Here we provide definitions for some of the more commonly used of these terms, including all those employed throughout this book.

Bansho and *bansho-keikaku*	Bansho can be translated into English as "use or organization of blackboard" or more literally as "board writing." Japanese teachers consider the blackboard an important instructional tool for organizing students' thoughts and they therefore take *bansho* very seriously. Planning how to organize the blackboard is usually called *bansho-keikaku* and Japanese teachers often discuss this aspect of their teaching as a part of lesson study
Donyu, tenkai, and *matome* (or *shumatsu*)	These terms refer to the three key parts of a lesson: introduction, development (or expansion), and summary. Lessons are often planned and discussed in these three stages.

Gakushu   Course of study published by the Ministry of Education in
shido yoryo   Japan.

Gengenho   Subtraction–subtraction method used by students to solve
                   a subtraction problem involving regrouping (e.g., In the
                   case of 12 minus 7, decompose 12 into 10 and 2 and decom-
                   pose 7 into 2 and 5. First, subtract one 2 from the other. Sec-
                   ond, subtract 5 from the remaining 10 to get the answer 5).

Genkaho   Subtraction–addition method used by students to solve a
                   subtraction problem involving regrouping (e.g., In the case
                   of 12 minus 7, decompose the number 12 into 10 and 2 and
                   then subtract 7 from the 10 to get an answer of 3. Then add
                   the 2 and the 3 to get the answer 5).

Hatsumon   Teacher's questions or actions designed to help provoke
                   students' deep thinking about a problem they are solving.

Hokaho   Supplement–addition method used by students to solve a
                   subtraction problem involving regrouping (e.g., In the case
                   of 12 minus 7, count up from an array of 12 objects starting
                   from the eighth object [i.e., by saying "8, 9, 10, 11, 12"]. Keep
                   track of the number of objects counted.

Isseijugyo   Instruction that aims for deep understanding by placing
                   students at the center of the activity through having them
                   present and discuss their ideas as a whole class.

Jirikikaiketsu   To solve, or struggle with, a problem on one's own. During
                   the course of a lesson Japanese students are often asked to
                   work for a while on their own on problems presented to
                   them. Japanese teachers believe that this independent work
                   helps students take advantage of the class discussions that
                   will follow during the *neriage* component of the lesson (de-
                   scribed later).

Jugyokenkyu   The word *jugyokenkyu* is made up of two words: *jugyo*,
                   which means lesson, and *kenkyu*, which means study or re-
                   search. Lesson study, as these two words indicate, consists
                   of the study or examination of teaching practice and stu-
                   dents' learning.

Ju no hosu   Supplementary numbers adding up to 10.

Kazoehiki   Counting–subtraction method used by students to solve a
                   subtraction problem involving regrouping (e.g., In the case

of 12 minus 7, count off, one by one, 7 objects from an array of 12 objects. Then count the number of left over objects).

Kenkyujugyo   Study lesson or research lesson. These are lessons prepared by teachers during the course of lesson study. These lessons are meticulously and collaboratively planned and prepared, publicly taught, and carefully discussed in order to achieve an overachieving lesson study goal.

Kenkyu no matome or *kenkyukiyo*   Summary of the study or research bulletin. These are reports written by teachers about their lesson study work. These reports contain lesson plans developed through lesson study cycles as well as descriptions of teachers' goals, rationales, approaches findings, and future tasks for their conduct of lesson study.

Kenshu-sokushin-soshiki or *kenshu-soshiki*   *Konaikenshu* promotional committee. The role of this committee is to help plan and organize meaningful and effective *konaikenshu* at a school, and to keep this work on track. Generally teachers either volunteer or are nominated to be members of this committee.

Kikanjunshi   The literal translation of this word is to walk around between the desks and inspect students. In Japanese lessons, after a teacher presents a problem to students, they are generally asked to work on the problem on their own. The teacher then walks around and monitors how the students are solving the problem. Doing *kikanjunshi* involves not only monitoring the students, but also collecting notes on their ideas and thinking about who to ask to come up to present his or her work, and in what order.

Kokaijugyo or *kokai-kenkyujugyo*   Lesson study open house. A lesson study open house involves a host school inviting teachers and other educators from neighboring schools to observe and discuss several study lessons. The goal is for the host school to present and further its lesson study achievements.

Konaikenshu   School-based in-service professional development. The first term in this expression, *konai*, means "in school," and the second term, *kenshu*, means "training." *Konaikenshu*, is a form of school-based in-service training that brings together the teaching staff of a school to work in a sustained and focused manner on a schoolwide goal.

Neriage   Part of a Japanese lesson that aims at polishing the learning
                 or achieving higher learning through whole class discus-
                 sion. Based on the collective ideas introduced by the stu-
                 dents for solving a problem and with the teacher's
                 facilitation, during the *neriage* portion of a lesson the class
                 discusses in depth the mathematical concepts targeted in
                 the lesson. During this *neriage* process, teachers try to
                 achieve consensus among the class for identifying what are
                 common misunderstandings as well as for what are correct
                 and what are optimal solution strategies.

Shidoan   Lesson plan.

Shiki   Expressions that use numbers, letters, and mathematical
                 symbols to describe solution strategies. Students are often
                 required to write out *shiki* to describe their work (solution
                 process). Diagrams, pictures, tables, graphs, and common
                 algorithms (vertical calculation method) often used by stu-
                 dents to describe their work are considered distinct from
                 the more formal *shiki*. Algorithms commonly used during
                 calculation processes are called *hissan* (pencil calculation
                 method) in Japanese.

Shokuinshitsu   Staff room. Teachers in Japan all have desks, teaching mate-
or kyoinshitsu rials, and supplies in a common staff room where they
                 spend most of their time when they are not teaching. The
                 space is for the teachers to plan lessons, correct homework,
                 hold meetings, relax, and socialize.

Takuto   The word *takuto* comes from the German word "taktstock"
                 (a baton for directing an orchestra) and it means to orches-
                 trate or facilitate a lesson. In order to achieve the goals of a
                 lesson, teachers must orchestrate or facilitate students' pre-
                 sentations and discussions. Effective *takuto* uses students'
                 voices, discoveries, and mistakes skillfully to encourage
                 students' discussions in order to achieve the lesson goal.

Tsumazuki   Students' mistakes that afford rich learning opportunities.
                 Japanese teachers often ask students to present their wrong
                 solutions or mistakes for all their classmates to benefit from
                 what can be learned from analyzing these errors. Japanese
                 teachers also believe that this careful examination of errors
                 can help reduce students' tendency to focus on just wanting
                 to find the right answer.

Yusaburi   A strategy for solidifying a student's already acquired
                    knowledge, particularly when this knowledge is simply
                    based on the memorization of a procedure. More specifi-
                    cally, this strategy entails the teacher disagreeing with or
                    questioning the child's presented idea in order to make
                    the child question him or herself. This disagreement is
                    usually done in front of the whole class in order to maxi-
                    mize its effect.

Appendix B
Methods Students Can
Use to Subtract 7 from 12

"Counting–subtraction" methods (*kazoehiki*): Counting off 7 one by one starting either with a group of 12 or a group of 2 and 10 (from which the 7 are counted off).

"Supplement–addition" method (*hokaho*): Count up from 8 while keeping track of the numbers counted.

"Subtraction–addition" method (*genkaho*): $12 - 7 = (10 + 2) - 7 = (10 - 7) + 2 = 3 + 2 = 5$

"Subtraction–subtraction" method (*gengenho*): $12 - 7 = (10 + 2) - (5 + 2) = (10 - 5) + (2 - 2) = 5$

A Proposed Model for How Best to Structure Problem-based Lessons.

Goals	Lesson steps	Teaching process and hatsumon	Anticipated students' reactions	Teacher's reactions and important points to remember	Evaluation (+ students, * teacher)
Desire for Learning	Grasping the problem Presenting the Problem	• Organizing previously learned knowledge. ○ Make clear what previously learned knowledge can be used for solving the new problem. • Recalling what students learned during the previous lesson. • Omitting some condition of the problem in order to stimulate the students' interest. ○ Using a concrete object to help the students grasp the situation of the problem and stimulate conversation with them when the teacher introduces the condition missing in the problem. ○ It will be nicer if the situation of the problem comes from the students' real life. ○ Making sure all the students understand the situation of the problem.	• "That looks easy." • "We need to use addition, multiplication ..." • "We can use something we learned before." • (Nodding) • "I wonder, what kind of number can we put in the blank?" • "I don't understand." • "This problem looks interesting to solve." • "This problem is similar to what we did before." • "I want to solve this problem." • "I think I can write down an expression but I don't know how to solve the problem." • "The expression for this problem is ..." • "I think the answer will be something like ..." • "If I use this I may be able to solve the problem."	• Help the students to recall previously learned knowledge. • Praise the students who are raising their hands and presenting their ideas in the classroom. • Ask students to read out loud. • Help the students to understand the situation of the problem clearly by discussing how it relates to their real life, using a concrete object (real object) or a half-abstract object (tiles, discs, etc.). • Try not to introduce the problem cold. Create an introduction to the lesson that motivates students' interest and curiosity without them noticing they are solving the problem. • Help the students to understand the situation of the problem and help them to notice what kind of method they can use to solve the problem. • Write down the expression on the blackboard and confirm what they have already learned and not learned.	(Interest, Attitude, Knowledge, Understanding) + Did the students positively recall what they learned before? (Observation of the students) + Did the students understand what kind of calculations they needed to use? (Presentation) + Did the students understand what they needed to fill in the blanks in order to make a complete problem? (Raising hands) + Were the students able to fill in the blanks using appropriate numbers. (Presentation)

(continued on next page)

241

APPENDIX C (continued)

Goals	Lesson steps	Teaching process and hatsumon	Anticipated students' reactions	Teacher's reactions and important points to remember	Evaluation (+ students, * teacher)
		• Setting up a problem that can be solved by individual students based on their level of academic ability. • Introduction of main problem.		• Confirm the necessary conditions of the problem in order to solve it. Sometimes changing the numbers used in the problem helps the students to understand the situation of the problem.	+ Were the students enthusiastically solving the problem? * Did the teacher understand the goal of the lesson? * Did the situation of the problem provided lead to various student solution methods?
Ability to learn	Students solving the problem on their own	• Let's think about how we can solve the problem! • We have not learned it yet but I wonder if we can solve the problem by thinking hard about it. • Let's use the previously learned knowledge to solve the problem! • If you find one way to solve the problem, try to find other way to solve it! (1) Thinking about an expression. (2) Understanding the problem and task clearly. (3) Solving the problem individually.	• "I don't know how to solve it." • "I might be able to solve it." • "I will try solving it." • "I wonder how I can solve it?" • "I will use something I learned before to solve it." • There are many different ways to solve the problem (1) Method 1: ... (2) Method 2: ... (3) Method 3: ...	• Ask the students to think about the problem using diagrams, half abstract materials, etc. • Ask the students to write down their various ideas on the handouts. • Provide some hint cards for the students having a hard time solving the problem. (Walk around and give advice) • If the hint cards did not help the students, ask them to talk to other friends in their groups. • Provide handouts designed to stimulate students' interests and help them with their problem solving process.	(Way of thinking, expression, manipulation) + Did the student quickly open their notebooks (handouts) and start to solve the problem? (Observation of the students) * Did the teacher prepare something in order to meet the students' individual differences. * Was the support provided by the teacher appropriate in helping the students to solve the problem?

			Assessment
	• One way to solve the problem • Many ways to solve the problem	• "I found this to be an interesting method to solve it." • Think out the best way to present an idea clearly in the class. • "Let's think again if my method is right."	• Use a class seating chart to help organize/categorize students' methods/thinking.	+ Did the students find their own solution to the problem? (Handout) + Did the students come up with many different ideas? (Students' seating chart and handout)
Ability that is gained through this learning activity	Neriage	• The students present their ideas using blackboard and notes (notebook & handout) • The students add their opinion to their friend's presentation. • Be able to identify similar ideas presented by their friends and be able to talk about what was impressive about those ideas. Basic form of neriage process: 1. Please write your ideas on the blackboard. 2. Please present your ideas. (Are there people who did it differently?)	• The students present their ideas one by one by identifying which of their solutions are different from the other ideas already presented. • "First, I did like this ... then I did like that ... , and I solved it." • "Looks like student A's method and student B's method are similar." • "It looks like student A's method is easier to calculate." • "My method is ..."	• Make clear which space the presenters can use on the blackboard and ask them to write freely. • Make sure to give a voice to students who have similar ideas but are not be able to present during the class. • If the students have miscalculations, the teacher informs them and asks them to correct. • Ask students to raise their hands to check how many of them have the same idea. If it is necessary, the teacher asks those students to provide additional explanations of the idea. • Praise each one of the presenters by telling the class that each idea was a well-thought-out idea.	(Expression/manipulation, knowledge/understanding) + Could students present their ideas clearly to other students? (Presentation)

(continued on next page)

APPENDIX C (*continued*)

Goals	Lesson steps	Teaching process and hatsumon	Anticipated students' reactions	Teacher's reactions and important points to remember	Evaluation (+ students, * teacher)
		3. If you have anything to add to what your friend just presented, please tell the class. 4. Please ask questions about your friend's presented idea. 5. Which one of the presented ideas are similar to your own idea? 6. What do you think are the good points about your friend's ideas that you also thought about? 7. Let's compare your own idea with your friend's presented ideas. 8. Why did you think so? 9. Which one of the solutions do you think is the best? 10. Which one of the solutions is better than the others? • Conducting a discussion on merits of ideas and methods.	• "I see." • "I wonder why he/she thought that way …" • "I wonder which one of the methods is better …" • "I understand many students' methods."	• Help the students to understand, that even if they have not yet learned the new concept, if they think hard they can find a way to solve the problem. • Help the students be clear about the focal points of the discussion that help them understand. • Focused on the "Merits of Individuality (*Ko no yosa*)": Be mindful how the different ideas presented in the classroom are a result of students' differences. • Focused on the "Merits of Mathematics (*Sansu no yosa*)": • What is useful? • What is easy to understand? • What is easy to carry out? • Which one helps expand and deepen ideas? • Which one is useful and applicable? • Which one is more accurate? • Which idea is beautiful? • By classifying, contrasting, finding similarities, and confronting ideas through discussion with students try to organize various ideas into one or two better ideas.	+ Could the students present their ideas in the class? Could they listen to other students' presentations and recognize the idea of others. (Presentation) + Were the students enthusiastically seeking to deepen their understanding? (Presentation)

			(Interest/Attitude, Way of thinking, Expression/Manipulation, Knowledge/Understanding)

Expanding knowledge (Practice problems)

- Preparing practice problems suited to achieving the goals of the lesson.
- Prepare practice problems using the same setting as in the main problem for the lesson, but with changed numbers.
- Organizing/Summarizing what the students learned during the lesson.
- Preparing practice problems that help the students to deepen their understanding of what they discussed during the *Neriage* process. Also, the problems should help students try to apply the new ideas that they learned through the *Neriage* process.

- "I understand how to solve the problem."
- "I think I can solve a similar problem."
- "I would like to use my friend's method which I thought is good."
- "I wonder if I can solve this problem differently (than what I did or what other students did) ..."
- "I want to try to solve more problems like those we worked on today."

- Think hard about the organization of the blackboard.
- Summarize the discussion and lead the students to understand the goal of the lesson.
- Facilitate the students' discussions about the methods presented from the standpoint of which is simpler, clearer, and more accurate.
- Praise the students from viewpoints in order to increase their desire for learning.
1. What they accomplished (e.g., were able to solve the problem, came up with a different idea, were able to understand other ideas, etc.)
2. What they are trying to do (e.g., want to present, try to listen, try to explain clearly, etc.) (Related to attitude for learning)
- Ask the students to solve the problem using some other methods and help them notice the merits of using certain methods.
- Ask the students to reflect on the process of solving the problem and ask them to summarize it in their own words.

(Interest/Attitude, Way of thinking, Expression/Manipulation, Knowledge/Understanding)
* Did the teacher achieve the goal of the lesson?
* Did the teacher notice each individual student's idea for solving the problem and progress of understanding of the lesson and did the teacher praise such progress?

(continued on next page)

APPENDIX C (continued)

Goals	Lesson steps	Teaching process and hatsumon	Anticipated students' reactions	Teacher's reactions and important points to remember	Evaluation (+ students, * teacher)
		• Listing new questions and unresolved problems that came out during the *Neriage* process and providing advance announcement for what the students will be learning in the next lesson. "Let's try to solve this problem by referring that what you learned from today's lesson."		• Provide similar practice problems to evaluate the students' understanding of the lesson.	+ Self reflect on to day's lesson. (Rating understanding and interest or writing on handouts.)

Important note: As they plan lessons that address their chosen goals, teachers can select the most suited instructional ideas from the "basic structure of a lesson" proposed herein

Author Index

Subject Index